# ELEMENTS OF HEBREW

# WILLIAM R. HARPER'S

# Elements of Hebrew
## BY AN INDUCTIVE METHOD

REVISED BY

## J. M. POWIS SMITH

THE UNIVERSITY OF CHICAGO PRESS
Chicago & London

*Library of Congress Catalog Card Number: 59-7625*

THE UNIVERSITY OF CHICAGO PRESS, CHICAGO 60637
The University of Chicago Press, Ltd., London W.C. 1

*Sixth Edition published 1885; revised 1921. Reissued 1959.*
*Fourth Impression 1968*

*Printed in the United States of America*

# FOREWORD

At last students can again obtain William Rainey Harper's *Introductory Hebrew Method and Manual* and *Elements of Hebrew*, textbooks which for generations have been used with great success in the teaching of biblical Hebrew. It was with regret that we saw them withdrawn and it is with enthusiasm that we welcome their return. No other textbooks have been able to win the respect and popularity that the Harper books have always had. Pupils and teachers alike can testify that they furnish an excellent and enduring means for gaining a knowledge of Hebrew.

The inductive method employed by Professor Harper is based on sound educational principles. From the very first lesson the student has the incentive of a feeling of definite accomplishment. The constant repetition of the biblical material both establishes and fortifies the student's knowledge of the Hebrew language.

The grammar, as presented in the *Elements of Hebrew*, is neither oversimplified nor belabored with involved and wordy complexity. Essential principles are enunciated briefly, clearly, and soundly, with ample illustration. They can be grasped and retained easily.

The aids to instruction incorporated in the *Introductory Hebrew Method and Manual*, used in conjunction with the *Elements*, are a teacher's delight. In addition to the discussion of the biblical words in the reading lesson, there are exercises that are distinctive for establishing a real appreciation of Hebrew style and syntax. The volume also contains the vocalized text of Genesis I–VIII for reading purposes, the unvocalized text of Genesis I–IV for practice in vocalizing, and the transliterated text of Genesis I to afford the student a check on his work during the early lessons. In addition to the usual vocabularies necessary for the lessons, the *Manual* also contains the frequency lists developed by Professor Harper to help the student master vocabulary rapidly and efficiently by learning first the words most frequently used in the Bible. Such accessories are valuable aids to the teacher, for they make possible greater flexibility in method so that materials can be adapted to the needs of the class.

These books were written long ago by Professor Harper, the first president of the University of Chicago, on the basis of his successful experience both with classes and with his famous correspondence courses. They have met the test of time and are surprisingly modern. As his employment of the educationally sound inductive method and his development of frequency lists in vocabulary demonstrate, Professor Harper could be said to be ahead of his time. Judiciously and carefully revised by Professor J. M. P. Smith, these books are regarded by many as still the best tools for the learning and teaching of biblical Hebrew. While it is true that Hebrew studies have progressed in the interim and that consequently at some points minor improvements might be made if and when a revision is undertaken, there is no serious obstacle to the use of these volumes as now reproduced.

With the present increasing interest in biblical Hebrew, the reintroduction of these fine textbooks will afford an opportunity for increasing numbers of students to learn Hebrew quickly and well, whether in class or privately.

RAYMOND A. BOWMAN

UNIVERSITY OF CHICAGO
October 1958

# PREFACE

The sixth edition of Harper's ELEMENTS OF HEBREW appeared in 1885. Since that time it has served the needs of large numbers of students beginning the study of Hebrew, and has gained for itself a secure position among elementary text-books. But during the past thirty-five years much progress has been made in the study of Hebrew grammar, of which Harper's ELEMENTS remained unaware. The late President Harper himself was, of course, fully conscious of this, and frequently expressed his eagerness to bring out a new edition of the ELEMENTS. The pressure of official duties, however, and his premature death denied him this privilege.

The value of the Harper manner of approach to the study of Hebrew has been so clearly demonstrated in the experience of successive generations of students that the perpetuation of the text-books in which it is embodied seems called for. To this end the present revision has been undertaken. Effort has been made to preserve the form and method of the original as far as possible. The changes incorporated in the new edition are only such as seem demanded by the present status of our knowledge of Hebrew and Semitic grammar. The more important of these changes may be noted here.

(1) The half-open syllable has been eliminated, as was suggested by Sievers (*Metrische Studien*, vol. I, p. 22), and approved by Gesenius-Kautzsch (*Hebr. Grammatik*, 28th ed., 1909). (2) A beginning has been made along the line of bringing Hebrew grammar into accord with the results of the modern study of phonetics. This involves some marked changes in the treatment of the Hebrew vowel-system; but it seems well to make this departure, even in a book for beginners, since beginners are entitled to protection from known errors; and further because many students in our best colleges are learning the newer phonetic principles and will welcome them as old friends when they find them in this new field. (3) A frank acceptance has been accorded the biliteral explanation of the so-called ע״ע and ע״ו

verbs and nouns.   This point of view seems more nearly in accordance with the facts, and likewise makes the study of these forms simpler for beginners.   The biliteral hypothesis has not been carried as far here as it might well be in a more advanced grammar, its application being confined to the more apparent cases, for the sake of simplicity.

It remains to express my sense of obligation to two of my colleagues.   Professor Ira Maurice Price has read the work both in manuscript and in proof, and has done much to insure accuracy in printing.   To Professor Martin Sprengling, who read the book in manuscript, I am especially grateful for numerous and valuable suggestions, the acceptance of which will, I trust, greatly increase the worth of the book.   Its errors are my own; I cannot hope to have escaped error in the presentation of a subject beset with so much that is problematical.   "To err is human; to forgive, divine!"   I can hope only that the present edition may give a new lease of life to this work of my greatest teacher.

J. M. Powis Smith.

The University of Chicago, Jan. 1, 1921.

# PREFACE TO THE SIXTH EDITION

The first edition of the ELEMENTS was issued in July, 1881; the second, in October, 1882; the third, in February, 1883; the fourth, in November, 1883; the fifth, in November, 1884. All these editions, the first excepted, were printed from one set of plates, with only such changes and additions, from time to time, as the use of the same plates would permit. The peculiar circumstances of publication explained, although they could not excuse, the incomplete, and often imperfect, treatment accorded in these editions to very many of the subjects. While the present edition lays no claim to completeness, or to freedom from error, it will certainly be found more nearly complete and perfect than preceding editions. The author can only regret that regular and special duties of a most exacting nature, have not permitted him to give that amount of time, or that attention to the preparation of the book, which justice to the subject, to those who may use the book, and to himself, demanded.

The present edition, which contains nearly one hundred additional pages, and is entirely re-written, differs considerably from the former editions, and radically from other grammars now in common use. Some of the distinguishing features of the grammar deserve, perhaps, special mention:

1) For the purpose, not of aiding the beginner to pronounce, but of teaching the exact force and value of the several consonant- and vowel-sounds, a minute system of transliteration has been employed, by which the attention of the student is directed from the very beginning to the details of the vowel-system. Too little, by far, is made in Hebrew study, of the vowel-system, without a correct knowledge of which all effort is merely groping in darkness.

2) A tolerably exhaustive treatment, more complete perhaps than any that has yet appeared in English, is given of the various vowel-sounds. Each sound is treated separately, the laws which regulate its occurrence and the grammatical forms in which it appears being carefully noted.

3) **Certain** important distinctions, not heretofore generally recognized by American teachers, are indicated throughout the grammar; *e. g.*, (*a*) the tone-long é ( ﬞ ), heightened from ă, which is seen in Segholates, in ל״ה Imperfects and Participles, and elsewhere; (*b*) the naturally long *e* (‍ﬞ ) contracted from *ay*, which occurs in plural nouns before the pronominal suffixes ךָ, הָ, and in certain Imperfects before נָה; (*c*) the ô obscured from â, as distinguished from the ô = *aw*.

4) Instead of adopting a new Paradigm-word for each class of weak verbs, the verb קֹטֵל is retained, with such variation as the particular weak verb under consideration demanded; *e. g.*, עָטֵל for the פ׳ guttural verb, קֹטֵט for the ע״ע verb, קוּל for the ע״ו verb. There can be no objection to this method. Many grammarians have adopted it in the treatment of noun-formation. Experience has shown that, in this way, men learn the verb more rapidly and more thoroughly.

5) In the treatment of the strong verb, the student is referred, in every case, to the primary form or ground-form from which the form in use has arisen in accordance with the phonetic laws of the language. That treatment which starts with stems having the form which occurs in the Perf. 3 m. sg., or Impf. 3 m. sg., is, at the same time, unscientific and unsatisfactory. The bugbear of Hebrew grammar is the weak verb. Nor will it be otherwise so long as the effort is made to explain the forms of weak verbs from those of the strong verb. How absurd, for example, to derive יָקוּם from a form like יִקְטֹל; but how simple to derive it from a form like יְקְטֹל, the ground-form of יִקְטֹל. Together with the form in use, the student should learn also the primary form from which the usual form is derived. This method will furnish a knowledge of the language, which will be not only more scientific, but also more lasting.

6) Particular attention is given to the subject of noun-formation, and on this is based the treatment of noun-inflection. The same method which would teach the primary forms of verbal stems, will also teach the primary forms of noun-stems.

7) That fiction of Hebrew grammarians, the connecting-vowel, has

been practically discarded. The Hebrew has no connecting-vowels. The vowels incorrectly called connecting-vowels are the relics of old case- or stem-endings. These case- or stem-endings, summarily disposed of in current grammars under the head of "paragogic" vowels, are restored to the position which their existence and occurrence demand.

But it is asked, What has a beginner to do with all this? Why should a grammar which proposes only to consider the "elements" of the language, take up these subjects? While this may do for specialists, of what service is it to him who studies Hebrew only for exegetical purposes? Our reply is this :—

1) The experiment of teaching men something about Hebrew grammar, of giving them only a superficial knowledge, has been tried for half a century; and it has failed. Men instructed in this manner take no interest in the study, learn little or nothing of the language, and forget, almost before it is learned, the little that they may have acquired. If for no other reason, the adoption of a new system is justified by the lamentable failure of the old to furnish any practical results.

2) Those who take up the study of Hebrew are men, not children. Why should they not learn, as they proceed, the explanation of this or that fact? Why should the student be told that the Infinitive Construct (קְטֹל) is formed from the Absolute (קָטוֹל) by rejecting the pretonic qāmĕç? Is it not better that he should learn at once that the ō of the Construct is from ŭ, while the ô of the Absolute is from â, and thus be enabled to grasp all the more firmly those two great phonetic laws of the language, *heightening* and *obscuration?*

3) The best way, *always,* to learn a thing is the right way, even if, at first, it is more difficult. If there *is* a difference between the ō of the Imperfect, Imperative and Infinitive Construct on the one hand, and the ô of the Infinitive Absolute and Participles on the other, what is gained by passing over it in silence?

4) In order to learn any subject, the student must be interested in that subject. Is he not more likely to be interested in an accurate, scientific treatment, than in an arbitrary, superficial treatment?

The treatment adopted in the ELEMENTS is an inductive one, so

far as it was possible to make it such.   In the discussion of each subject there are first given sufficient data, either in the way of words
taken from the text, or of Paradigms, to form a basis for the work.
The words cited are from the early chapters of Genesis, with which
the student is supposed to be familiarizing himself, as the subjects
are being taken up.   Where these chapters furnished no suitable
example, a word is taken from some other book, the chapter and verse
being cited in each case.   It is intended that the student shall feel
in all his work that he is dealing with the actual facts of the language,
and not with hypothetical forms.   After the presentation of the
"facts," the principles taught by these facts are stated as concisely
as possible.   While the book is an elementary treatise and, for this
reason, does not aim to take up the exceptions and anomalies of the
language, it will be found to contain a treatment of all that is essential, and to include everything of importance which can be classified.
In the treatment of the strong and weak verbs, a list is given under
each class of the more important verbs belonging to this class.   This
list may be used as an exercise, or merely for handy reference.

The author lays no claim to originality so far as concerns the material employed; there is indeed little room for originality in this line.
In the matter, however, of arrangement, and of statement, he con-
fidently believes that a kind of help is here afforded the student which
cannot be found elsewhere.

In the work of preparation, the best and latest authorities have
been freely used.   Special acknowledgment is due the grammars of
Bickell, Gesenius (Kautzsch), and Davidson; but valuable aid has
been received from those of Green, Nordheimer, Kalisch, Land,
Ewald, Olshausen, König, Stade, and Böttcher.

For his assistance in the preparation of the manuscript for the
printer, and for many valuable suggestions, the author is indebted to
Mr. Frederic J. Gurney, of Morgan Park.   He desires also to express
his thanks to Mr. C. E. Crandall, of Milton, Wis., for aid rendered by
him in the verification of references and in the revision of the proof-
sheets, and to Rev. John W. Payne, of Morgan Park, Ill., for the
skill and care exhibited in the typographical finish and accuracy of
the book.   He is under obligations, still further, to Professors C. R.

Brown, of Newton Centre, S. Burnham, of Hamilton, E. L. Curtis, of Chicago, and F. B. Denio, of Bangor, for useful suggestions and corrections.

It is generally conceded that in America we are on the eve of a great revival in the department of Semitic study. It is the author's hope that this volume may contribute something toward this greatly needed awakening. Trusting that the new edition may be received with the same favor as those which have preceded it, and that its shortcomings will be as far as possible overlooked, he places the book, although with many misgivings, in the hands of those who favor the Inductive Method.

W. R. H.

Morgan Park, Ill., Sept. 1, 1885.

# TABLE OF CONTENTS

## PART FIRST—ORTHOGRAPHY.

### I. THE LETTERS.

xv

# PART FIRST—ORTHOGRAPHY

# I. The Letters

## *1. Alphabet*

| | Sign. | Equivalent. | Name. | Num. Value. |
|---|---|---|---|---|
| 1 | א | ' | 'Å-lĕf | 1 |
| 2 | בּ | b | Bêθ | 2 |
| • | ב | v | ] | |
| 3 | גּ | g | Gí-mĕl | 3 |
| | [ג | ğ | ] | |
| 4 | דּ | d | Då-lĕθ | 4 |
| | [ד | đ= | tk in *this*] | |
| 5 | ה | h | Hê | 5 |
| 6 | ו | w | Wåw | 6 |
| 7 | ז | z | Zá-yĭn | 7 |
| 8 | ח | ḥ | Ḥêθ | 8 |
| 9 | ט | ṭ | Ṭêθ | 9 |
| 10 | י | y | Yôd | 10 |
| 11 | כּ | k | Käf | 20 |
| | [ך | χ | ] | |

| | Sign. | Equivalent. | Name. | Num. Value. |
|---|---|---|---|---|
| 12 | ל | l | Lå-mĕd | 30 |
| 13 | מ | m | Mêm | 40 |
| 14 | נ | n | Nûn | 50 |
| 15 | ס | s | Så-mĕχ | 60 |
| 16 | ע | ' | 'Å-yĭn | 70 |
| 17 | פּ | p | Pê | 80 |
| | [פ | f | ] | |
| 18 | צ | ṣ | Så-dê | 90 |
| 19 | ק | ḳ | Ḳôf | 100 |
| 20 | ר | r | Rêš | 200 |
| 21 | שׁ שׂ | š, ś | Šîn, Śîn | 300 |
| 22 | ת | t | Tåw | 400 |
| | [ת | θ=*th* in *cloth*] | | |

1. The Hebrew language has twenty-two letters; these are consonants and are written from right to left.

2. The vowels in the "names" of the letters, given above, are sounded according to the English equivalents given in § 5. The "equivalents" for the consonants given above are rather to be regarded as symbols suggestive of the characters they represent than as exact reproductions.

3. The equivalent of each sign is the initial letter of its name.

4. The six consonants written with a dot in them are also written without the dot; but then they are changed in pronunciation, viz., ב=v; ג = ğ; ד = đ; כ = χ; פ = f; ת = θ; see § 12.

3

## 2. Remarks on the Pronunciation of Letters

1. אֵת = 'ēθ (1:1)[1]; הָאָרֶץ = hâ-'ă-rĕṣ (1:1); אֱלֹהִים = 'ᵉlô-hîm (1:1); תְּהוֹם = θᵉhôm (1:2).

2. עַל = 'ăl (1:2); עֶרֶב = 'é-rĕv (1:5); רְקִיעַ = râ-ḳî(ă)' (1:6).

3. אֶחָד = 'ĕ-ḥâd (1:5); חֹשֶׁךְ = ḥō-šĕχ (1:2); מְרַחֶפֶת = mᵉră-hé̆-fēθ (1:2).

4. קָרָא = ḳâ-râ' (1:5); כִּי = kî (1:4); בֹּקֶר = bō-ḳĕr (1:5).

5. טוֹב = ṭôv (1:4); מִתַּחַת = mĭt-tă̆-ḥăθ (1:7); הַקָּטֹן = hăḳ-ḳâ-ṭōn (1:16).

6. בְּרֵאשִׁית = bᵉrē'-šîθ (1:1); וַיַּעַשׂ = wăy-yă̆-'ăś (1:7); חֹשֶׁךְ = ḥō-šĕχ (1:2).

7. עֵץ = 'ēṣ (1:11); תּוֹצֵא = tô-ṣē'(1:12); יִסְגֹּר = yĭs-gōr (2:21).

8. וְאֵת = wᵉ'ēθ (1:1); וְבֹהוּ = wâ-vō-hû (1:2); וְרוּחַ = wᵉrû(ă)ḥ (1:2).

1. א ( ' ) is a laryngeal stop, made by bringing the edges of the larynx together, thus shutting off the emission of the breath; ה (h) is a "rough breathing," like h in *how*.

2. ע ( ' ) is a sound peculiar to the Semitic and made far down in the larynx; it is so difficult of utterance that no attempt is made to reproduce it here.

3. ח (ḥ) was a deep laryngeal; it is now generally pronounced like *ch* in the German *Buch*.

4. ק (ḳ) is a *k*-sound, but pronounced farther back on the palate than כ (k).

5. ט (ṭ) is a dental sound made with the tip of the tongue higher up than in the pronunciation of ת (t)[2].

6. שׁ (š) is pronounced like the English *sh;* שׂ (ś) is an ordinary *s*-sound, now indistinguishable from ס (s).

7. צ (ṣ) is a sharp hissing *s*-sound; more emphatic than the ordinary ס (s).

8. ו (w) is pronounced like *w* in *water*, and not like our *v*.

9. The spirant כ (χ) is pronounced like weak German *ch* in *Kirche*.

10. The spirant ג (ğ) is pronounced like *g* in German *Tage*.

---

[1] The chapter and verse in Genesis, in which a given word is found; are thus indicated; 1:1—meaning chapter 1, verse 1; 2:3—meaning chapter 2, verse 3, etc.

[2] In ordinary practice, ט and ת are scarcely, if at all, to be distinguished.

### 3.  Remarks on the Forms of Letters

1. בְּרֵאשִׁית בָּרָא אֱלֹהִים אֵת הַשָּׁמַיִם וְאֵת
2. (1:12) תּוֹצֵא | (1:2) פְּנֵי (1:2) פְּנֵי (1:1) אֱלֹהִים | כִּי (1:4)
(1:11) עֵץ | (1:20) עוֹף | (1:4) בֵּין (1:2) הַמַּיִם | (1:2) חֹשֶׁךְ
3. (3:24) דֶּרֶךְ; (1:2) פְּנֵי (1:28), בִּדְגַת (1:16); כּוֹכָבִים
(1:11) זֶרַע; (1:4) בֵּין (1:3) וַיְהִי; (1:2) חֹשֶׁךְ (1:2), הָיְתָה
(1:6), רָקִיעַ (1:5); יוֹם (2:21), יִסְגֹּר (1:2); מַיִם (1:4), טוֹב
תּוֹצֵא (1:12); חֹשֶׁךְ (1:4), עֵשֶׂב (1:11).

1. Words are written from right to left, and may not be divided; when it is necessary to fill out a line, certain letters (א, ה, ל, ם, ת) are extended.

2. Five letters (כ, מ, נ, פ, צ) have two forms; the second (ך, ם, ן, ף, ץ) is used at the end of words.

3. Certain letters, very similar in form, are to be carefully distinguished: ם, ב, כ; ג, נ; ד, ר, ך, ה, ח, ת; ו, י; ז, ן; ט, מ; ם, ע; צ; ש, שׂ.

### 4.  The Classification of Letters

|  | Labials. | Labio-Dentals. | Dentals. | Palatals. | Velars. | Laryngeals |
|---|---|---|---|---|---|---|
| Stops | כ ב |  | ט ת ד |  | ק כ ג | א |
| Fricatives | ו | פ ב | ת ד צ שׂ ס ז שׁ | י | כ ג | ע ח ה |
| Nasals | מ |  | נ |  |  |  |
| Lateral |  |  | ל |  |  |  |
| Rolled |  |  | ר |  |  |  |

Hebrew words consist of consonants and vowels as in all other languages. The use of the breath is fundamental in the production of these sounds. Vowels are produced by the relatively free, unobstructed emission of the breath, the modifications of vowel-sound being caused by varying positions of the vocal organs. Consonants, on the other hand, involve either a total or a partial obstruction of the breath. The Hebrew consonants, therefore, are classified on two bases: (1) the use of the breath in their production, (2) the vocal organs employed.

1. The first classification includes five groups of sounds:

*a.* The *Stops* which involve a complete stoppage of the breath.

*b.* The *Fricatives* produced by the friction of the breath escaping through some narrow passage.

**Remark.**—The Fricatives ב, ג, ד, כ, פ, ת may for convenience be designated spirants.

*c.* The *Nasal* sounds in which the breath is emitted through the nose.

*d.* The *Lateral* sound (ל *l*) in which the breath escapes along openings on one or both sides of the tongue.

*e.* The *Rolled* sound (ר *r*) in which the tongue rapidly taps the teeth or the ridge of the teeth, thus successively obstructing and freeing the passage of air.

2. The second classification, based on the organs of speech employed, falls into six sub-divisions:

*a.* The *Labials* proper involve the closing or partial closing of the lips.

*b.* The *Labio-Dentals*, a special variety of labials, are made by allowing the breath to escape with the front teeth placed upon the lower lip.

*c.* The *Dentals* are made with the tip of the tongue touching, or in close proximity to, the front teeth. Of these some bring the tip of the tongue close to the front teeth, or in contact with them, while with others the contact or approach is a little farther back on the tongue. The difference between ב and ב, ת and ת, ג and ג, פ and פ, ד and ד, כ and כ is that in the stops the breath is fully checked, while in the spirants the breath is allowed a partial outlet.

    *d.* The *Palatal* consonant (י__*y*) involves the approach toward the highest part of the palate of that part of the tongue which is opposite the top of the palate.

    *e.* The *Velars* involve contact between the tongue and the soft palate (velum). Of these ק is made the farthest back.

    *f.* The *Laryngeals* involve action of the larynx which is not as yet clearly understood.

    **Note 1.**—A third classification is generally recognized by students of phonetics: viz., *voiced* and *unvoiced* consonants. The former involve vibration of the vocal cords, the latter do not. Examples of voiced consonants are ב, ד, and of unvoiced, פ, ת. But for further details of phonetics the student may refer to G. Noël-Armfield, *General Phonetics for Missionaries and Students of Languages* (Cambridge: Heffer & Sons, 1915).

## II. Vowels

### 5. The Vowel-Signs[1]

1. בְ, רָא, שָׁ, אָ, הָ, אָ, תָה, וּ; הַשׁ, מֵ, עַל, הַמ, חַת, מַב

2. שִׁית, הִים, הִי, כִּי, דִּיל, נִי; יֵם, יִק, מַת, מִק, לַם, יֵשׁ

3. רֶר, נֵי, דֵּל, בֵּין, מֵ, שֵׁ; רָץ, שֶׁךְ, פֵּת, רְב, קֶר, שֵׁר

4. הוּ, רוּ, וּו, יוּ, צוּ, בוֹ, דוּ; כָל, לְק, רֶם, יִק, יֵל

5. הוֹם, יוֹם, אוֹר, ־ל, תָ־, שֹׁל; כָּל־, שָׁם, אָךְ, עָב

6. בְ, וְ, יְ, פְ, תֶ, מְ; אֲ, עֲ; אֱ, הֱ; קָ, הָ

1. ◌ָ is pronounced as *â* in *âll*; ◌ַ like *ă* in *class*.

2. ◌ִי is pronounced as *i* in *machine*; ◌ִ (i. e., without a following ◌ִי), as *i* in *pin*.[2]

3. ◌ֵי or ◌ֵ is pronounced as *ey* in *they*; ◌ֶ as *e* in *met*.

4. וּ is pronounced as *oo* in *moon*; ◌ֻ as *u* in *put*.[2]

5. וֹ or ◌ֹ is pronounced as *o* in *note*; ◌ָ practically the same as *â* in *âll*, the same sign being used for both sounds.

6. *a.* ◌ְ is a very quickly uttered sound, as *e* in *below*, when the word is pronounced rapidly, so as to slur over the *e* and run the *b* and *l* almost (but not quite) together; thus—*b'low*, not *below*, nor *blow;* p*°lice*, not *police*, nor *plice.*

*b.* ◌ֲ (a combination of ◌ַ and ◌ְ) is a little fuller in sound than ◌ְ, and with a slight *ă* quality.

*c.* ◌ֱ (a combination of ◌ֵ and ◌ְ) is a little fuller in sound than ◌ְ, and with a slight *ĕ* quality.

*d.* ◌ֳ (a combination of ◌ָ (ŏ) and ◌ְ) is a little fuller in sound than ◌ְ, and with a slight *â* or *ŏ* quality.

### 6. The Vowel-Letters

Before the introduction[3] of vowel-signs (§ 5.), certain weak consonants, א, ה, ו, י, were sometimes used to indicate the vowel-sounds, and hence were called *vowel-letters:*

---

[1] All *letters* in Hebrew are consonants; the alphabet contains no vowels. To supply the lack of vowels the above system of vowel-signs was introduced.

[2] Sometimes ◌ִ is written where ◌ִי was intended, and ◌ֻ where ו was intended; in such cases ◌ִ is pronounced as ◌ִי (*i* in *machine*), and ◌ֻ as ו (*oo* in *moon*).

[3] These signs were introduced between the sixth and eighth centuries A. D.

1. קאם[1] = ḳâm; היתה = hȧ-yᵉθȧ (1 : 2); חיה = ḥȧy-yȧ (1 : 20).

2. תהו = θō-hû (1 : 2); רוח = rû(ă)ḥ (1 : 2); היו = hȧ-yû (1 : 15);
אור = 'ôr (1 : 3); טוב = ṭôv (1 : 4); יום = yôm (1 : 5).

3. אלהים = 'ᵉlô-hîm (1 : 1); ראשית = rē'-šîθ (1 : 1); שלישי =
šᵉlî-šî (1 : 13); פני = pᵉnê (1 : 2); שני = šᵉnê (1 : 16); בין =
bên (1 : 4).

4. יהיה = yĭh-yê (1 : 29); מקוה = mĭḳ-wê (1 : 10); אהלה =
'ŏhᵒ-lô (12 : 8).

1. The a-sound was indicated, when medial, by the laryngeal א;
when final, by the laryngeal ה.

Note 1.—Medial a (ă or â) was indicated rarely; final â was
generally, though not uniformly, indicated.[2]

Note 2.—The letter א, when the final letter of a root, does not
belong here; since, in this case, it is not a vowel-letter, but has merely
lost its consonantal character.

2. The sounds û and ô were indicated by ו.

Note.—Medial û and ô were generally indicated; final û and ô
were always indicated.

3. The sounds î and ê were indicated by י.

Note.—Medial î and ê were generally indicated; final î and ê
were always indicated.

4. The sounds ê and ô, when final, were frequently indicated by ה.

Note 1.—Only *long* vowels were thus indicated, and, with but
few exceptions, besides â, only the naturally long (§ 30.) vowels.

Note 2.—Vowels indicated thus are said to be written *fully;*
when not thus indicated, they are said to be written *defectively.*

Note 3.—Briefly stated, the use of the vowel-letters may thus
be put:

The vowels î and ê, medial and final, are represented by..........י.
The vowels û and ô, medial and final, are represented by........ו.
Final vowels, except î and û, are represented by..............ה.

Note 4.—In the later books of the Old Testament the *full* writing
is more common than in the earlier books, the tone-long vowels (§ 31.)
being often thus represented.

---

[1] Hos. 10 : 14.   [2] *Cf.* קלֹך (3 : 10); אָכְלָה (3 : 11).

### 7. The Classification of the Vowel-Sounds

The primary vowel-sounds in Hebrew are represented by the three vowels ă (--), ĭ (--), and ŭ (--). Of these ă is made with the widest opening of the vocal organs; ĭ is made with a narrower opening and with the breath striking the front of the hard palate; ŭ is also made with a narrow opening, but farther back in the mouth, and with rounding of the lips.

Closely related to the foregoing are five other sounds, viz., ĕ (--), ē (--), å ( , ), ŏ (--), and ō (--). Of these, ĕ is midway between ă and ĭ, and may arise from either by *deflection*. Likewise å and ŏ are midway between ă and ŭ, and are so closely alike as to be represented by the same sign; å comes from ă under the influence of the tone by a *rounding* of the lips, while ŏ comes from ŭ without tonal influence by a lowering of the back of the tongue, which produces a greater opening as for the ă sounds—this may also be designated as *deflection*. The remaining two vowels, ē and ō, arise from ĭ and ŭ, respectively, under the influence of the tone; each of them is made farther back on the palate than its corresponding short vowel. Hence we shall speak of ē and ō as *lowered* respectively from ĭ and ŭ.

In addition to these vowel-sounds, there are two other classes, viz., those made by *lengthening* the primary vowel-sounds and those made by *reducing* them to their lowest terms.

The naturally long vowels are of three classes, viz., (1) those arising from *contraction*, e. g., ă + w = ô; (2) those arising in *compensation* for the quiescence or loss of a consonant, e. g., in יֹאמַר the א has quiesced causing ă to become â, which was then rounded to ô; (3) those which acquired their length in the earliest stages of the language and are found as characteristic of certain formations, e. g., the ô of the Ḳăl active participle which has been rounded from â.

The *reduced* vowels are of two classes, viz., (1) the simple Šᵉwâ which is a neutral sound to which any one of the short vowels may be reduced, and (2) the compound Šᵉwâ which has a distinct form for each of the three short vowels, viz., --: from ă, --: from ĭ, and --: from ŭ.

The vowel-sounds, therefore, may be classified according to (1) their organic formation, (2) their quantity, (3) their nature, (4) their value:

  1. Classified according to their *organic formation*, they are:

    *a.* A-class, including the *a*-vowels and those derived from them.

    *b.* I-class, including the *i*-vowels and those derived from them.

    *c.* U-class, including the *u*-vowels and those derived from them.

  2. Classified according to their *quantity*, they are:

| | *a*-class. | *i*-class. | *u*-class. |
|---|---|---|---|
| *a. Short,* | ◌ַ ◌ֶ | ◌ִ ◌ֵ | ◌ֻ ◌ָ(ŏ) |
| *b. Long,* | ◌ָ | י◌ִ, י◌ֶ or ◌ֵ, י◌ֶ | וּ, ◌ֻ or ◌ֹ |
| *c. Reduced,* | ◌ֲ ◌ֳ | ◌ֲ ◌ֳ | ◌ֲ ◌ֳ |

**Note.**—The vowels ◌ַ and ◌ֶ are sometimes called doubtful; because, not infrequently, they are the defective writing of a long vowel.

  3. Classified according to their *origin* or *nature*, they are:

    *a. Pure*............ă;      ĭ;      ŭ.

    *b. Deflected*.........ĕ from ă;   ĕ from ĭ;   ŏ from ŭ.

    *c. Attenuated*........ĭ from ă;

    *d. Tone-Long*.......â from ă;   ē from ĭ;   ō from ŭ.

    *e. Naturally Long*...
      â;      î;      û.
      ô from â;   ê;      ô.
      ê ( = י◌ֶ or ה◌ֶ )

    *f. Reduced*.......... ᵉ and ᵃ;  ᵉ and ᵉ;  ᵉ and ᵒ.

  4. Classified according to their *value* in inflection, they are:

    *a. Changeable*—viz., (1) all short vowels not followed by a consonant in the same syllable; (2) tone-long; (3) reduced.

    *b. Unchangeable*—viz., (1) short vowels followed by a consonant in the same syllable; (2) naturally long.

    **Note.**—*Changeable* and *unchangeable* here apply only to changes of *quantity*, not of quality.

### 8. The Names of the Vowels

The following table presents the arrangement of the vowel-sounds according to their quantity (§ **7.** *d*), and at the same time gives the technical name of each sound.

| Class. | Long. | | | Short. | | Reduced. |
|---|---|---|---|---|---|---|
| A-Class | ◌ָ â, å | Ḳâmĕṣ | ◌ַ ă | Pă𝜃åḥ | ◌ֱ e | Simple Šᵉwâ |
| | ◌ֶ ê | Sᵉ̆gôl | | | ◌ֲ a | Ḥâṭēf-Pă𝜃åḥ |
| I-Class | ◌ִ î | Ḥîrĕḳ | ◌ִ ĭ | Ḥîrĕḳ | ◌ֱ e | Simple Sᵉwâ |
| | ◌ֵ ê, ē | Ṣērê | ◌ֶ ĕ | Sᵉ̆gôl | ◌ֱ e | Ḥâṭēf-Sᵉ̆gôl |
| U-Class | וּ û | Šûrĕḳ | ◌ֻ ŭ | Ḳĭbbûṣ | ◌ֱ e | Simple Šᵉwâ |
| | ◌ֹ ô, ō | Ḥôlĕm | ◌ָ ŏ | Ḳâmĕṣ-Ḥâṭûf | ◌ֳ o | Ḥâṭēf-Ḳâmĕṣ |

### 9. Simple and Compound Šᵉwâ

1. וְ originally וְ; בְּ originally בְּ; רְקִיעַ (1 : 15), but רְקִיעַ (1 : 6).
2. אֲשֶׁר (1 : 7); יַעֲזֹב־ (2 : 24); אֱלֹהִים (1 : 1); מוֹעֲדִים (1 : 14); לְקָחָהּ (2 : 23).

1. Simple Šᵉwâ (◌ְ) is a neutral sound which may arise from any of the short vowels and represents the minimum of vowel-sound. (For transliteration and pronunciation see § 5. f.)

2. Compound Šᵉwâ (◌ֲ, ◌ֱ, ◌ֳ) is a more audible sound than simple Šᵉwâ (§ 5. 6. b. c. d.), and is found, instead of simple Šᵉwâ, chiefly under laryngeals. Each of the three classes of vowels has its own distinctive compound Šᵉwâ.

### 10. Vocal Šᵉwâ

1. בְּרֵאשִׁית (1:1); תְּהוֹם (1:2); הָיְתָה (1:2); יִשְׁרְצוּ (1:20).
2. וַיְהִי = wăy-hî (1:3); בִּרְקִיעַ = bĭr-ḳî(ă)ʿ (1:15); מַלְאוּ = mĭl-'û (1:28); בִּדְגַת = bĭd-ğă𝜃 (1:28); וַיְכָל = 'wăy-ḵăl (2:2); עָבְדָהּ = 'ŏv-dåh (2:15).
3. יַעֲזֹב־ = yă'ᵃ-zŏv (2:24); לְקָחָהּ = lŭḳº-hå (2:23); יַעֲלֶה = yă'ᵃ-lê (2:6).

1. Vocal Šᵉwâ is always *initial, i. e.,* it goes with the *following* vowel to form a syllable.

2. Certain forms in which Šᵉwâ seems to waver between two sylla-

bles, and is consequently called *medial* by many grammarians, are to be treated as follows:

*a.* Forms with wâw-conversive (§ **70.**), where the dâḡēš-fŏrtē has disappeared, were originally pronounced like wăy-yᵉhî; but with the loss of the second yôḏ the vocal Šᵉwâ also disappeared; hence such forms are better pronounced as wăy-hî, etc., ay being treated as a diphthong.

*b.* Similarly Šᵉwâ is silent in such forms with prefixed prepositions as bǐr-ḵî(ằ)ʽ and lim-ʼô-rôθ and in forms like mil-ʼû.

**Note.**—This pronunciation is attested by such forms as לְנְפֹּל[1] and חְשְׁפִי.[2] That there was more or less variation in such cases, however, is clear from the variation in the use of dâḡēš-lēnē in spirants after such a Šᵉwâ, from the fact that the Hebrew uses the same sign for a vocal Šᵉwâ and a silent Šᵉwâ, and from the testimony of the transliterations in the older strata of the Septuagint (§ **11.**). *Cf.* similar variations in spoken English, *e. g.*, tol-e-ra-ble and tol-rᵉble, con-side-ra-ble and con-sid-rᵉble; ath-letic and ath-e-letic.

*c.* In such forms as יַעֲזֹב, etc., the Šᵉwâ is only a helping vowel and does not affect the general situation; *cf.* the similar situation in such forms as שָׁלַחַתְּ, where the coming in of paθaḥ-furtive does not increase the number of syllables.

*d.* In forms with spirants after a so-called medial Šᵉwâ, the absence of the dâḡēš is a survival from an earlier stage when a vowel-sound was heard before the spirant; *cf.* again שָׁלַחַתְּ, in which the presence of the later păθăḥ-furtive does not change the older hard sound of the *t*.

### 11. Silent Šᵉwâ

1. וַיִּקְרָא = wăy-yǐḳ-rằʼ (1:5); וַיִּבְדֵּל = wăy-yăv-dēl (1:7); מַבְדִּיל = măv-dîl (1:6).

2. *a.* חֹשֶׁךְ (1:4); בְּתוֹךְ (1:6); הַהֹלֵךְ (2:14).

    *b.* אַתְּ = ʼătt; נָתַתְּ = nâ-θătt; קָטַלְתְּ = ḳằ-ṭălt.

**Remark.**—בְּרֵאשִׁית (1:1); וּבֵין (1:4); טוֹב (1:4); יוֹם (1:5); רָאשִׁים (2:10).

---

[1] Jer. 51:49.    [2] Isa. 47:2.

The simple Šᵉwâ (⸺), aside from its use to indicate a vowel-sound (§ 9.), appears frequently where it has no sound. It occurs thus:

1. Under all consonants standing in the *middle* of a word and closing a syllable (§ 26.).

2. Under a final letter, when that letter

    *a.* Is Kăf; or

    *b.* Is a consonant containing Dăǧeš-fŏrtē or lēnē, or preceded by another consonant with Šᵉwâ.

3. Under an *initial* consonant in שְׁתֵּי.

**Remark.**—The weak letters א, ה, ו, י, when quiescent, or used as vowel-letters (§ 6.), do not, of course, receive this silent Šᵉwâ.

**Note 1.**—Šᵉwâ under an *initial* consonant, whether of a word or of a syllable, is always *vocal*.

**Note 2.**—Šᵉwâ under a final consonant, whether of a word or of a syllable, is always *silent*.

# III.  Other Points

## 12.  Dåğĕš-Lēnē

1. בְּרֵאשִׁית (1:1); הָיְתָה (1:2); וְבֹחוּ (1:2); בְּתוֹךְ (1:6);
עַל־פְּנֵי (1:2); בּוֹ פְרִי (1:29); יִסְגֹּר (2:21); מַבְדִּיל (1:6).

2. בְּדֹנַת = bĭd-ğăθ (1:28); לְעׇבְדָהּ = l'ŏv-dåh (2:15).

3. בְּצַלְמוֹ בְּצֶלֶם (1:27); וּנְקֵבָה בָרָא (1:27); כִּי בְיוֹם (2:17);
רְדוּ בִדְנַת (1:28); תִּגְּעוּ בּוֹ פֶּן (3:3).

1. The letters ב, ג, ד, כ, פ, ת, have two sounds.  Their hard
sound (b, g, d, k, p, t) is indicated by a point called Dåğĕš-lēnē, which
they regularly receive whenever they do not immediately follow a
vowel-sound.

**Note 1.**—As fricatives they are pronounced: ב = v; ד = d
= th in *those;* פ = f in *fat* (cf. *ph* in *philosophy*); ת = θ = th in *thin;*
כ = χ, like German *ch* in *Kirche*, but made farther forward; ג (= ğ
in German *Tage*) is not in ordinary practice distinguished from ג (= g).

**Note 2.**—To distinguish these six fricatives from the rest of the
class thus named, we shall call them *Spirants*.  The term spirant is
commonly used in a wider sense than this, but for practical purposes
we may confine it here to this definite usage.

2. These spirants without Dåğĕš-lēnē usually follow a vowel-
sound, but sometimes the absence of the Dåğĕš persists even after
the preceding vowel has disappeared.

**Note.**—The soft sound of these letters after preceding vowels
is due to the failure to shut off completely the emission of the breath
involved in the pronunciation of the vowel which would result in a
*stop* (ד, ת, etc., cf. § 4.).  Cf. the common Irish pronunciation of
*lady* as *laḍy*, and *better* as *bĕθĕr*.

3. When by a disjunctive accent (§ 23. 2. *a*) one of these letters
is cut off from whatever may precede it, as at the beginning of a
chapter, verse, or section of a verse, it does not immediately follow a
vowel and hence takes Dåğĕš-lēnē.

### 13. *Dåḡēš-Fŏrtē*

1. הַשָּׁמַיִם = hăš-šå-mă-yĭm (1 : 1); הַמַּיִם = hăm-mă-yĭm (1 : 7);

   הַיַּבָּשָׁה = hăy-yăb-bå-šå (1 : 9); הַמְּאֹרֹת = hăm-mᵉ'ô-rôθ
   (1 : 16).

2. חַוָּה = hăw-wå (3 : 20); מִתַּחַת = mĭt-tă-ḥăθ (1 : 7); הַבְּהֵמָה
   = hăb-bᵉhē-må (1 : 25); הַדַּעַת = hăd-dă-'ăθ (2 : 17).

1. The doubling of a letter is indicated by a point in its bosom, called Dåḡēš-fŏrtē. Consonants may be doubled, however, only when they immediately follow a full vowel.

2. The point in Wåw and in the spirants is always Dåḡēš-fŏrtē, if preceded by a full vowel.

**Note 1.**—Dåḡēš-fŏrtē in a spirant serves also as Dåḡēš-lēnē, doubling the *hard*, not the *soft*, sound of the spirant.

**Note 2.**—A syllable whose final consonant has Dåḡēš-fŏrtē is called *sharpened* (§ **26.** 3).

**Note 3.**—A doubled letter is regularly preceded by a short vowel; this is generally a *pure* (§ **29.** 1–3) vowel, seldom a deflected (§ **29.** 4, 5) vowel.

### 14. *Omission of Dåḡēš-Fŏrtē*

1. וַיְכַל (2:2) *for* וַיִּכַל; וַיֵּצֶן (2:16) *for* וַיִּצֶן; אִם (2:24) *for* אִם.

2. וַיְהִי (1:3) *for* וַיְהִי; חַיְתוֹ (1:24) *for* חַיְתוֹ; לְקְחָה (2:23) *for*
   לְקְחָה.

3. הָאוֹר (1 : 4) *for* הָאוֹר; הַחֹשֶׁךְ (1 : 4) *for* הַחֹשֶׁךְ; הַהֹלֵךְ
   (2 : 14) *for* הַהֹלֵךְ.

1. Dåḡēš-fŏrtē is *always* omitted from a final vowelless consonant, there being nothing in this case to support the doubling.[1]

2. It is often omitted from medial consonants which have only a Šᵉwå to support them. (But a spirant may not thus lose Dåḡēš-fŏrtē.)

3. It is always omitted from the laryngeals, א, ה, ח, ע, and ר.

**Note 1.**—When Dåḡēš-fŏrtē is omitted from a laryngeal and no compensation made for the loss by the strengthening of the preceding vowel, the Dåḡēš is said to be implied or understood.

---

[1] The only exceptions to this statement are אַתְּ *thou* (f.), and נָתַתְּ *thou* (f.) *didst give.*

**Note 2.**—Dåğēš may be thus implied in ח, ה, and ע, but not in א and ר.

**Note 3.**—The syllable preceding a consonant in which Dåğēš-fŏrtē is thus implied is really a closed syllable.

### 15. Kinds of Dåğēš-Fŏrtē

1. מִתַּחַת (1:7) *for* מִן־תַּחַת; יִקָּווּ (1:9) *for* יִנְקָווּ; נָתַתִּי (2:21) יִקַּח (3:22) *for* מִן־מֶן־נוּ ; נָתַנְתִּי (1:29) *for* יִלְקַח.

2. הַטֵּאת (4:7); מִתְהַלֵּךְ (3:8); יְכֻלּוּ (2:1); יְקַדֵּשׁ (2:3); כִּנּוֹר (4:21).

3. לְקָחָה־זֹּאת (2:23); אֲעֶשֶׂה־לֹּו (2:18); עֹשֶׂה־פְּרִי (1:12).

4. הַלְּבֶן (17:17); הַצְּפִינוֹ (Ex. 2:3); מִקְּדָשׁ (Ex. 15:17).

5. חָדְלוּ (Judg. 5:7); וְיַחֵלּוּ (Job 29:21); יְצַתּוּ (Isa. 33:12).

6. אֵלֶּה (2:4); לָמָּה (4:6); הֵנָּה (6:2); [הֵמָּה].

1. When the doubling represents the combination of two similar, or the assimilation of two dissimilar consonants, the Dåğēš-fŏrtē is called *compensative.*

2. When the doubling is characteristic of a grammatical form, the Dåğēš-fŏrtē is called *characteristic.*

3. When by its use the initial letter of a word is joined to the final vowel of a preceding word, the Dåğēš-fŏrtē is called *conjunctive.*

4. When it is inserted in a consonant with Šᵉwâ, which is preceded by a short vowel, to make the Šᵉwâ audible, the Dåğēš-fŏrtē is called *separative.*

5. When the doubling strengthens or emphasizes the final tone-syllable of a section or verse, the Dåğēš-fŏrtē is called *emphatic.*

6. When the doubling gives greater firmness to the preceding vowel, the Dåğēš-fŏrtē is called *firmative.*

### 16. Mǎppîḳ and Râfê

1. לְאִשָּׁה (2:15); לְשָׁמְרָה (2:15); לְעָבְדָה (2:15); לְמִינָה (1:24); זַרְעָהּ (3:6); עָמָהּ (3:6); זַרְעָהּ (3:15).

2. לְמָיִם (1:6); בְּדֹנַת (1:26); לְקָחָה (2:23); וּמֵחֶלְבֵּהֶן (4:4);
וַיַּהַרְגֵהוּ (4:8).

1. Măppîķ (מַפִּיק extender) is a point placed in final ה, when this letter is used as a consonant, and not as a vowel-letter.

Note.—Măppîķ is written in MSS. also in א,[1] ו and י.

2. Râfê (רָפֶה rest) is a horizontal stroke placed over a letter, to call particular attention to the *absence* of Dâḡēš or Măppîķ.

## 17. Măķķēf

1. זַרְעוֹ־בוֹ (1:5); וַיְהִי־עֶרֶב (1:3); יְהִי־אוֹר (1:2); עַל־פְּנֵי
(1:11).

2. יִמְשָׁל־בָּךְ (3:16); כָּל־נֶפֶשׁ (1:21); אֶת־הָאוֹר (1:4); אֵת הָאוֹר
וְשֵׁם־הַנָּהָר (2:13).

1. Măķķēf (מַקֵּף binder) is a horizontal stroke placed between two words, to indicate that they are to be pronounced together and accented as if they formed but a single word.

2. If the former of two words, joined by Măķķēf, should contain a long vowel in a closed syllable (§ 26. 2), such a vowel gives way to a short vowel, or receives Mếθěḡ (§ 18. 4).

## 18. Mếθěḡ

1. הַכּוֹכָבִים (1:9); תֵּרָאֶה (1:7); הָרָקִיעַ (1:3); וַיְהִי־אוֹר
(1:16); הָאַרְבָּעִים (18:29).

2. בְּהִבָּרְאָם (2:4); תּוֹלְדוֹת (1:21); שָׁרְצוּ (1:2); הָיְתָה (2:4);
תֹּאכֵלוּ (3:1).

3. לְקָחָה (2:23); נַעֲשֶׂה (2:3); לַעֲשׂוֹת (1:26); הָאֲדָמָה (1:25);
יַעֲשׂוּ (3:7).

4. בְּתוֹךְ־הַגָּן (3:3); עֵץ־הַגָּן (3:2); וְשֵׁם־הַנָּהָר (2:13);
תֵּת־כָּחָהּ (4:12).

---

[1] A Măppîķ in א is found in printed texts in Gen. 43:26; Lev. 23:17.

5. יִהְיֶה (1:29); יִהְיוּ (2:25); בִּהְיוֹתָם (4:8); יָחֱיֶה (17:18);
וֶהְיֵה (20:7).

6. וַיֵּצֵא (4:16); וַיִּשָּׁבַע לוֹ (24:9); פַּדֶּנָה אֲרָם (28:2).

Mĕθĕǧ (מֶתֶג *bridle*) is a perpendicular line placed on the left side
of a vowel-point, to indicate that the syllable to which it belongs has
a secondary accent.[1]  The following are its chief uses:

1. On the second syllable before the tone, but generally on the
third, if the second is closed (§ **26.** 2).

2. With a long vowel followed by a vocal Šᵉwâ pretonic.

3. With all vowels before compound Šᵉwâ.

4. With a long vowel in a closed syllable, before Măķķēf.

5. With the first syllable of all forms of הָיָה and חָיָה in which
the ה and ח have Simple (*i. e.*, silent) Šᵉwâ.

6. With an unaccented ⸗ in a final syllable; and to insure the
distinct enunciation of a vowel which otherwise might be neglected.

### 19.  Ḳᵉrê and Kᵉθiv

1. הוֹצֵא (8:17) = הוֹצֵא; וַיִּשֶׂם (24:33) = וַיּוּשֶׂם; בֶּגֶד (30:11)
= בְּגָד.

2. הוֹצֵא (8:17), read הָיְצֵא; וַיִּשֶׂם (24:33) = וַיּוּשֶׂם; בְּגָד
(30:11), read בָּא גָד.

3. הוּא, to be read הִיא; יְהוִֹה, to be read אֲדֹנָי; יְהוָה, to be
read אֱלֹהִים; נַעַר, to be read נַעֲרָה.

The Hebrew text was first written with consonants only.  Not
until somewhere between 600 and 800 A. D. were the vowels written
with the consonants.  Sometimes the vowels call for a different pronunciation from that indicated by the consonants; but usually the
vowels agree with the consonants as to pronunciation.

1. Kᵉθiv (כְּתִיב, *written*) is the term applied to the pronuncia-

---

[1] Mûnăḥ (‧) is sometimes substituted for Mĕθĕǧ.

tion of a word that is called for by the consonants of the text as distinguished from the vowels written with them.

2. Ḳᵉrê (קְרִי, *to be read*) is the term applied to the pronunciation of a word called for by the vowels supplied by the Massoretes (the name applied to those students of the Hebrew text who established the traditional pronunciation represented by the present vocalization of the text).

3. Some words are always read otherwise than as they are written. These are said to have a "perpetual Ḳᵉrê."

# IV. The Accents

## 20. *The Place of the Accent*[1]

1. רֵאשִׁית (1:1); בָּרָא (1:1); שָׁמַיִם (1:1); הָאָרֶץ (1:1); חֹשֶׁךְ (1:2).

2. רֵאשִׁית (1:1); מָקוֹם (1:9); שָׁמַיִם (1:1); מַיִם (1:6); תַּחַת (1:9).

3. רֵאשִׁית (1:1); בָּרָא (1:1); מַבְדִּיל (1:6); יִקְרָא (2:23); מִתְהַלֵּךְ (3:8).

מַאֲכָל (2:9); יִקְרָא (1:5); אֶחָד (1:5); רָקִיעַ (1:6); תַּצְמִיחַ (3:18).

4. אֶרֶץ (1:10); חֹשֶׁךְ (1:2); דֶּשֶׁא (1:11); שֶׁרֶץ (1:20); עֵדֶן (2:8). אֶבֶן (1:20); נֶפֶשׁ (1:20); עֵשֶׂב (1:11); עֶרֶב (1:5); תֹהוּ (1:2); (2:12).

1. The accent or tone may rest on the ultima, in which case the word is called Mǐlră'; or on the penult, in which case the word is called Mǐl'ēl; but never on the antepenult.

2. So far as the syllabification of a word is concerned, a closed syllable with a long vowel, or an open syllable with a short vowel, is, as a rule, accented (§ 28. 1. 2).

3. Uninflected words, and words receiving in inflection no endings, are accented on the ultima.

4. Nouns of the class called Seğolates, which are really monosyllabic (§ 89.), usually accent the characteristic vowel and not the helping vowel.

**Note 1.**—The place of the accent in *inflected* words, involving appendages, must be studied in connection with the subject of verbal and nominal inflection.

---

[1] The place of the accent is indicated in this grammer by the the use of the accent ⸗. Words which are not thus indicated are to be accented on the ultima.

21

**Note 2.**—The term "accent" is used of the sign marking the syllable which receives the stress of voice; the term "tone" is used of the *stress* of voice.

### 21. Shifting of the Tone

1. קָרָא לָיְלָה (1:5); עָשָׂה פְרִי (1:11); תֹּאכַל לֶחֶם (3:19).

2. אַתָּה (4:7), but אַתָּה (3:11); אָנֹכִי (7:4), but אָנֹכִי (4:9).

3. וַיֹּאמֶר (1:3); וַיְבָרֶךְ (1:22); וַיִּיצֶר (2:7); וַיָּקֶם (4:8).

4. וְהִצַּלְתִּי, וְהוֹצֵאתִי, וְהֵבֵיתִי (Ex. 3:20); וְאָכַלְתָּ (3:18); (Ex. 6:6).

1. The tone is often shifted from the ultima to the penult of a word which is followed closely by a monosyllable, or by a dissyllable accented upon the penult.

2. The tone is sometimes shifted in the case of words standing at the end of a clause or section, *i. e., in pause* (§ 38.).

3. Wāw Conversive with the Imperfect usually causes shifting of the tone from the ultima to the penult when the latter is an open syllable (§ 73.) and the former is closed.

4. Wāw Conversive with the Perfect often causes shifting of the tone from the penult to the ultima (§ 73.).

### 22. The Table of Accents

#### 1. DISJUNCTIVES

**Class I.—Emperors**

| | | | |
|---|---|---|---|
| 1. סִלּוּק׃ Sĭllûk.......... אֶ | | 3. סְגֹלְתָּא Sᵉḡōltå........ אֱ |
| 2. אֶתְנָח 'Aθnåḥ......... אֱ | | 4. שַׁלְשֶׁלֶת Šalšéleθ...... אֱ |

**Class II.—Kings**

| | |
|---|---|
| 5. זָקֵף קָטֹן Zåḵēf ḵåṭōn.. אֶ | 7. רְבִיעַ Rᵉvî(ă)'.......... אֶ |
| 6. זָקֵף גָּדוֹל Zåḵēf gåḏôl... אֱ | |

**Class III.—Dukes**

| | |
|---|---|
| 8. פַּשְׁטָא Påšṭå.......... אֱ | 11. תְּבִיר Tᵉvîr........... אֶ |
| 9. יְתִיב Yᵉθîv........... אֶ | 12. זַרְקָא Zărḵå.......... אֱ |
| 10. טִפְחָא Ṭĭfḥå.......... אֱ | |

Class IV.—Counts

13. גֵּרֶשׁ Gĕrĕš............א

14. גְּרְשַׁ֞יִם Gᵉrǎšayim......א

15. לְגַרְמֶהּ׀ Lᵉḡarmĕh[1]....א׀

16. פָּזֵר Pāzēr............א

17. קַרְנֵי פָרָה Ḳărnê Fårå..א

18. תְּלִישָׁא גְדוֹלָה Tᵉlišå Gᵉdôlå....א

2. CONJUNCTIVES

Class V.—Servants

19. מֵרְכָא Mĕrχå..........א

20. מֵרְכָא כְפוּלָא Mĕrχå χᵉfûlå......א

21. מוּנַח Mûnăḥ..........א

22. דַּרְגָּא Dărgå............א

23. קַדְמָא Ḳădmå........א

24. מַהְפַּךְ Măhpăχ.......א

25. תְּלִישָׁא קְטַנָּה Tᵉlišå Ḳᵉṭănnå.......א

26. יְרַח בֶּן־יוֹמוֹ Yĕrăḥ bĕn yômô.......א

27. מְאַיְלָא Mᵉʾăy-yᵉlå[2]......א

### 23. Remarks on the Table of Accents

1. The "Accents" were designed to have a threefold use:

a. To serve as musical notes in the cantillation of the Law and the Prophets in the synagogue;

b. To indicate the tone-syllable (i. e., the syllable which is to be accented) of every word;

c. To show the relation sustained by each word to the other words in a clause or sentence.

2. Every accent is used as a sign of interpunction (§ 23. 1. c), to separate or join the several words of a sentence:

a. Disjunctives (those numbered 1–18 in the Table) mark a separation.

b. Conjunctives (those numbered 19–27 in the Table) mark a connection.

3. The Disjunctives vary in strength or power, and are accordingly divided into four ranks: Emperors, Kings, Dukes, Counts.

4. Those accents numbered 9 and 18 are pre-positive, i. e., written

[1] Made up of Mûnăḥ and Pᵉsîḳ.
[2] Used for Mĕθĕḡ with words which have Sillûḳ or 'Aθnăḥ.

only on the first letter of a word, wherever the tone-syllable of that word may be.

5. Those accents numbered 3, 8, 12, 25 are *post*-positive, *i. e.*, written only on the last letter of a word, wherever the tone-syllable of that word may be.

6. The post-positive accents are repeated whenever their word is accented on the Penult, or has Păθăḥ-furtive (§ **42.** 2. *d*) under the last letter.

7. Sïllûḳ may be distinguished from Mĕθĕǧ (§ **18.**), Păšṭă from Ḳădmă, and Y⁽θîv from Măhpăχ by their position.

### 24. The Consecution of the More Common Accents

1. : הָאָֽרֶץ . . . . . . . . . . . . . . . . . . . . . . . . . . . . . . . . . . . . Gen. 1 : 1.

2. : הָאָֽרֶץ . . . . . . . . . אֱלֹהִים . . . . . . . . . . . . . . . . . . . . . . Gen. 1 : 1.

3. : כֵּֽן . . . . . . . . . . . . . . . לָרָקִיעַ . . . . . . . הָרָקִֽיעַ . . . . . . . Gen. 1 : 7.

: עַל־הָאָֽרֶץ . . . . . . וְכִבְשֻׁהָ . . . . . . . אֱלֹהִים֒ . . . . . . . Gen. 1 : 28.

1. Every verse (Păsûḳ) is separated from the verse following by the sign **:**, called Sôf Păsûḳ (*end of the verse*); while the last word of every verse has on its tone-syllable the accent ⌐⌐, called Sïllûḳ, which, in form, is like Mĕθĕǧ (§ **18.**).

**Note.**—Since Sïllûḳ always stands on the last tone-syllable of a verse, while Mĕθĕǧ never stands on a tone-syllable, they are easily distinguished.

2. If the verse contain *two* primary sections, Sïllûḳ marks the end of the *first*, while the end of the second is indicated by ⌐⌐, 'Aθnăḥ.

**Note 1.**—In the study of the accentuation of a verse one must begin with Sïllûḳ, *i. e.*, at the end of the verse.

**Note 2.**—These accents have only relative power. The pauses marked are logical pauses.

3. If the verse contain *three* primary sections, Sïllûḳ marks the end of the first; 'Aθnăḥ, the end of the second; while the end of the third is indicated by ⌐⌐, called S⁽ǧôltă.

**Note.**—For an explanation of the repetition of ⌐⌐, see § **23.** 6.

4. : הַמָּיִם......אֱלֹהִים......תְהוֹם........וָבֹהוּ...Gen. 1:2

5. *a.* הַלָּיְלָה...........לְהַבְדִּיל.........הַשָּׁמַיִם..Gen. 1:14.

*b.* הַיַּבָּשָׁה.............אֶחָד..וַיֹּאמֶר אֱלֹהִים...Gen. 1:9.

6. : הָאָרֶץ...הַשָּׁמַיִם.....אֱלֹהִים....בְּרֵאשִׁית...Gen. 1:1.

: הַחֹשֶׁךְ......הָאוֹר......אֶת־הָאוֹר כִּי־טוֹב...Gen. 1:4.

...אֱלֹהִים...אֹתָם.Gen. 1:28....וֹאת....הַנָּחָשׁ..Gen. 3:14.

4. When a *primary* section is large enough to be divided, or to contain a *secondary* section, the end of this secondary section, whether it stand in the primary section ruled by Sĭllûḳ or 'Aθnåḥ, is most frequently marked by ֔, called Zåḳēf ḳåṭōn.

5. *a.* In secondary sections containing but a single word, where Zåḳēf ḳåṭōn would have been expected, Zåḳēf gåđôl, ֕, is generally found instead.

*b.* A secondary section of less importance than that which is indicated by Zåḳēf ḳåṭōn is marked by ֗, called Rᵉvî(ă)'.

6. The pause required by the rhythm before Sĭllûḳ and 'Aθnåḥ is marked by a disjunctive ֖, called Ṭĭfḥå; that before Sᵉgōltå, by ֮, called Zårḳå.

**Note.**—For the consecution of the remaining disjunctives see the Table of Consecution of Accents (§ 25.).

7. : וְאֵת הָאָרֶץ.........(1:1); : עַל־פְּנֵי הַמָּיִם.........(1:2);

: וּבֵין הַחֹשֶׁךְ........(1:4).

8. בָּרָא אֱלֹהִים.........(1:1); עַל־פְּנֵי תְהוֹם........(1:2);

קָרָא לָיְלָה......(1:5).

9. כִּי עָשִׂיתָ זֹּאת.......(3:14); אֲשֶׁר בְּתוֹךְ־הַגָּן......(3:3).

7. The Conjunctive accent which always accompanies Sĭllûḳ is ֥, called Mĕrχå.

8. The Conjunctive accent which always accompanies 'Aθnåḥ is ֣, called Mûnåḥ.

9. The Conjunctive accent which always accompanies Sᵉgōltå is likewise Mûnåḥ.

## 25. A Table Showing the Consecution of the Accents

### REMARKS ON THE TABLE

1. The Consecution of Sïllûḳ and 'Aθnâḥ, with the exception of the first conjunctive, is the same.

2. The *third* disjunctive preceding Sïllûḳ and 'Aθnâḥ, the *second* preceding Sᵉġōltâ and Zâḳēf ḳâṭōn, and the *first* preceding Rᵉvî(ă)ʽ is Gérēš, after which the consecution is the same for all.

3. This Gérēš may be entirely omitted, in which case the servant of the preceding disjunctive will be present and will assume the functions of Gérēš.

4. After Ḳădmâ the consecution may proceed either with Tᵉlîšâ Ḳᵉṭănnâ (and its Mûnâḥ's) or, if there is a slight emphasis, with the disjunctive Tᵉlîšâ Ġᵉdôlâ (and its Mûnâḥ's).

5. Words standing between the Tᵉlîšâ Ḳᵉṭănnâ or the Tᵉlîšâ Ġᵉdôlâ and the beginning of the section, will receive Mûnâḥ if they are closely related, but Pâzēr if there is a great emphasis. Words standing between Pâzēr and the beginning of the verse will receive Mûnâḥ.

**Note.**—Instead of Mûnâḥ, Lᵉġărmēh (*i. e.*, Mûnâḥ with Pᵉsîḳ (|–⊤–)) is substituted if there is a slight emphasis on the word.

6. Instead of Pâzēr, preceded by Mûnâḥ, there may be substituted Ḳărnê Fârâ, which is always preceded by Yĕrăḥ bĕn yômô. Other words will have Mûnâḥ.

Note 1.—This table exhibits in general the features of the prose system. There are, however, many exceptions. The poetic system is entirely different.

Note 2.—A few accents, occurring but seldom, are omitted from the table.

Note 3.—This very brief treatment of the accent aims only to introduce the student to a subject, which demands much careful study and investigation for its mastery. Reference may be made to Wickes, *A Treatise on the Accentuation of the Twenty-One so-called Prose Books of the Old Testament* (1886); *Idem, A Treatise on the Three so-called Poetical Books of the Old Testament, Psalms, Proverbs and Job* (1881).

# V. Syllables

## 26. Kinds of Syllables

1. יְהִי (1:2); פְּנֵי (1:2); וְרְבְֿהוּ (1:2); תְֿהוּ (1:2); בְּרָא (1:1); (1:3).

2. מַזְרִיעַ (1:11); טוֹב (1:4); בֵּין (1:4); מַבְֿדִיל (1:6); לִמְשֹׁל (1:18).

1. Syllables which end in a vowel-sound are called *open*.
2. Syllables which end in a consonant are called *closed*.

**Note 1.**—A *closed* syllable whose final consonant is doubled is called *sharpened*.

**Note 2.**—What seems to be an unaccented *open* syllable, with a short vowel, is of frequent occurrence; this is commonly called a half-open syllable; but it is better treated as closed (§ 10.).

## 27. Syllabification

1. אֲשֶׁר (1:7); רְקִיעַ (1:20); וּֿמֵֿחָלְֿבֵֿהֶן (4:4).

2. וּֿבֵין (1:4); אֱלֹֿהִים (1:1); בְּרֵאֿשִׁית (1:1); יִֿשְֿׁרְֿצוּ (1:20).

3. עָרֶב (1:5) for עֶרֶב; יֶרֶב (1:22) for יִֿרְֿבֶּ; וַֿיֶּֿשֶׂת (9:21).

1. A word contains as many syllables as it has vowels; but Păθăḥ-furtive (§ 42. 2. *d*), and Š͏ᵉwâ do not form syllables.

2. Syllables must *begin* with a consonant, the only exception being the prefixed conjunction וּ; they *may* begin with two consonants, the first always having under it a vocal Š͏ᵉwâ.[1]

**Remark.**—Syllables often occur which apparently begin with a Š͏ᵉwâ. These are cases in which Š͏ᵉwâ creeps in after a laryngeal as a transitional or liaison element linking the two syllables together and facilitating pronunciation of the laryngeal. The Š͏ᵉwâ is better treated as belonging with the preceding laryngeal.

---

[1] There is a single exception to this remark, viz., שְׁתֵּי (Gen. 4 : 19) in which the Š͏ᵉwâ is silent.

3. Syllables may end in *two* consonants, but only when these are strong. The harshness resulting from this combination is generally avoided by the insertion of a helping vowel (§ **36.**).

### 28.　*Quantity of the Vowel in Syllables*

1. בָּרָא (1:1); בְּרֵא־שִׁית (1:1); מֵ־עַל (1:7); הָ־אֹור (1:4); הָ־יְתָה (1:2).

2. אֵת (1:1); מַבְ־דִּיל (1:6); מִקְ־וֵה (1:10); וַיִּקְ־רָא (1:5); מֵ־עַל (1:7).

3. הַשָּׁמַיִם (1:1); לְאִשָּׁה (2:22); אִמֹּו (2:24); יָקֻם (4:15).

4. (*a*). הַ־חֹשֶׁךְ (1:4);

   (*b*). נַעֲשֶׂה (1:26);

   (*c*). בִּרְקִיעַ (1:14); מָלְאוּ (1:22);

   (*d*). וַאֲדֹנָי (18:12).

5. בֵּית (6:14); מַיִם (1:6); יֵרֶב (1:22); נַעַר (19:4).

1. The vowel of an unaccented open syllable must be long.

2. The vowel of a closed syllable must be short, unless it has the tone; when it has the tone, it *may be* long.

3. The vowel of the sharpened syllable is short, unless it has the tone; it is pure, *i. e.*, ă, ĭ, ŭ, and not deflected, *i. e.*, ĕ or ŏ.

4. Short vowels are often found in what appear to be unaccented open syllables, and are often called half-open syllables; but they are better treated as closed syllables. For example in (*a*) dåğēš-fŏrtē is implied or understood, thus making the syllable closed; in (*b*) the laryngeal once had no vowel (*cf.* (²תַּעֲדֶה ;יְיֹּאסֹר¹[Isa. 61:10]; נֶחְמָד [2:9]; and the Šᵉwâ is therefore only a secondary helping-element and does not affect the syllabification; in (*c*) the Šᵉwâ is to be treated as silent (*cf.* § **10.**); in (*d*) the laryngeal was once vocal and closed the syllable, and the short vowel persists even though the laryngeal has become quiescent (*cf.* § **10.**).

5. The vowel of an open accented syllable may be short.

---
¹ 1 Kgs. 20:14.　　　　² Isa. 61:10.

# VI. Euphony of Vowels[1]

## 29. *Short Vowels*

1. *a.* יַבְדֵּל (1:4); יַבָּשָׁה (1:9); יַמִּים (1:10); חַיָּה (1:20); מַזְרִיעַ (1:11).

   *b.* אַף (1:7); מֵֽ־עַל (1:25); וְהַב־ (2:12); גַּן (2:8); חַיַּת־ (3:1).

   *c.* שַׁבַּת (2:3); לָקַח (2:22); דָּבַק (2:24); לָקַח (3:23); יַצְמַח (2:9).

   *d.* הֱשִׁיאַנִי (3:13); אַיִן (2:5); הַדַּעַת (2:9); פַּעַם (2:23); בֵּיתָה (15:5); שָׁמַיְמָה (24:32).

   *e.* מַאֲכָל (1:26); יַעֲלֶה (2:6); לַעֲבֹד (2:5); נַעֲשֶׂה (2:9).

2. *a.* הִנֵּה (1:29); אִשְׁתּוֹ (2:24); אִמּוֹ (2:24); יִרֶב (1:22); יִבֶן (2:22).

   *b.* [קְטֵל]; יִקְרָא (1:5); הַמְטִיר (1:18); לִמְשֹׁל (2:5); נִפְקְחוּ (3:5).

3. *a.* וַיְכֻלּוּ (2:1); עֵירֻמִּים (3:7); לֻקַּח (3:23); יֻקַּם (4:24); [חֻקָּה].

---

1. The pure short ă is found:

   *a.* In unaccented closed, or sharpened syllables;

   *b.* In the closed syllable with secondary accent of nouns in the construct state, and a few monosyllabic nouns and particles;

   *c.* In the accented closed syllable of many verbal forms.

   *d.* (1) As the accented characteristic vowel of laryngeal and ע״י Seǧolates (§ 89.); (2) before the suffix נִי, and (3) sometimes before the locative ending הָ‍.

---

[1] This treatment is not intended to be exhaustive; it will be found practically complete, however, so far as general principles are concerned.

*e.* In a closed syllable with Mé$\theta$ĕǧ (§ **18.** 3) before a compound Šᵉwâ.

2. The pure short ĭ is found:

*a.* In unaccented closed, and especially sharpened, syllables, and in some accented open syllables (§ **28.** 5); but

*b.* That ĭ (‑‑) which comes by attenuation or thinning (§ **36.** 4) from an original ă must be distinguished from an original ĭ, although it is subject to the same rules as the latter.

3. The pure short ŭ is found almost exclusively in unaccented sharpened syllables.

4. ‑אֶת (1:4); וַיְבָרֶךְ (1:22); וַיָּשֶׂם (2:8); וַיְגָרֶשׁ (3:24); וַתֵּלֶד (4:1).

וַיִּבֶן (2:22); יָרֶב (1:22); עֵזֶר (2:18); עֵשֶׂב (1:11); חֹשֶׁךְ (1:2); נֶחְמָד (2:9); [וַיֶּעְטַל]; עֲבָד; אֶרֶץ; יֶדְכֶם (9:2).

5. ‑כָּל (1:21); אָכְלָה (1:29); כָּתְנוֹת (3:21); רָחְבָּהּ (6:15); [הָקְטַל].

עֲבָדָה (2:15); שָׁמְרָה (2:15); ‑אָכָל (3:11); יֶעֱזֹב (2:24).

4. The short *e*-sound ‑‑ (ĕ), as a deflection from ă or ĭ, is found:

*a.* In unaccented closed syllables in general.

*b.* As an unaccented vowel in certain forms with wâw conversive.

*c.* As a helping-vowel in Seǧolate nouns.

*d.* As the characteristic accented vowel in Seǧolate forms.

*e.* In unaccented closed syllables before laryngeals.

**Note 1.**—There is also to be noticed the character of the ‑‑ which appears in certain particles, *e. g.*, פֶּן, אֲשֶׁר, etc., and pronominal forms (כֵּן; כֶם; תֶּן; תֶּם; אַתֶּם); the origin of which is obscure.

5. The short *o*-sound ‑‑ (ŏ), deflected from and more common than ‑‑ (ŭ) and sustaining to ‑‑ and ‑‑ (ō) the same relation that is sustained by ‑‑ (ĕ) to ‑‑ (ĭ) and ‑‑ (ē), is found in unaccented closed syllables.

### 30. *Naturally Long Vowels*

1. *a.* נָע (4 : 14) = nâ'; שָׁת (4 : 25) = šâθ; [קָל = ḳâl].

   *b.* גַּנָּב=gănnâv¹; מַתָּן=mắttân²; כָּתַב=kʻθâv³; קָרֵב=ḳʻrâv.⁴

   *c.* אֱלֹהִים (1 : 1) = 'ᵉlôhîm *for* 'ᵉlâhîm; יֹאמֶר (1 : 3) = yô'měr *for* yâ'měr; גָּדֹל (1 : 16)=gâdôl *for* gâdâl; אָכֹל (2 : 16) = 'âχôl *for* 'âχâl.

2. *a.* וִיהִי = וְיהִי (1:6); יִיצֶר = יִיצֶר (2:7); יִישָׁן = יִישָׁן (2:21).

   *b.* יָמִין = yâmîn⁵; חָסִיד = ḥâsîd⁶; מָשִׁיחַ = mâšî(ă)ḥ.⁷

   *c.* פִּילֶגֶשׁ⁸; קְטֹור *for* קִיטֹור

   *d.* עָשִׂית (3 : 13) *for* עָשִׂיתָ (עָשִׂיתָ); צִוִּיתִי (3 : 17) *for* צִוִּיתִי (צִוִּיתִי).

   *e.* הִשִּׂיא (3:13); הִגִּיד (3:11); יַלְבִּשֶׁם (3:21); הִמְטִיר (2:5); הַבְדִּיל (1:18).

   *f.* מֵקִים (9 : 9); תָּשִׂים (6 : 16);

3. *a.* קוּם¹¹; יְקוּם¹⁰; תָּשׁוּב (3 : 19);

   *b.* הוֹסַד=הוּסַד¹²; בְּהוּ = בֹּהוּ (1 : 2); תְּהוּ = תֹּהוּ (1 : 2); הוּקַם¹³.

   *c.* אָרוּר (3 : 14); עָרוּם (3 : 1); הַבּוּרָה (4 : 23); כְּרוּב (3 : 24); רְכוּשׁ (12 : 5).

Naturally long vowels have arisen either (1) from contraction of a vowel and semivowel (*i. e.*, *y* or *w*), or (2) as the characteristic of certain nominal and verbal forms, or (3) in compensation.

   1. Naturally long â (◌ָ, seldom אָ), comparatively rare, is found:

     *a.* In certain forms of middle-vowel verbs (§ 89.) of which it is characteristic.

     *b.* In certain nominal forms, of which it is characteristic (§§ 94, 95.).

---

¹ Ex. 22 : 1, 6, 7.    ² Gen. 34 : 12; 2 Kgs. 11 : 18.    ³ Esth. 4 : 8.
⁴ 2 Sam. 17 : 11.    ⁵ Gen. 13 : 9.    ⁶ Ps. 30 : 5.
⁷ 1 Sam. 2 : 10.    ⁸ Gen. 19 : 28.    ⁹ Judg. 19 : 2.
¹⁰ Ex. 21 : 19.    ¹¹ Gen. 13 : 17.    ¹² Ezra 3 : 11.
¹³ Ex. 40 : 17.

*c.* Naturally long â, in the great majority of instances, was rounded to ô (§ **30.** 6).

2. Naturally long î (י ‿, sometimes ‿), is found:

*a.* As the contraction of *iy* (§ **83.** *f*).

*b.* In certain nominal forms of which it is characteristic (§ **94.**).

*c.* In certain nominal forms in which it is compensative (§ **95.**).

*d.* In certain ל״ה forms, before consonant-additions (§ **85.**).

*e.* In Hifʻil forms, in which ē would naturally have been expected.

*f.* In certain forms of middle-vowel verbs.

3. Naturally long û (ו, sometimes ‿) is found:

*a.* As characteristic of certain middle-vowel Ḳal forms (§ **89.**).

*b.* As the contraction of *uw*, whenever the combination *uw* would be final; in certain פ״ו Hŏfʻäl forms (§ **83.**); and in certain middle-vowel and ע״ע Hŏfʻäl forms, which seem to follow the analogy of פ״ו forms.

*c.* As characteristic of certain nominal forms, including the Ḳal passive participle.

4. *a.* בֵּין (1 : 4); בַּיִת¹; עֵינַיִם (3 : 6).

*b.* תֵּיטִיב (4 : 7) = têṭîv *from* תֵּיטִיב; הֵינִיקָה (21 : 7) *from* הֵינִיקָה.

*c.* עֲשֵׂה (6 : 14) = ʻᵃśê *from* עֲשֵׂי; מִקְוֵה (1 : 10) = mĭḳwê *from* מִקְוֵי.

*d.* צִוִּיתִי (3 : 11)].; הָרְאֵת⁴; צִוִּיתִי³; הִכֵּיתִי² [*cf.*

*e.* דְּמֵי (1 : 2) = pᵉnê *from* פְּנֵי; שְׁנֵי (1 : 16); עֵינֵי (3 : 7); פְּנֵי (4 : 10).

*f.* מֵישָׁר⁷ *from* מֵישָׁר; אֵיתָן⁶ *from* אֵיתָן; מֵיטָב⁵ *from* מֵיטָב.

5. *a.* תְּפוּצֶינָה¹²; תַּעֲשֶׂינָה⁸; תִּבְכֶּינָה⁹; תְּסֻבֶּינָה¹⁰; תִּצְלֶינָה¹¹.

*b.* [סוּסִיהָ]; פָּנֶיךָ (4 : 6); אַפֶּיךָ (3 : 19); חַיֶּיךָ (3 : 14).

*c.* הַשָּׂדֶה (2 : 5); עֲשֵׂה (1 : 11); יַעֲשֶׂה (18 : 25).

---

¹ Gen. 12 : 15.　　　² Ex. 3 : 10.　　　³ Deut. 3 : 21.　　　⁴ Deut. 4 : 35.
⁵ 1 Sam. 15 : 9.　　⁶ Gen. 49 : 24.　　⁷ Isa. 26 : 7.　　　⁸ Deut. 1 : 44.
⁹ Ruth 1 : 9.　　　¹⁰ Gen. 37 : 7.　　¹¹ 1 Sam. 3 : 11.　　¹² Zech. 13 : 7.

**4.** Naturally long ê (written ‏יָ‎, yet sometimes ‏ַ‎ and ‏הָ‎) comes from the contraction of *ay* or *ai*, and is found:

*a.* In the inflection of ‏עָ"ו‎ Seğolates (§ 84.).

*b.* In the Hif'il forms of verbs originally ‏פָ"י‎.

*c.* In the Imperative (2 m. sg.) of verbs ‏לָ"ה‎ (§ 85.); and in the construct state of nouns ending in ‏הָ‎ (ê) (§ 110.).

*d.* In ‏לָ"ה‎ perfects before consonant additions (§ 85.).

*e.* In the plural construct ending of masc. nouns, ‏לָ"ה‎ (§ 110.).

*f.* In the penult of a few nominal formations.

**Note.**—The ê of *d* very frequently yields to î, especially in *active perfects*.

**5.** Besides ê, there is another naturally long *e*-sound, which likewise arises out of *ay*. It is written ‏יֶ‎ and ‏הֶ‎ and may, for the sake of distinction, be transliterated as *ệ*. It is found:

*a.* In ‏לָ"ה‎ Imperfects and Imv's before the fem. plur. termination ‏נָה‎ (§ 85.); and, after the analogy of these forms, also as a separating vowel in similar middle-vowel and ‏עָ"ע‎ forms.

*b.* In the forms of plural nouns before the pronominal suffixes ‏ךָ‎ and ‏ךְ‎ (§ 111.).

*c.* In the absolute forms of nouns from ‏לָ"ה‎ roots and in the Ḳăl Impf. and the Participles of ‏לָ"ה‎ verbs.

**6.** *a.* ‏אָכֹל‎ (2 : 16) = 'ăχôl *for* 'ăχâl; ‏יֵצֵא‎ (2:10) = yôṣē', *for* yâṣē'; ‏רֹמֵשׂ‎ (1 : 26) = rômēś *for* râmēś; ‏סוֹבֵב‎ (2 : 13) = sôvēv *for* sâvēv.

*b.* ‏יֹאמֶר‎ (1 : 3) = yô'mĕr *for* yâ'mĕr; [‏יִקֹּל‎ = yĭḳḳôl *for* yĭḳḳâl].

*c.* ‏אֱלֹהִים‎ (1:1)='ĕlôhîm; ‏דּוֹר‎ (6 : 9); ‏עוֹלָם‎ (3 : 22); ‏שָׁלוֹם‎ (26 : 31).

*d.* ‏יְעוֹפֵף‎ (1 : 20) = yᵉʻôfēf; ‏יִתְבֹּשָׁשׁוּ‎ (2 : 25) = yĭθbôšăšû.

*e.* ‏הֲקִמֹתִי‎ (6 : 18); ‏הֲשִׁיבֹתִיךָ‎ (28 : 15); ‏סַבֹּתִי‎[1]; ‏קָלֹּות‎[2].

**7.** *a.* ‏יוֹם‎ (1 : 5); ‏תוֹךְ‎ (1 : 6) = θôχ [*cf.* ‏וְתָוֶךְ‎].

*b.* ‏תֹּסֵף‎ (4 : 2) = tôsĕf; ‏הוֹלִידוֹ‎ (5 : 4); ‏נוֹרָא‎[3].

---

[1] 1 Sam. 22 : 22.                    [2] Nahum 1 : 14.                    [3] Isa. 18 : 2.

c. תּוֹלְדוֹת (2 : 4); מוֹעֵד (1 : 14).

d. אֹהֳלֹה (12 : 8); זַרְעוֹ (1 : 11); בּוֹ (1 : 11); לְמִינוֹ (1 : 11).

8.    תֵּרָאֶה (1 : 9); הֶעָרִים (19 : 25, 29); בְּעָנָן (9 : 13, 14, 16); מְבֹרָךְ[1]

6. Naturally long ô, for the most part written defectively, is in many cases only the rounding of a naturally long â (§ 30. 1). This is the case:

a. In the forms of the Infinitive Absolute (§ 70. 1. b), and in the Ḳăl Active Participle (§ 71. 1. a).

b. In the Ḳăl Imperfect of verbs פ״א (§ 82.), and in the Nïf'ăl of middle-vowel verbs (§ 89.).

c. In a large number of nominal formations (§§ 94, 95.).

d. In so-called Pôlēl (or Pô'ēl), and Hïθpôlēl (or Hïθpô'ēl) forms.

e. In the separating vowel used before consonant terminations in the Perfects of ע״ע and middle-vowel verbs (§§ 88, 89.).

7. There is, however, a second naturally long ô, which is the result of the contraction of au or aw. This is found:

a. In a large number of monosyllabic nouns from middle-vowel stems.

b. In the Nïf'ăl and Hïf'ïl of verbs originally פ״ו (§ 80. 3. b).

c. In many פ״ו nominal formations (§§ 99, 101.).

d. In the contraction of âhû = ô (seldom written ֹה).

8. Vowels strengthened in compensation for the loss of a consonant are unchangeable, like naturally long vowels.

Note 1.—Naturally long vowels are usually written fully (§ 6. 4. N. 2), and are thus distinguished from tone-long vowels. There are many cases, however, in which the distinction can be determined only from a knowledge of the grammatical form in which the vowel stands.

Note 2.—Naturally long vowels are unchangeable. The exceptions to this rule are so few as scarcely to deserve notice.

[1] Num. 22 : 6.

### 31. Tone-Long Vowels

1. *a.* אָדָם (1:26); אֶחָד (1:5); אָכְלָתְ (3:11); יִצְמָח (2:5); תָּוֶךְ (15:10).

  *b.* יַבָּשָׁה (1:9); בְּהֵמָה (1:26); חַיָּה (1:28); בָּרָא (1:1); מָוֶת[1] (1:1); הָאָרֶץ (1:1); הִשְׁקָה (2:6); יִקְרָא (1:5).

  *c.* רָקִיעַ (1:6) *for* רְ־קִיעַ; בָּרָא (1:1) *for* בַּרָא; יִקְרֵא (2:23); תִּפָּקַחְנָה (3:7); מָ־קוֹם (1:9) *for* מַקוֹם; תָּשׁוּב (3:19); וָבְהוּ (1:2).

  *d.* תִּפָּקַחְנָה (3:7); בָּנֶיהָ[2]; צִוִּיתִיךָ (3:11); אָכְלָתְ (3:11); צָפֹנָה (13:14); לַיְלָה (1:5).

A short vowel (־ַ, ־ִ, ־ֻ), when it would stand in close proximity to the tone, frequently becomes long, ă becoming å, ĭ becoming ē, ŭ becoming ō. These vowels are called, from their origin, *tone*-long.

1. Tone-long å, instead of an original ă, is found:

  *a.* In a closed *tone*-syllable,
    (1) in the absolute state of nouns;
    (2) in pause (§ **38.**);
    (3) in a few Seğolates from middle-vowel roots;

  *b.* In an open *tone*-syllable,
    (1) in the more recent feminine ending ־ָה (from ăθ) (§ **109. 2.** *b*);
    (2) in ל"ה and ל"א verbal forms (§§ **85, 86. 1.** *a*);
    (3) in some Seğolate nouns;

  *c.* In an open *pretone*-syllable; *always*, except as indicated in § **32. 2.**

  *d.* In an open *posttone*-syllable,
    (1) in the case of the pronominal ending תָּ, and frequently the suffixes הָ and ךָ;
    (2) in the feminine plural termination נָה, and the locative ending, ־ָה (*directive*) (§ **108.**).

---

[1] Deut. 19:6.      [2] Ruth 1:3.

2. *a.* [זָקֵן ;לָבַשׁ ;וַיִּבֶשׁ] רָמֶשׂ (1:26); הָלַךְ (2:14); ־ֶ

(2:11); יִתֵּן (1:17); תֵּת (4:12); תֵּן (4:42); יֵצֵא (4:16);

שֵׁב (20:15); יְקַדֵּשׁ (2:3); יַבְדֵּל (1:4); יִשְׁכֵּן (3:24);

יִתְחַבֵּא (3:8); מִתְהַלֵּךְ (3:8); זָקֵן (19:4); עָקֵב (3:15);

מָגֵן (15:1); עָרֵל (17:14); שָׁלֵם (15:16); עֵץ (2:16); שֵׁם

(2:11); אֵת (1:1); כֵּן (1:7); בֵּן (4:25); עֵשָׂב (1:11);

עֵזֶר (2:18); סֵפֶר (5:1); יֵצֶר (6:5); עֵדֶן (2:8).

*b.* בְּהֵמָה (1:24); נְקֵבָה (1:27); תַּרְדֵּמָה (2:21); לֵבָב (Dt.

28:28); שֵׁנִי (1:8); יֵצֵא (4:16); וַיֵּשֶׁב (4:16) *for* יֵשֵׁב;

יֵדַע (4:17) *for* יֵדַע.

3. *a.* מָשֹׁל (1:18); יִשְׁבֹּת (2:2); יִסְגֹּר (2:21); קָטֹנְתִּי (32:11);

יָכֹלְתִּי (30:8); אָדֹם (25:30); עָמֹק [1]; כֹּל (1:30).

*b.* שֹׁהַם (1:5); בֹּקֶר (1:2); חֹשֶׁךְ (1:2); בֹהוּ (1:2); תֹהוּ

(2:12).

*c.* יְבָרֶךְ [4]; מְבָרֶךְ [3]; go-rᵉšû [2]; גֹּרְשׁוּ.

2. Tone-long ─, instead of short ─ or ─, is found:

 *a.* In a closed *tone*-syllable; always, except in a few monosyllabic particles. Worthy of notice is its occurrence,

  (1) in the Ḳăl Perfect of many stative verbs (§ 64. 2), and in the Ḳăl Active Participle (§ 71. 1. *a*);

  (2) in the Ḳăl Imperfect and Imperative of נָתַן (§ 81.), and of verbs originally פ"ן (§ 83.);

  (3) in Nĭf'ăl, Pĭ'ēl, Hĭf'ĭl and Hĭθpă'ēl forms in which the ĭ, whence ē comes, was originally ă (§§ 59. 1. *b*, 60. 1. *b*);

  (4) in many monosyllabic and dissyllabic nominal formations;

  (5) in *i*-class Segŏlates (§ 92.).

 *b.* In an open *pretone* (or *ante-pretone*) syllable, always instead of ĭ, as,

  (1) in nominal formations;

---

[1] Lev. 13:3.　　[2] Ex. 12:39.　　[3] Num. 22:6.　　[4] 2 Sam. 7:29.

(2) in the preformative of the Ḳăl Impf. of פ"ן verbs (§ **83. 2. a**).

3. Tone-long — (ŏ), instead of —, is found:

    *a.* In a closed *tone*-syllable. Worthy of notice is its occurrence,

        (1) in the Ḳăl Infinitive Construct, Imperative, and Imperfect (§ **66. R. 2**);

        (2) in the Ḳăl Perfect of a few stative verbs (§ **64. 3**);

        (3) in a few nominal forms (§ **93. 1.** *c*);

    *b.* In an open *tone*-syllable, in *u*-class Seġolates.

    *c.* In an open *pretone*-syllable.

**Note 1.**—Tone-long vowels are correctly written defectively; in the later language the incorrect *full* writing is frequent.

**Note 2.**—The tone-long vowel, arising from the rejection of Dăġēš-fŏrtē from a following laryngeal, is unchangeable.

### 32. *Reduced Vowels*

1. *a.* מָ־אוֹר (1 : 16) *from* גְּ־דֹל ;גְּ־דָלִים (1 : 16) *from* מְאֹרֹת ;גְּ־דֹל. עֲ־וֹנִי *from* עָ־וֹן.

    *b.* עֲ־זַבְתֶּם[2] *for* עֲ־שִׂיתֶם ;עֲ־זַבְתֶּם *for* עֲ־שִׂיתֶם[1].

    *c.* גֶּ־אַלְתִּיךָ[3] *for* הָ־רְגוּ ;גְּ־אַלְתִּיךָ *for* הָ־רְגוּ (4 : 25).

2. *a.* תֵּלְדִי ;יִשְׁרְצוּ *for* הָיָתָה ;הָיְתָה (1 : 2) *for* יִשְׁרְצוּ (1 : 20) *for* תֵּלְדִי ;נָתְנָה (3 : 12) *for* נָתָנָה (3 : 16).

    *b.* דְּמֵי (1 : 16); שְׁנֵי (1 : 2); פְּנֵי ;רָקִיעַ (1 : 20) *from* רְקִיעַ (4 : 10).

    *c.* יֹדֵעַ (3 : 5) *from* יֹדְעֵי ;צֹעֵק ;צֹעֲקִים (4 : 10) *from* יָדַע.

    *d.* גְּחֹנְךָ (3 : 14); קֹלְךָ (3 : 10); אֲכָלְכֶם (3 : 5); אֹכַלְךָ (2 : 17); זַרְעֵךְ (3 : 15).

**Remark.**—בְּ originally בַּ; לְ orig. לַ; כְּ orig. כַּ; וְ orig. וַ.

3. *a.* אֲדָמָה (2:6); אֲשֶׁר (1:7); אֱלֹהִים (1:1); אֲרוּרָה (3:17); נָעֳמִי[4].

---

*b.* ‏בְּסָעֲרָה‎ ;‏תְּאַלְּצֵהוּ‎[2] ;‏שְׁבָלֵי‎ ;‏לְקָחָה‎ *for* (2 : 23) ‏לְקָחָה‎ [3]

*c.* ‏וְזָהָב‎ (2 : 12); ‏וּלְהַבְדִּיל‎ (1 : 18); ‏וְשָׁקָה‎ (27 : 26); ‏וַיִּקְרַב־‎ [4]


A short vowel, or a tone-long vowel, gives way to Šᵉwâ, either simple or compound, when it would stand in an open syllable at a distance from the tone. The change may be called reduction (§ 36. 3). Reduced vowels are found:

1. In what would be the *antepretone*-syllable,
    *a.* In the inflection of nouns (§ **36**. 3. *b*).
    *b.* Before the grave termination in the inflection of verbs (§ 63. R.4).
    *c.* In many verbal forms to which a pronominal suffix is attached.
2. In what would be the *pretone*-syllable,
    *a.* In the inflection of verbs, before ‏הָ‎, ‏וּ‎ and ‏יִ‎ (§ **36**. 3. *a*).
    *b.* In the formation of the construct state of nouns (sg. and pl.).
    *c.* In the nominal inflection of participial forms.
    *d.* Before the suffixes ‏ךָ‎, ‏כֶם‎ and ‏כֶן‎, when attached to nouns and to certain verbal forms.

**Remark.**—In many particles which originally had ‏_ַ‎, there is found ‏_ִ‎, but before the tone the original ă often becomes ‏_ָ‎ (§§ **47**. 5; **49**. 4).

3. The simple Šᵉwâ (§ 9. 1) may represent the vowel-sound of any class. But the compound Šᵉwâ (§ 9. 2) has three distinct forms, one for each class, and is found:
    *a.* Chiefly under laryngeals (§ **42**. 3). But sometimes also,
    *b.* Under a letter which is, or should be, doubled.
    *c.* Under a letter preceded by the prefix ‏וּ‎.

**Note 1.**—The Šᵉwâ under a laryngeal, if vocal, *must* be compound Šᵉwâ; since a simple Šᵉwâ standing under a laryngeal is *always* silent.

**Note 2.**—The Ḥâtēf Sᵉġôl never appears anywhere but under laryngeals.

**Note 3.**—Simple Šᵉwâ is always vocal (1) at the beginning of a word, (2) under a consonant with dåġēš-fŏrtē, (3) after another Šᵉwâ, except in the case of a final consonant.

---

[1] Zech. 4 : 12.　　　[2] Judg. 16 : 16.　　　[3] 2 Kgs. 2 : 1.　　　[4] Ps. 55 : 22.

### 33. The A-Class Vowels

In accordance with the foregoing statements (§§ 29–32.) it is seen that the A-class vowels include:

1. The pure short $-\!\!\!-$ (ă).

2. The attenuated $-\!\!\!-$ (ĭ), arising in unaccented closed, and especially sharpened, syllables.

3. The short $-\!\!\!-$ (ĕ) which is deflected from ă, either with or without the tone.

4. The naturally long $-\!\!\!-$ (â), which has come from contraction or from compensative lengthening, or from a lengthening characteristic of nominal forms.

5. The naturally long $-\!\!\!-$ (ô), which has come by rounding from a naturally long â.

6. The tone-long $-\!\!\!-$ (å), which has arisen from an original ă through the influence of the tone.

7. The simple $-\!\!\!-$ (ᵉ), which is a reduction of $-\!\!\!-$, through the influence of the tone.

8. The compound $-\!\!\!-$ (ᵃ), which occurs instead of $-\!\!\!-$ according to the usage mentioned in § 32. 3. a. d.

9. The naturally long $-\!\!\!-$ (ê) which is probably diphthongal in character.

### 34. The I-Class Vowels

In accordance with the foregoing statements (§§ 29–32.) it is seen that the I-class vowels include:

1. The pure short $-\!\!\!-$ (ĭ), now found chiefly in unaccented closed, and especially sharpened, syllables.

2. The deflected $-\!\!\!-$ (ĕ), found in unaccented closed syllables.

3. The naturally long $-\!\!\!-$ (î), from iy, see â, § 33. 3.

4. The naturally long $-\!\!\!-$ (ê), which is diphthongal in its character, coming, as it always does, from the contraction of ai or ay.

5. The tone-long $-\!\!\!-$ (ē), which has come from an original $-\!\!\!-$, through the influence of the tone.

6. The simple $-\!\!\!-$ (ᵉ), cf. § 33. 7.

7. The compound $-\!\!\!-$ (ᵉ), occurring instead of $-\!\!\!-$ chiefly under laryngeals.

### 35.  The U-Class Vowels

In accordance with the foregoing statements (§§ **29–32.**), it is
seen that the U-class vowels include:

1. The pure short ◌ֻ (ŭ), now found chiefly in sharpened syllables.

2. The deflected ◌ֻ (ŏ), found chiefly in unaccented closed syllables.

3. The naturally long וּ (û), from *uw;* and see â, **§ 33. 3.**

4. The naturally long וֹ (ô), which is diphthongal in its character,
coming, as it always does, from the contraction of *au* or *aw.*  [On the
ô rounded from â, see **§ 33. 4.**]

5. The tone-long ◌ֹ (ō), which has arisen from an original ◌ֻ,
through the influence of the tone.

6. The simple ◌ֳ (ᵒ), see **§ 33. 7.**

7. The compound ◌ֳ (ᵒ), occurring instead of ◌ֳ chiefly under
laryngeals.

### 36.  Changes of Vowels

1. *a.* אֶרֶץ (1 : 24); דְּבַר *from* דָּבָר; צַדֶּקֶת *from* (16 : 2) צְדָקָה
*from* אֶרֶץ; סֵפֶר *from* סְפַר.

*b.* הָרַג (4 : 25) *from* דְּבַר; הָרְגוּ *from* (15 : 1) דְּבָרִים
קָטַל; שָׁמַיִם *from* (1 : 1) הָקֵם; הַקְטֵל[1], *but* הָקֵם
*from* קָטַל.

*c.* שָׁרְצוּ (1 : 21) שָׁרְצוּ; מָשְׁלוּ *for* מָשְׁלוּ.

*d.* בְּרָאתִי (1 : 1); קָרָאת (17 : 19) קָרָאת (1 : 5); יִקְרָא; בָּרָא (6 : 7).

*e.* אַתָּה (3 : 11); יִצְמָח (2 : 5); שָׁמַיִם (1 : 17); לַמָּיִם (1 : 6).

2 *a.* שָׁרֶץ *but* שָׁרְצוּ (1 : 21); תֹּאכַל *but* (2 : 16) תֹּאכְלוּ (3 : 1)
*for* תֵּלְדִי *but* תֵּלֵד (1 : 20); יִשְׁרְצוּ; תֹּאכְלוּ (3 : 16);
יַהַרְגֵנִי (4 : 14). יַהַרְגֵהוּ *but* (4 : 8); יַהֲרֹג *for*) יַהֲרֹג.

*b.* גָּדֹל *but* פָּנִים; פְּנֵי *but* (1 : 2); רָקִיעַ *but* רָקִיע (1 : 20); *but*
בָּשָׂר *but* מָאֹרֹת (1 : 16); מָאוֹר *but* (1 : 16); גְּדֹלִים
בְּשָׂרִי (2 : 23).

---

¹ Deut. 22 : 4.

In the formation of stems and the inflection of words, the following vowel-changes occur:

1. Tone-long vowels are found,

*a.* Usually when in nouns an original short vowel comes under the tone, either in open or closed syllables.

*b.* When a short vowel would stand in an open syllable before the tone. This is characteristic of nominal formations.

*c.* When in verbs an originally ante-pretonic short vowel becomes pretonic, in an open syllable.

*d.* When a following weak consonant becomes quiescent.

*e.* When an originally short vowel comes to stand in pause.

Under such circumstances, ă is usually *rounded* to å; ĭ is *lowered* to ē, and ŭ to ō (see §§ 33–35.).

**Note.**—*Cf.* German *ălle*, but English *âll*.

2. *Reduction* is the process by which a vowel is minimized or compressed to its smallest proportions. *Cf. heaven*, pronounced *hev'n*, but Anglo-Saxon *heofon; even*, pronounced *ev'n*, but Anglo-Saxon *efen* and *ebhan;* also the initial *a* in *America* when pronounced quickly. This process takes place,

*a.* When an ultimate — (ă), — (ĭ), or — (ŭ) in the inflection of *verbs* loses the tone; as when personal terminations consisting of a vowel, or pronominal suffixes connected by a vowel, are added.

*b.* When a penultimate vowel, in the inflection of *nouns*, no longer stands immediately before the tone, as in the formation of the construct state, when terminations of gender and number are appended, and when pronominal suffixes are added.

**Note 1.**—Herein consists the great difference between verbal and nominal inflection, that in verbal, the ultimate vowel, in nominal, the penultimate vowel is changed.

**Note 2.**—In some *verbal* forms, the vowel of whose ultima is unchangeable, the penultimate vowel is reduced.

**Note 3.**—In some *nominal* forms, the vowel of whose penultima is unchangeable, the ultimate vowel is reduced.

**Note 4.**—Only vowels standing in an open syllable may be reduced. Naturally long vowels are never reduced.

3. a. (1:18) הִבְדִּיל *but* הִבְדִּיל ;יֵשׁ *originally* (2:2) יִשְׁבַּת

b. [קָטֵל *but* ,וַיַּקְטֵל] ;(2:3) יְקַדֵּשׁ *but* קֻדַּשׁ ;בַּת[1] *but* בָּתֵּי.[2]

c. יְלַדְתִּיךָ[3]; דְּמָכֶם *for* (9:5) ;דַּמְכֶם *for* (24:30) דְּבָרֵי
דְבָרֵי.

4. a. הִקְפִצוּ[4]; אָכְלָה *for* (1:29) אָכְלָה ;הַקְטֵל *for* הַקְטֵל].

b. יֶעְטַל *for* יַעְטַל ;נַעְטַל *for* נֶעְטַל ;הֶעְטִיל *for* הַעְטִיל].

c. אֶרֶץ (1:24); עֶרֶב (1:5); רֶמֶשׂ (1:24); רֶחֶם (20:18).

5. אֵת (*with*), ־אֶת (4:1); אִתְּךָ (6:18); יָנְקָם = יָקָם (4:15).

6. a. לְמִינָה *for* (1:24) לְמִינָה.

b. וִיהִי *for* (1:6) וְיְהִי=wǐy-hǐy; תֹּהוּ *for* (1:2) תֹהֻן = θōhǔw.

c. בֵּין (1:4) *for* בַּיִן=bǎy(ǐ)n; לְמִינוֹ *for* (1:11) לְמִינֵהוּ; בּוֹ
בְּהֻן (1:11) *for*, etc., etc.

d. קָם (*from* קָם); נָקוֹם (*from* נָקַם); גָּדוֹל (*from* גָּדַל);
הַקְטִיל (*from* הִקְטִיל).

7. קוֹטֵל קָטֵל; *from* גָּדַל שׁוֹפְטֵי; *from* גָּדֵל שָׁפְטֵי.

8. a. בִּרְקִיעַ (1:26); לִמְאֹרֹת (1:15); בִדְגַת (1:14);
בָּחֳרִי[5] כִּדְמוּתֵנוּ; (1:26) לֵאמֹר *for* (1:22) לַעֲבֹד; (2:5);

b. יַהַרְגֻהוּ *for* (4:8) יַהַרְגֵהוּ]; נֶעְטָלָה *for* נָעְטְלָה].

9. a. עֶרֶב (19:4); בַּיִת (2:23); פַּעַם (1:11); זֶרַע (1:5); בְּהֻן
(1:2).

b. מֶמְשֶׁלֶת *for* (1:16) מֶמְשָׁלֶת; מְרַחֶפֶת *for* (1:2) מְרַחֶפֶת.

c. יֵרָב *for* (1:22) יֵרְב; וַיַּעַשׂ *for* (1:7) וַיֵּעַשׂ; יָבֶן
יָבֵן *for*.

---

[1] Ex. 2:1.   [2] Ruth 2:8.   [3] Ps. 2:7.   [4] Ps. 1:2.
[5] Ezek. 20:5.

3. *Attenuation* is a thinning of — (ă) to — (ĭ). It is the same change as that seen in *sang, sing; tango, attingo;* and in *master* which becomes *mister,* when used as a proclitic title (*cf.* Oxford Dictionary, s. v. *Mr.*). It takes place,

*a.* In closed syllables containing preformatives: as in the Ḳăl Imperfect, the Nĭf'ăl and Hĭf'ĭl Perfects.

*b.* In sharpened syllables: as in the Pĭ'ēl Perfect, and various nominal formations.

*c.* In closed syllables which have lost the tone, especially in the construct plural of nouns and before grave suffixes.

4. *Deflection* involves a change of quality in vowels, whereby ă becomes ĕ, ĭ becomes ĕ, and ŭ becomes ŏ. The same change is seen in the Greek and Latin forms, *mihi* and *meus, bulbus* and βολβός, *nummus* and νόμος. It often takes place,

*a.* When they would stand in an unaccented closed syllable.

*b.* When they would stand before a laryngeal with Šᵉwâ.

*c.* When ă stands as the original vowel of a Segolate form.

5. Original short vowels usually stand unchanged in sharpened syllables.

6. *Lengthening* (or contraction) takes place,

*a.* When two similar vowels, generally by the dropping of a consonant, come together.

*b.* When a vowel and a semi-vowel come together; then $i+y=\hat{i}$, $u+w=\hat{u}$.

*c.* When ă or å is followed by ĭ or y, or by ŭ or w; then $a+i$ or $y=\hat{e}$, $a+u$ or $w=\hat{o}$.

*d.* As characteristic of certain verbal and nominal forms.

7. *Rounding* is a process applied not only in producing å from ă, but also in changing the vowel â to ô. The same change is seen in the Anglo-Saxon *hām, hame,* or *haam* becoming *home; stān,* becoming *stone.*

8. A vocal Šᵉwâ must always be followed by a full vowel, rather than by another Šᵉwâ. Hence:

*a.* At the beginning of a word, an original short vowel, that ordinarily is reduced to Šᵉwâ, will remain without reduction if followed by a Šᵉwâ, yielding only to such attenuation or deflection as may be necessary; ă is commonly attenuated to ĭ, but if the Š͏ᵉwâ is compound, the short vowel is assimilated to it.

*b.* In the middle of a word, where a compound Š͏ᵉwâ stands as helping-vowel under a laryngeal, when inflectional change brings a vocal Š͏ᵉwâ immediately after the compound Š͏ᵉwâ, the latter in every case gives place to the corresponding short vowel (or a deflection of it) as helping-vowel.

9. When two vowelless consonants would come together at the end of a word, a helping-vowel is usually inserted between them to aid in pronunciation. The helping-vowel practically constitutes a new syllable, but the nature of the vowel treatment in many cases shows that the new syllable was not fully recognized—(*cf.* § 27.). This helping-vowel is generally ĕ, but with a laryngeal it is usually ă, with ˋ‿ it is ĭ, and with ˎ‿ it is generally ŭ. The most common instances of this are:

*a.* The large class of nouns called Seǧolates (§ 92.).

*b.* A class of feminine formations resembling Seǧolates.

*c.* Certain short verbal forms (§ 85. *l*).

**Note.**—The use of a helping-vowel is common in carelessly spoken English; *e. g., elm* becomes *ellum; prism=prisum; film= fillum; Henry=Henery; athletic=atheletic,* etc.

### 37. *Tables of Vowel-Changes*

The following tables summarize the various possible vowel-changes:

**TABLE I**

| | |
|---|---|
| $i+i$ or $i+y$ | = î |
| $a+y$ | = ay |
| $a+i$ or $a+y$ | = ê |
| $a+y$ | = ê̆ |
| $a+a$ | = ô |
| $a+a$ | = â |
| $a+w$ | = aw |
| $a+u$ or $a+w$ | = ô |
| $u+u$ or $u+w$ | = û |

## TABLE II

original *a* attenuated to ĭ which then is treated
  like an original.........................ĭ
original *a* retained as.....................ă
original *a* rounded to.....................å
original *a* deflected to....................ĕ
original *a* reduced to.....................ᵉ
original *a* reduced to.....................ᵃ

original *i* deflected to....................ĕ
original *i* retained as.....................ĭ
original *i* lowered to......................ē
original *i* reduced to.....................ᵉ
original *i* reduced to.....................ᵉ

original *u* deflected to....................ŏ
original *u* retained as.....................ŭ
original *u* lowered to......................ō
original *u* reduced to.....................ᵉ
original *u* reduced to.....................ᵒ

### 38. *Pause*

1. אִשְׁתֶּֽךָ (3:17); בַּעֲבוּרֶֽךָ (2:25); נִפְתָּֽחוּ (7:11); יִתְבֹּשָֽׁשׁוּ
(3:17).

2. זֶֽרַע (2:5); יִצְמָֽח (3:11); אָכַֽלְתָּ (1:5); לָֽיְלָה (1:2); הַמָּֽיִם
(1:29) for זֶֽרַע (=וְזֶרַע); הָֽבֶל (4:2) for הֶֽבֶל (=הֲבֵל).

3. אָֽתָּה (3:11) for אַתָּה; אָנֹֽכִי (3:10) for אָנֹכִי.

4. תָּמֽוּת (2:17); *but* וַיָּֽמָת (11:28); *and* וַיָּֽמָת (5:5, 8, 11, 14, 17,
etc.).

The pause at the end of a verse or clause, indicated by the more
powerful accents (§ **23**. 3), causes certain changes:

1. Šᵉwâ yields to its original vowel, and this, if short, undergoes the
customary tonal change and is accented.

Note.—The Šᵉwâ standing before the suffix ךָ, yields to its original—, which becomes ê (§ **30**. 5).

2. A short vowel becomes tone-long. The — in Seǧolates in pause becomes —.

3. The tone is frequently shifted from the ultima to the penult.

4. The tone which, in short forms, is on the penult is given to the ultima.

# VII.  Euphony of Consonants

## 39. *Assimilation*

1. מִקֶּדֶם מִן־כָּל־; מִכָּל־ (2:2) *for* מִן־תַּחַת; מִתַּחַת (1:7) *for* (2:8).

יִנָּטַע (2:8) *for* יִטַּע; יִנָּפַח (2:7) *for* יִפַּח; יִנָּתֵן; יִתֵּן (1:17) *for* .

2. אַחַדְתְּ *for* מְדַבֵּר ¹; מִתְדַּבֵּר (35:2); אַחַת (2:21) *for* הִטָּהָרוּ.

3. אֵיצַק² *for* אֶצֹק *for* יִקַּח; יִלְקַח (18:4); יִקַּח (2:15) *for* יִקַּח.

**Remark.**—שָׁכַנְתִּי³; נִחַמְתִּי (6:7); מִן־הָאָרֶץ (2:6); לִנְפֹּל⁴.

*Assimilation* of the final consonant of a closed syllable to the initial consonant of the following syllable takes place:

1. In the case of the weak נ, of the preposition מִן (§ 48. 1), and of the first radical of verbs פ"ן (§ 81.).

**Note.**—This is a very common thing in English, *e. g. irresistible* for *inresistible, illegible* for *inlegible.*

2. In the case of תְ of הִתְ (§ 59. 5. *b*) and rarely of ד.

**Note.**—*Cf. attract* for *adtract; attest* for *adtest; annotate* for *adnotate; appropriate* for *adpropriate.*

3. In the case of ל in לָקַח *to take* (§ 84. *g*) and י in a few פ"י verbs (§ 83.).

**Remark.**—The letter נ is *not* assimilated when it stands (1) in an accented syllable, or (2) before a laryngeal (except ח), or (3) after the preposition ל.

**Note.**—Assimilation is indicated by a Dåǧēš-fŏrtē in the following consonant, which, however, is rejected from final consonants (§ 14. 1).

## 40. *Rejection*

1. *a.* (נ)שְׂאֵת (4:12); (ל)קַחַת (4:11); (נ)גֶשׁ־ (19:9); (נ)תֵת (4:7).

*b.* (י)לֶכֶת (11:31); (י)דַעַת (2:9); (י)דַע (20:7); (י)לֶדֶת (4:2).

---

¹ Num. 7 : 89.  ² Isa. 44 : 3.  ³ Ex. 25 : 8.  ⁴ Num. 14 : 3.

c. נַחְנוּ (42:11) *for* אֲנַחְנוּ; ¹אָכָל *probably for* מְאָכָל.

2. לָאוֹר (1:5) *for* לְהָאוֹר; יַבְדֵּל (1:7) *for* יְהַבְדֵּל.

3. תָּמוּתוּ (42:20) *but* תְּמוּתוּן (3:3); הָיָה (2:10) *for* הָיִי.


The consonants most liable to rejection are the laryngeals א and ה, the dentals ל and נ, and the vowel-letters ו and י. These are often rejected:

1. From the beginning of a word when there is no vowel beneath to sustain them,

    *a.* In the case of נ of verbs פ״ן (§ 81.) and of ל in לְקַח in the Ḳăl Imv. and Infinitive Construct.

    *b.* In the case of ו or י of verbs פ״ן in the same forms.

    *c.* In a few isolated cases.

2. From the middle of a word when preceded only by a Š°wâ.

3. From the end of a word, by ordinary attrition, as in the case of ן of the plural ending וּן; and of a final י in verbs ל״ה (§ 85.).

**Note 1.**—On the rejection of א and ה, see also § 43.

**Note 2.**—On the rejection of ו and י, see also § 44.

### 41. Addition, Transposition, Commutation

1. ⁶אֶתְנַן; ⁵אֶשְׁכֹּל; ⁴אַזְכָּרָה; ³אֶזְרוֹעַ *and* ²זְרוֹעַ.

2. נִתְשַׁחֲוֶה; נִשְׁתַּחֲוֶה ⁸ *for* הִתְשַׁמֵּר; הִתְשַׁמֵּר ⁷ *for* הִשְׁתַּמֵּר.

3. *a.* הִתְצַיַּד ¹⁰ *for* הִצְטַיֵּד; הִתְצַדֵּק ⁹ *for* הִצְטַדֵּק.

    *b.* עָשׂוּו ¹² *for* עָשׂוּי; וְצַר ¹¹ *for* קוּם; קוּם *for* (2:8) יָצַר.


1. The *addition* of a letter sometimes takes place at the beginning of a word to avoid harshness in pronunciation, as in the case of

    א, called prosthetic, when used in the formation of nouns.

2. The *transposition* of letters, of frequent occurrence in the province of the lexicon, occurs in the grammar only in the case of ת of the Hĭθpă'ēl of verbs when it would stand before a sibilant fricative.

---

¹ Ex. 3 : 2.    ² Ex. 6 : 6.    ³ Jer. 32 : 21.    ⁴ Lev. 2 : 2.
⁵ Gen. 14 : 13.    ⁶ Deut. 23 : 19.    ⁷ Mic. 6 : 16.    ⁸ Gen. 22 : 5.
⁹ Gen. 44 : 16.    ¹⁰ Josh. 9 : 12.    ¹¹ Ruth 4 : 7.    ¹² Ex. 3 : 16.

3. The *commutation* of letters, of frequent occurrence in the province of the lexicon, occurs in the grammar in the case of

    *a.* ת and ט in the Hĭθpă'ēl stem.

    *b.* ו and י in פ"ו, middle-vowel and ל"ה forms (see § **44.** 1. *a—e*).

### 42. The Peculiarities of Laryngeals

1. *a.* הָרְקִיעַ (1:7); הָאֲדָמָה (1:25); הָעוֹף (1:22); וַתֵּרֶאָה (1:9).

    *b.* מְרַחֶפֶת (1:2); הַהוּא (2:12); הַחַיָּה (1:21); הַחֹשֶׁךְ (1:4); [פֻּעַל].

2. *a.* וַיִּרָא (1:4); יַעֲלֶה (2:6); לַעֲבֹד־ (2:5); נַעֲשֶׂה (1:26); יַעֲזֹב־ (2:24).

    *b.* יִפַּח (2:7); יִטַּע (2:8); יַצְמַח (2:9); יֵדַע (4:25); [קְטַח].

    *c.* נֶחְמָד (2:9); יֶחֱזַק (41:56); תֶּחְדַּל[1]; הֶעֱבַדְתַּנִי[2].

    *d.* רוּחַ (1:2); רָקִיעַ (1:6); מַזְרִיעַ (1:11); זֶרַע (1:29); רְקִיעַ (1:15).

3. *a.* שְׁאֵלָה[3] *from* šă'ălâ; אֱלֹהִים (1:1) *from* 'ilâh; חֳלִי[4] *from* ḥŏlî.

    *b.* עֲבֹד־ (2:5); עֲשׂוֹת (2:4); אֱמֹר (1:22); הֱיוֹת (2:18); *cf.* וְהָיָה (12:2). [הֶעֱטַל]⁵; פָּעֳלֶךָ; אֶעֱשֶׂה (2:18); יַעֲלֶה (2:6); נַעֲשֶׂה (1:26).

**Remarks.—** יַהַרְגֻהוּ (2:9); נֶחְמָד (2:24); יַעֲזֹב־ (2:24) *but* יִשְׁבֹּת (2:2); וְהַעֲמַדְתָּ[8] (4:8); הֶעֱמִיד[6] *and* הֶעֱמַדְתָּ[7] *but* יַהַרְגֻהוּ *for*

The laryngeals, in the order of their strength beginning with the weakest, are א, ע, ה, ח. ר shares some of their characteristics. They have the following peculiarities:

1. They refuse to be doubled (*i. e.*, to receive Dåḡēš-fŏrtē). But here a distinction must be made between,

    *a.* א and ר, which entirely reject the doubling, and require a strengthening of the preceding vowel (§ **36.** 2. *b*); and

---

¹ Deut. 23 : 23.    ² Isa. 43 : 24.    ³ Ex. 3 : 22.    ⁴ Deut. 28 : 61.
⁵ Ruth 2 : 12.    ⁶ Num. 5 : 18, 30.    ⁷ Ps. 31 : 9.    ⁸ Num. 3 : 6; 8 : 13.

*b.* ע, ח, and ה, of which ע sometimes, ח and ה nearly always, receive a so-called Dåḡeš-fŏrtē *implied,* and allow a preceding vowel to remain short.

2. They take, particularly before them, the *a*-vowels; hence,

*a.* The vowel ◌ַ (ă) is chosen instead of ◌ִ (ĭ) or ◌ֶ (ĕ), especially when ă was the original vowel.

*b.* The vowel ◌ַ (ă) is chosen instead of ◌ֵ (ē) or ◌ֹ (ō), especially when ă was a collateral form.

*c.* The vowel ◌ֶ (ĕ), arising by deflection from ă, is chosen for the sake of dissimilarity.

*d.* The vowel ◌ַ steals in between a heterogeneous long vowel and a final laryngeal as an aid in pronunciation. This ◌ַ is called Păθăḥ-*furtive;* it is a mere transition-sound and does not make a syllable. It disappears when the laryngeal ceases to be final.

**Note 1.**—The letter ר (1) does not receive Dåḡeš-fŏrtē, and (2) often shows a preference for ◌ַ, and is consequently frequently classed for convenience with the laryngeals.

**Note 2.**—A final א is not a consonant, nor is final ה, unless it contain Măppîḳ (§ 16. 1).

3. They have a decided preference for compound Š⁴wâ. Hence there is found under laryngeals,

*a.* A compound Š⁴wâ, rather than a simple Š⁴wâ, in the place of an original vowel; and in this case the compound Š⁴wâ of the class to which the original vowel belonged, is used.

*b.* An *inserted* compound Š⁴wâ for facilitating the pronunciation; and here,

    (1) an initial laryngeal takes ◌ֲ, except in the case of א, and of ה and ח in the verbs הָיָה and חָיָה, which prefer ◌ֱ;

    (2) a medial laryngeal takes that Š⁴wâ which corresponds to the preceding vowel.

**Remark 1.**—Thus where in *strong* forms there is found a silent Š⁴wâ, in *laryngeal* forms there is usually found a compound Š⁴wâ as a helping-vowel, which does not affect the syllabification.

**Remark 2.**—Under the strong laryngeals, especially ח, the use of the compound Šᵉwâ for the facilitation of pronunciation is not so general.

**Remark 3.**—When a compound Šᵉwâ would stand before a simple Šᵉwâ, the former always gives way to a vowel (§ 36.).

**Remark 4.**—The combination ־ְ ־ֲ often yields to ־ִ ־ַ, when removed to a distance from the tone.

### 43. *The Weakness of* א *and* ה

1. *a.* בָּרָא (1:1); יִקְרָא (1:5); תּוֹצֵא (1:24).

    *b.* רְאָשִׁים (1:1) *for* רֵאשִׁית; רָאשִׁים; רֵאֲשִׁית (2:10) *for* רָאשִׁים;
לֵאמֹר (1:22) *for* לִקְרֹאת; לִקְרַאת (15:10) *for* לִקְרַאת;
יֹּאמֶר (1:3) *for* יֹאמַר; כֵּאלֹהִים (3:5) *for* כֵּאלֹהִים.

**Remarks.**—יְרֵשִׁית; וָאֹכַל (3:12) *for* אֹכֵל; חֵטְא; ¹וַיִּרְא (1:4); ²רֵאשִׁית *for* רֵאשִׁית.

2. *a.* בַּיּוֹם; לְהַחְשֵׁךְ (1:5) *for* לְהָאוֹר; לַחְשֶׁךְ (1:5) *for* לְהָאוֹר; לָאוֹר (1:18).

    *b.* תֵּהָרְאֶה (1:9) *for* תֵּרָאֶה; יְהָבְדֵל (1:7) *for* יַבְדֵּל.

    *c.* אֹתוֹ (2:3); בֹּהוּ (1:11) *for* בּוֹ; לְמִינָהוּ (1:11) *for* לְמִינוֹ; אֹתָהוּ *for* אֹתוֹ.

The letters א and ה, being exceedingly weak, not only occasion change, but likewise suffer change:

1. א loses its consonantal power and is said *to quiesce* or *to be silent*,

    *a.* Always, when it stands at the end of a word; here belong all forms of a ל״א character.

    *b.* Often, when it stands in the middle of a word; then,

      (1) a preceding vowelless consonant receives its vowel;

      (2) or, it loses its compound Šᵉwâ after a preceding vowel. The Šᵉwâ disappears as soon as א quiesces and the preceding short vowel is strengthened in compensation for the loss of the א.

**Remark 1.**—A final א, preceded by a simple Šᵉwâ is otiose.

---

¹ Deut. 15 : 9.          ² Deut. 11 : 12.

**Remark 2.**—A quiescent א is frequently elided from the middle of a word.

2. The consonant ה at the end of a word is always distinguished from the vowel-letter ה by the presence of a Măppîḳ (§ **16.** 1).   But on account of its weakness it is often entirely lost,

*a.* In the case of the article after an inseparable preposition (§ **47.** 4).

*b.* In Hîf'îl, Hŏf'ăl and Hĭθpă'ēl verbal forms after a preformative of gender or person.

*c.* From between two vowels, which then contract.

**Note.**—The ה of ל"ה verbs and nouns (§ **85.**) is *always* a vowel-letter and has no connection with the ה here considered.

### 44. The Weakness of ו and י

1. *a.* יֵלֶךְ (4:23) *for* וְלֶךְ (*cf.* וְלָךְ 11:30); יָשַׁב [*cf.* יֵּשֶׁב (4:16)] *for* וְשֶׁב.

*b.* קָיֶם; יִתְיַלְדוּ[2] *but cf.* הִתְוַדַּע (45:1).

*c.* יִרְבִּין; עָשׂוּתָ *for* עָשִׂיתָ *for* עָשִׂיתָ; עָשׂוּי.

*d.* יִישָׁן (2:21) *for* יְוֹשַׁן; יִיצֶר (2:7) *for* יְוֹצֶר.

2. *a.* הֲעַת (3:22) *for* וְדַע; צֵא (8:16) *for* וְצֵא; יֵצֵא (4:16) *for* יְוֹצֵא.

*b.* הָיָה (2:10)=håyå; יַעֲלֶה (2:6)=yăʻǐlê.
הִשְׁקָה (2:6)=hĭšḳå; יִהְיֶה (1:29)=yĭhyê.

The semi-vowels, or vowel-consonants, ו and י, occasion a very large number of changes:

1. *Commutation of* ו *into* י *takes place,*

*a.* Almost always at the beginning of a word, the exceptions being very few.

*b.* Frequently in the Pĭʻēl of middle-vowel verbs, and generally in פ"ן verbs after הִתְ of the Hĭθpă'ēl.

---

¹ Ruth 4 : 7.    ² Num. 1 : 18.    ³ Ex. 3 : 16.    ⁴ Deut. 8 : 13.

*c.* Whenever it is retained as the third radical in verbs ל״ה, both when final and when medial (§ 85. 3).

*d.* When it would follow *i* in a closed syllable, as in the Ḳäl Imperfect of verbs פ״ן which have a פ״י treatment (§ 83.).

2. *Elision takes place,*

*a.* Of an initial נ when supported only by Šᵉwâ, as in certain פ״ן Inf's Construct and Imv's (§ 83.); and also when in the Ḳäl Impf. the נ, following ĭ, does not go over to י, according to 1. *d* above.

*b.* Of a final נ and י in verbs called ל״ה, the original vowel following them having been previously lost; in this case the vowel preceding, nearly always ă, is rounded to â in Perfects, and becomes ê in Imperfects and Participles (see for details, § 85.).

3. *a.* נוֹדַע (21:41); תּוֹצֵא (1:11) *for* תַּוֹצֵא; תֵּיטִיב (4:7) *for* תֵּיטִיב.

אַפֶּךָ (3:19); חַיֶּיךָ (3:14) *for* ḥăy-yăy-kå; ¹תַּעֲשֶׂינָה.

*b.* עֹשֵׂה (6:14) = ꜥśê *for* עָשִׂי; פְּנֵי (1:2) = pᵉnê *for* פָּנַי.

*c.* יִיצֶר (2:7) יְוֹשֵׁן=יִישַׁן; יִישַׁן (2:21) *for* יוֹשֵׁן; הוּסַד² *for* יִיצֶר.

4. *a.* וּנְקֵבָה (1:27); וּלְמִקְוֵה (1:10); וּמִלְאוּ (1:22); וּבֵין (1:4).

*b.* ³(יִשְׁתַּחֲוֶה) יִשְׁתַּחֲוּ *for* יִשְׁתַּחֲוּ (18:2) יִשְׁתָּחוּ; תָּהֹן *for* תָּהוּ (1:2).

*c.* פָּנָיו; אַפֵּיהוּ *for* אַפֵּיהוּ (2:7) אַפָּיו; תִּיהוּ⁻*for* תִּיהוּ; וּשְׁמַעְתָּיו⁴ (4:5).

5. *a.* יִקָּווּ (1:9); יָצֶר (2:8); יָלַד (4:18); יָדַע (4:1); יֶלֶד (4:26);
וָבֹהוּ (1:2).

*b.* עָשׂוּי⁵; גּוֹי⁶; see also the cases under 4. *c*, above.

*c.* שָׁלוֹתִי⁷; חַוָּה (3:20); יוּלַד (4:18).

3. *Contraction takes place,*

*a.* Of vowelless נ or י with a preceding ŏ, as

(1) in the פ״ן Nif'al and Hif'il (§ 83.), and the פ״י Hif'il
(§ 84. 2);

---
¹ Deut. 1 : 44.                                        ² Ezra 3 : 11.
³ In these cases a helping ⸺ is inserted (§ 30. *m*).        ⁴ Deut. 1 : 17.
⁵ Ex. 3 : 16.            ⁶ Deut. 4 : 7.                      ⁷ Job 3 : 26.

(2) before נָה in לְ"הּ Imperfects and Imv's, and before הַ
and הָ in plural of nouns (§ 30. 5); here *ay* gives ִי_ (*ê*).

*b.* Of final ו or י with a preceding *a*, in forms that are closely
tied to the following word, as

(1) in the Imperative of verbs לְ"הּ (§ 85. 1. *f*);

(2) in the Construct plural ending ִי_ (=*ay*)(§ 111. 3. *b*).

*c.* Of ו or י with a preceding *u* or *i* respectively, when a consonant follows, as in the פ"ו Höph'ăl (§ 83. 3. *c*), and in the Ḳăl Impf.
of פ"ו and פ"י verbs.

4. *Vocalization of* ו *to* וּ *takes place,*

*a.* At the beginning of a word in the case of the conjunction וּ
(§ 49. 2).

*b.* At the end of a word, whenever ו would be preceded by a
consonant, as

(1) in the case of לְ"הּ (or לְ"ו) Seğolates (§ 92. 2. *c*);

(2) in certain short forms of the imperfect. But

*c.* The reverse takes place, viz., change of וּ to ו, especially in
the case of the suffix הֶן, when it is attached

(1) to verbal forms ending in a vowel, and

(2) to the plural ending used before suffixes, viz., ִי_, of
which, however, the י is lost (being only orthographically
retained), and the ă rounded to â (§ 111.) as an assimilation to the ו.

5. *The consonantal force of* ו *or* י *is retained,*

*a.* When as radicals they stand at the beginning of syllables.

*b.* When a heterogeneous vowel, except ă, precedes.

*c.* When they would receive Dåğeš-förtē (§ 83.), and in a few
exceptional cases.

# PART SECOND—ETYMOLOGY

# VIII. Inseparable Particles

## 45. *The Article*

1. הַשָּׁמַיִם (1:1); הַמַּיִם (1:2); הַיַּבָּשָׁה (1:9); הַיּוֹם (1:14); הַלַּיְלָה (1:14).

2. הַחֹשֶׁךְ (1:4); הַחַיָּה (1:21); הַהוּא (2:12); הַהֹלֵךְ (2:14).

3. הָאָרֶץ (1:1); הָעוֹף (1:7); הָרָקִיעַ (1:22).

4. ⁴הֶעָוֹן; ³הֶהָרִים; ²הֶחָזָק; ¹הֶחָג

Remark 1.—הַיְאֹרָה ⁶ *for* הַיְאָרָה; הַמְיַלְּדֹת ⁵ *for* הַמְיַלֶּדֶת.

Remark 2.—הָעָם; ⁸ הָהָר ⁷ *for* הֶהָר; הָאָרֶץ (1:1) *for* הֶאָרֶץ; הָאָרֶץ *for* הֶעָם.

Remark 3.—לָאוֹר (1:5) *for* לְ + הָאוֹר; לַחֹשֶׁךְ (1:5) *for* לְ + הַחֹשֶׁךְ.

1. The usual form of the Article is הַ with a Dåĝēš-fŏrtē in the following letter. . . . . . . . . . . . . . . . . . . . . . . . . . . . . . . . . . . . . . . . . . .   הַ·

2. Before the strong laryngeals ה and ח which may be doubled by implication (§ 42. 1. *b*), it is. . . . . . . . . . . . . . . . . . . . .   הַ

3. Before the weak laryngeal א and before ר, and generally before ע, which cannot be doubled (§ 42. 1. *a*), ־ִ is rounded to ־ָ. . . . . . . . . . . . . . . . . . . . . . . . . . . . . . . . . . . . . . . . . . . . . . . . .   הָ

4. Before הָ, and before an unaccented הָ, עָ, the ־ָ is deflected to ־ֶ (ĕ) for the sake of dissimilarity. . . . . . . . . . . . . . . . .   הֶ

Remark 1.—The Dåĝēš-fŏrtē of the Article may of course be omitted from vowelless consonants (§ 14. 2).

Remark 2.—The words for *earth, mountain, people* irregularly change their vowel after the Article.

Remark 3.—The ה of the Article is elided after the prepositions לְ, כְּ, בְּ (§ 43. 2. *a*) and the vowel is given to the preposition.

¹ 1 Kgs. 8:65.   ² Num. 13:18.   ³ Gen. 7:19.   ⁴ 1 Sam. 25:24.
⁵ Ex. 1:19.   ⁶ Ex. 1:22.   ⁷ Ex. 3:12.   ⁸ Gen. 14:16.

### 46. Hē Interrogative

1. (4:9). הֲשֹׁמֵר אָחִי אָנֹכִי ;(3:11) הֲמִן־הָעֵץ ... אָכַלְתָּ

2. הַאֵלֶּה וְקָרָאתִי לָךְ ;(30:15) הַמְעַט קַחְתֵּךְ אֶת־אִישִׁי אִשָּׁה[1]

3. (17:17). הַלְּבֶן מֵאָה שָׁנָה יִוָּלֵד ;הֶהָיְתָה[2] ;הֶאָמַר[3]

In direct, and likewise indirect, interrogation, a particle is used
called Hē Interrogative:

1. It is usually written with Ḥâṭēf Păθăḥ . . . . . . . . . . . . . . . הֲ

2. Before vowelless consonants, and laryngeals, it is written   הַ

3. Before laryngeals with ־ָ, it is written (§ 31. 2. c) . . . . . . . הֶ

while rarely, especially with letters which have simple Š°wâ, it is
written with Dâĝēš-fŏrtē separative (§ 15. 4) . . . . . . . . . . . . . . הּ׳

Note.—Frequently no sign of interrogation appears; then the
context must be depended upon to reveal the interrogative character
of the statement.

### 47. The Inseparable Prepositions

1. (1:14). לְהַבְדִּיל ;(1:11) לְמִינוֹ ;(1:6) בְּתוֹךְ ;(1:1) בְּרֵאשִׁית

2. כִּדְמוּתֵנוּ ;(1:18) לִמְשֹׁל ;(1:15) לִמְאוֹרֹת ;(1:14) בִּרְקִיעַ
(1:26).

3. בְּחָרִי[4] ;(1:22) לֵאמֹר for לְאֱמֹר ;(2:5) לַעֲבֹד ;(2:3) לַעֲשׂוֹת

4. (1:10); לַיַּבָּשָׁה ;(1:7) לָרָקִיעַ ;(1:5) לַחֹשֶׁךְ ;(1:5) לָאוֹר
בַּיּוֹם (1:18).

5. לָדַעַת ;(1:29) לָכֶם ;(1:6) לַמַּיִם (3:22).

Remark 1.—לַאדֹנָי (17:7, 8); כֵּאלֹהִים (3:5); לֵאלֹהִים (18:30, 32).

Remark 2.—לַיהוָה proper writing for (4:3) לַאדֹנָי.

Three prepositions, לְ, כְּ, בְּ, are always prefixed to the words

---

[1] Ex. 2:7.     [2] Job 34:31.     [3] Joel 1:2.     [4] Ex. 11:8.

which they govern.   Their vowel was, originally, ─; but now they
are found written:

1. Ordinarily, with simple Šᵉwâ reduced from ă . . . . . . . . . . .    ─ְ

2. Before consonants having simple Šᵉwâ, with ĭ attenuated
from ă . . . . . . . . . . . . . . . . . . . . . . . . . . . . . . . . . . . . . . . . . . . . . . . .    ─ִ

3. Before laryngeals having compound Šᵉwâ, with the corre-
sponding short vowel . . . . . . . . . . . . . . . . . . . . . . . . . . . . ─ֲ, ─ֱ, ─ֳ (ŏ)

4. Before the Article, with the vowel of the Article . . . . ─ַ or ─ָ (å)

5. Before a tone-syllable, sometimes with tone-long . . . . . . . . ─ָ (å)

**Remark 1.**—The א of אֲדֹנָי Lord and אֱלֹהִים God loses its
consonantal force after the prepositions (§ 43. 1. *b*).

**Remark 2.**—The word יְהֹוָה, which is written יְהֹוָה, *i. e.*, with
the vowels of אֲדֹנָי, rather than יַהְוֶה as it should be written,
appears with the preposition as לַיהֹוָה (to be pronounced לַאדֹנָי).

Note 1.—The original ─ַ of the prepositions is usually reduced
to ─ְ, or rounded to ─ָ (å); it is retained before laryngeals with ─ֲ,
but assimilated to ─ֱ before ─ֱ, and to ─ֳ (ŏ) before ─ֳ.

Note 2.—For prepositions with pronominal suffixes, see § 51. 3, 4.

### 48.   The Preposition מִן

1. מִן־הָאָרֶץ (2:6); מִן־תַּחַת *for* מִתַּחַת (1:7); מִקֶּדֶם (2:8)
*for* מִן־קֶדֶם.

2. מִן־אִישׁ (6:14); מֵעַל (1:7) *for* מִן־עַל; מֵאִישׁ (2:23) *for* מִן־אִישׁ.

The preposition מִן *from*, is really the construct state of an ancient
noun and is written separately, chiefly before the Article; elsewhere
it is *prefixed* and appears:

1. Usually with its נ assimilated (§ 39. 1) . . . . . . . . . . . . . . . . .    מִ·

2. Before ה, rarely with Dăḡēš-fŏrtē implied (§ 42. 1. *b*) . . . .    מֵ
but before other laryngeals, with ─ lowered (§ 36. 2. *b*) . . . . . .    מֵ

Note.—On the form of מִן before pronominal suffixes, see § 51. 5.

### 49. Wåw Conjunctive

1. וְאֵת (1:1); וְהָאָרֶץ (1:2); וְלַחֹשֶׁךְ (1:5); וְשָׁנִים (1:14); וְשָׁמַיִם (2:4).

2. וּלְמִקְוֵה (1:10); וּבְעוֹף (1:26); וּמִלְאוּ (1:22); וּבֵין (1:4); וּנְקֵבָה (1:27).

3. וַאֲנִי; וַעֲשִׂיתֶם[1]; וְהָיָה for וְהָיָה (12:2); וְהָיָה (24:12); וְעָשָׂה (6:17).

4. וְנָד (4:12); וָנָד (2:9); וְזֶרַע (1:24); וְרֶמֶשׂ (1:2); וָבֹהוּ (1:2).


The conjunction *and*, originally וְ, is now found written:

1. Ordinarily with simple Šᵉwâ (§ 32. 2. R.).............. וְ

2. Before בּ, מ, פ (§ 44. 4), and vowelless consonants..... וּ

3. Before laryngeals having compound Šᵉwâ, with the corresponding short vowel...........................−ֲ, −ֱ, −ֳ (ŏ)

4. Before a tone-syllable, sometimes with tone-long −ָ (§ 31. 1. c)................................................. (å)

**Note 1.**—וְ with יְהִי gives וַיְהִי (1:6).

**Note 2.**—On וָ, the strengthened form of וְ, which is called Wåw Conversive and is used with the Imperfect, see § 73.

---

[1] Deut. 4 : 6, 16, 23, 25.

# IX.  Pronouns

## 50.  The Personal Pronoun

1. The following are the forms of the Personal Pronoun:

| | | | |
|---|---|---|---|
| *He* | הוּא | *They* (m.) | הֵם, הֵמָּה |
| *She* | הִיא | *They* (f.) | הֵן, הֵנָּה |
| *Thou* (m.) | אַתָּה | *Ye* (m.) | אַתֶּם |
| *Thou* (f.) | אַתְּ | *Ye* (f.) | אַתֵּן, אַתֵּנָה |
| *I* | אֲנִי, אָנֹכִי | *We* | אֲנַחְנוּ, נַחְנוּ |

2. The following are pausal forms:

אֲנָחְנוּ; אָתָּה and אָתָּה; אָנִי, אָנֹכִי;

3. The following remarks on the forms of the Pronouns are to be noted:

*a.* הִיא *she* is written הוּא in the Pentateuch, except eleven times.

*b.* אַתָּה *thou* (m.) is written five times defectively אַתְּ.

*c.* אַתְּ *thou* (f.) was originally אַתִּי or אַתִּין; seven times Ḳᵉθîv has אַתִּי, which would be pronounced ătî.

*d.* אֲנִי *I* (c.) is more common than the longer form אָנֹכִי.

*e.* הֵנָּה *they* (f.) is more common than הֵן, the latter occurring only with prefixes.

*f.* אַתֵּן *ye* (f.) occurs but once,[1] אַתֵּנָה, but four times.[2]

*g.* אֲנַחְנוּ *we* is the usual form, נַחְנוּ occurring but six times,[3] and a form אָנוּ but once.[4]

Note 1.—The הָ which appears in several of the forms was perhaps originally demonstrative, but has lost its force.

Note 2.—The following comparative table of the personal Pronouns in the more important Semitic languages will be of interest:

[1] Ezek. 34:31.　　　　　[2] Gen. 31:6; Ezek. 13:11, 20; 34:17.
[3] Gen. 42:11; Ex. 16:7, 8; Num. 32:32; 2 Sam. 17:12; Lam. 3:42.
[4] Jer. 42:6 (Ḳᵉθîv).

63

| Arabic. | Assyrian. | Aramaic. | Hebrew. |
|---|---|---|---|
| huwă | šû | הוּא | הוּא |
| hiyă | šî | הִיא | הִיא |
| anta | atta | אנתה | אַתָּה |
| anti | atti˙ | אַנְתְּ or אַתְּ　אנתי | אַתְּ |
| ană | anāku | אֲנָא | אָנֹכִי |
| hum | šūnu | הִמּוֹן, אנון ,הִמּוֹ | הֵמָּה, הֵם |
| hunna | šîna | אנון, אנין | הֵנָּה, הֵן |
| antum | attuna | אַתּוּן, אַנְתּוּן | אַתֶּם |
| antunna | attina | אַתֵּין | אַתֵּנָה, אַתֵּן |
| naḥnu | anīni | אֲנַחְנָא | נַחְנוּ, אֲנַחְנוּ |

**Note 3.**—We may note here also the expression פְּלֹנִי אַלְמֹנִי, equivalent to *a certain one*, and used as an indefinite pronoun.[1]

## 51. *Pronominal Suffixes*

### Tabular View

| 1.<br>Separate Forms. | 2.<br>With אֵת. | 3.<br>With בְּ and לְ. | 4.<br>With כְּ. | 5.<br>With מִן. |
|---|---|---|---|---|
| **Singular** | | | | |
| 3 m. הוּ | אֹתוֹ | בּוֹ | כָּמוֹהוּ | מִמֶּנּוּ |
| 3 f. הָ | אֹתָהּ | בָּהּ | כָּמוֹהָ | מִמֶּנָּה |
| 2 m. ךָ | אֹתְךָ, אֹתָךְ | בְּךָ, בָּךְ | כָּמוֹךָ | מִמְּךָ<br>מִמֶּךָ |
| 2 f. ךְ | אֹתָךְ | בָּךְ | — | מִמֵּךְ |
| 1 c. ִי or נִי | אֹתִי | בִּי | כָּמוֹנִי | מִמֶּנִּי |
| **Plural** | | | | |
| 3 m. הֶם or ם | אֹתָם, אֶתְהֶם ,ם | בָּם, בָּהֶם ,כָּהֶם | כָּמוֹהֶם | מֵהֶם |
| 3 f. ן or הֶן | אֹתָן, אֶתְהֶן ,ן | כָּהֵן | כָּהֵנָּה | מֵהֶן<br>מֵהֶנָּה |
| 2 m. כֶם | אֶתְכֶם | בָּכֶם | כָּמוֹכֶם, כָּכֶם | מִכֶּם |
| 2 f. כֶן | — | בָּכֵן | — | מִכֶּן |
| 1 c. נוּ | אֹתָנוּ | בָּנוּ | כָּמוֹנוּ | מִמֶּנּוּ |

---

[1] *Cf.* Ruth 4 : 1; 2 Kgs. 6 : 8.

When a pronoun is to be governed by a verb, a noun or a preposition, a shortened form must be used:

1. The "separate forms," given above, are the fragments of the pronouns which are thus used. They are attached directly to nominal and verbal forms ending in a vowel, but a so-called connecting-vowel is employed with forms ending in a consonant.

*a.* The suffixes כֶם, כֶן, הֶם and הֶן always receive the accent and are termed *heavy;* all others are *light.*

*b.* י__ is used with nouns; נִי with verbs.

*c.* הֶם and הֶן are used with nouns in both singular and plural, but chiefly with the plural; ם and ן are used with verbs and singular nouns.

**Note.**—On the union of verbs with suffixes, see § 74.; on the union of nouns with suffixes, see §§ 112, 113.

2. When for any reason it is impossible, or undesirable, to attach the suffix directly to a governing verb, it may be written in connection with אֵת, the sign of the definite accusative, which, however, except before כֶם, assumes the form אֹת or אוֹת ('ôθ).

3. The prepositions בְּ and לְ restore and round their original — before the suffixes (except י__ and ךָ); this vowel

*a.* Contracts with הוּ and forms וֹ (ô), the ה falling out and å contracting with û; with ךָ the final å is dropped, the ă of the preposition is rounded to å, and ה is preserved as a consonant with măppîḳ, the resulting form being הָ—; but elsewhere,

*b.* It appears as å either before or under the tone.

**Note.**—While either בָּם or בָּהֶם may be used, only לָהֶם is found.

4. Between the preposition כְּ and the suffixes, there is generally found an inserted syllable מוֹ. This syllable is found in poetry also after בְּ and לְ (but not when suffixes are added).

5. The preposition מִן before most of the suffixes takes a special form; in some cases,

*a.* The final ן is assimilated: מִמֶּךָ for מִמֶּנְךָ; מִמֶּנִּי *for* מִמֶּנְנִי; מִמֶּנּוּ (*from us*) *for* מִמֶּנְנוּ.

*b.* The consonant of the suffix is assimilated backwards and represented in נ: מִמֶּ֫נּוּ (*from him*) for מִמֶּנְהוּ; מִמֶּ֫נָּה for מִמֶּנְהָ.

Note 1.—The ◌ֶ in מִמֶּ֫נּוּ, etc., is deflected from ◌ִ (§ 29. 4).

Note 2.—Many variant forms, besides those given, are found, especially in poetry.

### 52. The Demonstrative Pronoun

| | | | |
|---|---|---|---|
| 1.   זֶה *this* (m.) | { זֹאת *this* (f.) | (אֵל) אֵ֫לֶּה *these* (m. or f.) | |
| | { זוֹ, זֹה *this* (f.) | { הֵ֫מָּה or הֵם *those* (m.) | |
| 2.   הוּא *that* (m.) | הִיא *that* (f.) | { הֵ֫נָּה or הֵן *those* (f.) | |

1. *a.* זֶה; *cf.* זוֹ rounded from זָֽי.

*b.* זֹאת =zô'θ, for zâ'θ (§ 30. 6), *i. e.*, זָֽי with feminine ending ת, *cf.* the shorter forms זוֹ, זֹה.

*c.* אֵ֫לֶּה has Dăḡēš-fŏrtē *firmative;* אֵל occurs only eight times, and then always in the Pentateuch and with the article.

2. The personal pronouns of the third person are used as remote demonstratives.

8. The forms הַלָּזֶה (*masc.*), הַלֵּזוּ (*fem.*), and הַלָּז (*masc. and fem.*), *this,* represent a stronger demonstrative, appearing only in the singular. They are not commonly used,—the first occurring twice,[1] the second, once,[2] the third seven times.[3]

### 53. The Relative Particle

1. אֲשֶׁר *who, which, that.*

2. ־שֶׁ, sometimes ־שַׁ.

3. זוּ.

1. The more frequent relative was originally a noun in the construct state meaning *place:*

    *a.* It is indeclinable,

    *b.* It is really a mere sign of relation, indicating the presence of some kind of a subordinate clause, the precise nature of which is indicated by other words, or by the general context.

---

[1] Gen. 24 : 65; 37 : 19.            [2] Ezek. 36 : 35.
[3] Judg. 6 : 20; 1 Sam. 14 : 1; 17 : 26; 2 Kgs. 4 : 25; 23 : 17; Dan. 8 : 16; Zech. 2 : 8.

2. ·שֶׁ, or ·שַׁ is in no way connected with אֲשֶׁר, but is a distinct pronoun.  It is found:

*a.* Exclusively in the Song of Songs, and frequently in Ecclesiastes.

*b.* Occasionally in other books, as Judges, 2 Kings, 1 Chronicles, Job, and the later Psalms.

3. זוּ is in reality a demonstrative (*cf.* זֶה); but its chief use is as a relative (*cf.* the similar usage of the English *that*, Greek ὅς, etc.).  It is indeclinable.

### 54.  The Interrogative Pronoun

1. מִי *who?*   מָה *what?*

2. *a.* מַה־יִּקְרָא (2:19); מַה־זֹּאת (3:13); מַה־שְּׁמוֹ (Ex. 3:13).

*b.* מַה־הִיא ; מַה־הוּא[1] (31:36); מֶה הַטָּאתִי[2].

*c.* מָה־אֵלֶּה[3]; מָה רְאִיתֶם[4]; *also* מָה הֵנָּה (21:29).

*d.* מֶה־חָדֵל ; מֶה־חָטָאתִי (20:9); מֶה עָשִׂיתָ (4:10)[5].

1. מִי refers to persons; מָה, to things.

2. מָה is variously pointed, according to the character of the consonant which follows:

*a.* Before consonants which can be doubled, it is.........מַה·

*b.* Before strong laryngeals (ה and ח), it is.............מַה

*c.* Before weak laryngeals (א, ע, and ר) it is...........מָה

*d.* Before laryngeals with ־ָ, it is....................מֶה

Note 1.—The Dăgēš-fŏrtē following מַה is compensative (§ 15.1), arising from the assimilation of ה which was a consonant.

Note 2.—The forms מֶה and מָה are sometimes found before other letters than laryngeals.

Note 3.—In the majority of cases מַה is connected with the following word by Măkkēf, and with זֶה often forms a single word, מַזֶּה.

Note 4.—By means of אַי (*where?*) prefixed to the demonstrative זֶה or זֹאת, another interrogative is formed.[6]

---

[1] Num. 16:11.       [3] Num. 13:18.       [4] Zech. 1:9.       [5] Judg. 9:48.
[6] Ps. 39:5.         [2] *Cf.* Jer. 5:7; Eccles. 11:6; 1 Kgs. 13:12.

# X. The Verb

## 55. Roots

1. בְּרָא (1:1); מַבְדִּיל (1:6) *from* בָּדַל; מִתְהַלֵּךְ (3:8) *from*
הִלֵּךְ; הֲקִימֹתִי (9:17) *from* קָם; שָׁבַת (2:3); הִמְטִיר
פָּקַח *from* (3:7) תִּפָּקַחְנָה; מָטָר *from* (2:5).

2. בָּרָא (1:1) *he created;* שָׁבַת (2:3) *he rested;* לָקַח (2:22)
*he took.*

  הָלַךְ (3:8) *he walked;* שָׁמַע (3:17) *he heard;* פָּקַח (3:7) *he*
  *opened.*

3. מוּת (3:4) *to die,* מֵת *he died;* שִׂים (2:8) *to put,* שָׂם *he put.*

All words are derived from so-called roots; concerning these it may
be noted:

1. While there are a very few roots of *four* letters, most Hebrew
roots consist of three or two letters, called *radicals.*

2. The root is generally pronounced with the vowels of the third
person singular masculine of the Perfect tense (§ **57.** 3. N. 1), this
being the simplest of all verbal forms.

3. Biliteral roots of the middle-vowel classes are commonly pronounced with the vowel of the infinitive construct.

**Note 1.**—The root is not in itself a word; it exists solely in the
mind of the philologist. בְּרָא is a root, but the word is בָּרָא.

**Note 2.**—Many of the roots now appearing to be triliteral, were
once biliterals; their triliteral forms are a later development.

**Note 3.**—For many words there has as yet been found no root.

## 56. Classes of Verbs

1. *a.* קָדַשׁ (1:4); בָּדַל (1:18); מָשַׁל (1:18); דָּבַק (2:24); שָׁבַת (2:3);
  (2:3).

b. שָׁלַח (1:11); זָרַע (1:2); רָחַף (1:2); הָרַג (4:8); עָזַב (2:24); (3:22).

c. נָתַן (1:17); יָצַר (2:7); בָּרָא (1:1); בָּנָה (Lam. 3:5).

2. a. סבב (2:11); חלל (4:26); חָנַן (33:5); גְּלָלוּ (29:3).

b. מוּת (3:4); בִּין[1] קוּם (13:17); יָשִׂים (30:42).

Verbal roots vary in inflection according to the number and nature of the consonants of which they are composed. They are therefore classified as:

1. *Triliteral*, when composed of three consonants. These again subdivide into three classes:

   *a. Strong* verbs, *i. e.*, those containing no consonant which will in any way affect the vowels usually employed in a given inflection.

   *b. Laryngeal* verbs, *i. e.*, those containing one or more laryngeals, which involve certain variations in vocalization from the so-called strong verb.

   *c. Weak* verbs, *i. e.*, those containing one or more consonants which may suffer assimilation (נ__), contraction and elision (ו__ and י__), or quiescence (א__). Such changes in the consonants, of course, affect the vowels seriously.

2. *Biliteral*, when composed of two consonants. These subdivide into two classes:

   *a.* The so-called *ʿayin-doubled* (ע″ע) verbs, in which the consonantal element of the root is emphasized in inflection.

   *b.* The *middle-vowel* verbs, in which the vowel-element is emphasized.

### 57. Inflection

1. a. בָּרָא (1:1) *from* ברא; שָׁב (18:33) *from* שׁב; סֹב (Deut. 2:3) *from* סב.

b. וַיְקַדֵּשׁ (2:3) *from* קדשׁ; לָקַח (3:23) *from* לקח; יָלַד (4:26) *from* ילד; סוֹבֵב (2:13) *from* סב.

---

[1] Prov. 23 : 1.

*c.* וְנִפְקְחוּ (3:5) *from* פקח; הִמְטִיר (2:5) *from* מטר; הוּחַל

יָשַׁב (Jer. 6:8) *from* נוֹשָׁבָה; חָלַל *from* (4:26).

2. שֵׁרְצוּ (3:10) *I heard;* שָׁמַעְתִּי (2:2) *he will rest;* יִשְׁבֹּת

*hast thou eaten?* (3:11) אָכַלְתָּ; *they swarmed* (1:21)

(4:3) יָבֵא; (17:12) יִמּוֹל; *they were opened* (3:7) וַתִּפָּקַחְנָה.

3. יַהַרְגֵהוּ (4:8) *he will kill him;* תֹּאכְלֶנָּה (3:17) *thou shalt eat it.*

The inflection of a verb includes three things:

1. The formation of verb-stems, of which there are,

    *a.* The simple verb-stem, generally identical with the root.

    *b.* Verb-stems formed by strengthening the simple root in various ways, especially by doubling or repetition of one or more radicals.

    *c.* Verb-stems formed by the use of *prefixes.*

2. The addition to the verb-stem of affixes and prefixes for the indication of tense or mood, person, number, gender.

3. The various changes of the verbal forms, which take place when pronominal suffixes are attached as objects.

**Note 1.**—The Hebrew verb has for each stem (1) a Perfect tense, which indicates finished or completed action, (2) an Imperfect, which indicates unfinished action, (3) an Imperative (except in Passive stems), (4) two Infinitives, and (5) a Participle.

**Note 2.**—The Perfect and Imperfect, which may be called tenses, are inflected to distinguish number, person, and *gender.*

**Note 3.**—The Imperative is used only in the second person, masculine and feminine, singular and plural.

### 58. *The Verb-Stems*

1. (11:9) בָּלַל; שָׁב[1]; לָ־קַח (3:22); בָּ־רָא (1:1); שָׁ־בַת (2:3).

2. נִשְׁמַר *watch* נִבְנָה[4]; נִכְבַּד[2]; נָכוֹן (41:32); נָסַב; נָבְנָה[3]; one's self; נִשְׁפַּט *go to law one with another.* [וְנִקְטַל]

---

[1] Jer. 30 : 18.      [2] 2 Sam. 6 : 20.      [3] Num. 34 : 4.      [4] 1 Kgs. 6 : 7.

3. [קְטֵל]; דִּבֶּר (12:4); מִלֵּא¹; כִּלָּה (18:33); בֵּרַךְ (24:1);
שֵׁרֵשׁ root; שֹׁרֶשׁ uproot; לִמֵּד teach; לָמַד learn.

4. [קֻטַּל]; פֻּקַּד²; קֹרָא³; מְבֹרָךְ⁴; לָקַח he took; לֻקַּח he was
taken.

5. [הִקְטִיל]; הִפְקִיד (39:5); הֶחֱזִיק; הֵקִים⁵; הֵסֵב⁷.

6. [הָקְטַל]; הָפְקַד; הָמְלַךְ⁹; הֻגַּד¹⁰; הֻשְׁלַךְ¹¹.

7. [הִתְקַטֵּל]; הִתְהַלֵּךְ (6:9); יִתְעַצֵּב (6:6); אֶשְׁתַּמֵּר¹².

הִטַּהֲרוּ; יִתְדַּכְּאוּ for יִדַּכְּאוּ¹³ for נִצְטַדֵּק (44:16) נִתְצַדֵּק
for הִתְטַהֲרוּ.

There are in common use seven verb-stems, each representing a
different aspect or development of the primary meaning of the verb.

1. The simple verb-stem is called *Ķăl* (קַל), *i. e., light,* since it
presents the verb in its simplest form, not encumbered with the additions characteristic of the other stems.

2. *a.* The Passive of the Ķăl stem is called *Nif'ăl.*

Note.—In all stems other than the Ķăl, the stem name is formed
from the paradigm-verb used by the Arabic and the Jewish grammarians, viz., פָּעַל; thus the name of this stem = נִפְעַל.

*b.* The formal characteristic of this stem is the prefixed נ.

*c.* The meaning of the stem is usually passive, but it occurs also
with its original *reflexive* force, and sometimes as *reciprocal.*

3. *a.* The intensive active stem is called *Pi'ēl* (triliteral) or *Pôlēl*
(biliteral).

*b.* The formal characteristic of this stem is the doubling or repetition of the second radical of the root.

*c.* The stem is used as an intensive of the Ķăl, and expresses
various shades of meaning such as (1) intensity, (2) repetition, (3)

¹ Ex. 35 : 35.    ² Ex. 38 : 21.    ³ Isa. 48 : 8.    ⁴ Num. 22 : 6.
⁵ Judg. 7 : 8.    ⁶ Josh. 4 : 9.    ⁷ 2 Kgs. 16 : 18.    ⁸ Jer. 6 : 6.
⁹ Dan. 9 : 1.    ¹⁰ Josh. 9 : 24.    ¹¹ Dan. 8 : 11.    ¹² Ps. 18 : 24.
¹³ Job 5 : 4.    ¹⁴ Ezr. 6 : 20.

causation, and (4) a privative idea, in the case of Pïʻēls from nominal
forms.

4. *a.* The intensive passive stem is called *Pŭʻăl* (triliteral) or
*Pôlăl* (biliteral).

*b.* The formal characteristic of this root is the doubling or repetition of the second radical, with ŭ or ô under the first radical.

*c.* The regular usage of this stem is as a passive of the Pïʻēl;
but sometimes it serves as passive of the Ḳǎl.

5. *a.* The active causative stem is called *Hïfʻïl.*

*b.* The formal characteristic of this stem is the prefix ＿ﬣ,
which undergoes modification in inflection.

*c.* This stem serves as a causative of the Ḳǎl.

6. *a.* The passive causative stem is called *Hŏfʻăl.*

*b.* The formal characteristic is the prefix ＿ﬣ, which undergoes change in inflection.

*c.* The usage of this stem is as a passive of the Hïfʻïl.

7. *a.* The intensive reflexive stem is called *Hïθpăʻēl.*

*b.* The formal characteristic of this stem is the prefix ＿ﬤﬣ,
joined to the Pïʻēl stem.

*c.* This stem is used primarily as a reflexive of the Pïʻēl stem;
but it occurs also with (1) a reciprocal, (2) a passive force, and (3)
the force of the indirect Greek middle.

**Note.**—The ﬨ of the prefix is always *transposed* when it would
stand before ס, שׁ or שׂ; it is transposed and partly *assimilated*, becoming ט, when before צ; and it is completely assimilated before
ד, ט or ת.

# XI. The Triliteral Verb

## A. THE STRONG VERB

### 59. General View of the Triliteral Verb-Stems

**TABLE**

| | Original Form. | Form appearing in the Perfect. | Name. | Force. | Characteristics. |
|---|---|---|---|---|---|
| 1. | קָטַל | קָטַל | Ḳăl | Simple Root meaning | None |
| 2. | נִקְטַל | נִקְטַל | Nĭf'ăl | Reflexive, Reciprocal, Passive | נ |
| 3. | קַטֵּל | קִטֵּל | Pĭ'ēl | Intensive Active | Dåğēš-fŏrtē in 2d radical |
| 4. | קֻטַּל | קֻטַּל | Pŭ'ăl | Intensive Passive | Dåğēš-fŏrtē and ֻ |
| 5. | הַקְטִיל | הִקְטִיל | Hĭf'ĭl | Causative Active | (הֶ) הַ |
| 6. | הַקְטַל | הָקְטַל | Hŏf'ăl | Causative Passive | (הֻ) הָ |
| 7. | הִתְקַטַּל | הִתְקַטֵּל | Hĭθpă'ēl | Reflexive, Reciprocal | הִת and Dåğēš-fŏrtē |

## REMARKS

1. An original penultimate ◌ַ is attenuated to ◌ִ, in Nĭf'ăl, Pĭ'ēl, and Hĭf'ĭl.

2. An ultimate ◌ֵ is lowered to ◌ַ, in some Pĭ'ēl, Hĭf'ĭl and Hĭθpă'ēl forms.

3. An ultimate ◌ַ is anomalously lengthened to ◌ִי, in some Hĭf'ĭl forms.

4. An original penultimate ◌ַ is deflected to ◌ָ (ŏ) in the Hŏf'ăl.

73

## NOTES[1]

1. Only 6 verbs out of about 1400 have all seven stems, viz.: בָּקַע,
פָּקַד ,יָלַד ,יָדַע ,חָלָה ,גָּלָה.

2. 379 verbs are found in Ḳăl only; 40 in Nĭf'ăl only; 68 in Pī'ēl
only; 11 in Pŭ'ăl only; 58 in Hĭf'ĭl only; 6 in Hŏf'ăl only; 19 in
Hĭθpă'ēl only.

3. In all, 1090 verbs have a Ḳăl stem; 433, a Nĭf'ăl stem; 405, a
Pī'ēl stem; 188, a Pŭ'ăl stem; 503, a Hĭf'ĭl stem; 104, a Hŏf'ăl stem;
177, a Hĭθpă'ēl stem.

### 60. The Ḳăl Perfect (Active)

#### TABULAR VIEW

| | | |
|---|---|---|
| 1. *He killed* | קָטַל | the simple verb-stem. |
| 2. *She killed* | קָטְלָה = קָטַל | with הָ_ (originally ת_ָ), the usual feminine sign. |
| 3. *Thou* (m.) *killedst* | קָטַלְתָּ = קָטַל | with תָּ; *cf.* the pronoun אַתָּה *thou* (m.). |
| 4. *Thou* (f.) *killedst* | קָטַלְתְּ = קָטַל | with תְּ; *cf.* the pronoun אַתְּ *thou* (f.). |
| 5. *I killed* | קָטַלְתִּי = קָטַל | with תִּי, the affix of 1st person in all Perfects. |
| 6. *They killed* | קָטְלוּ = קָטַל | with וּ, the usual plural sign with verbs. |
| 7. *Ye* (m.) *killed* | קְטַלְתֶּם = קָטַל | with תֶּם; *cf.* the pronoun אַתֶּם *ye* (m.). |
| 8. *Ye* (f.) *killed* | קְטַלְתֶּן = קָטַל | with תֶּן; *cf.* the pronoun אַתֶּן *ye* (f.). |
| 9. *We killed* | קָטַלְנוּ = קָטַל | with נוּ; *cf.* the pronoun אָנוּ ,אֲנַחְנוּ *we.* |

[1] Young's *Introduction to Hebrew*, pp. 16, 17.

## REMARKS

1. The pronominal elements used in the inflection of the Perfect are always *af*-fixed to the stem.

2. The inflection of the verb exhibits distinctions for number, person and *gender*. Special forms for the feminine occur in the 2d and 3d person sing., and in the 2d person plur.

3. *a.* The original vowels of the Ḳal Perfect are ă—ă (קָטַל). In the form קָטַל, the ă under the tone remains unchanged, while the ă in the open syllable before the tone is rounded to â. The same vowel change takes place in forms 3, 4, 5 and 9.

*b.* In forms 2 and 6, the vowel-terminations הָ_ (=*she*) and וּ (=*they*) draw the preceding consonant away from the ultimate vowel (ă) of the stem; the change of this vowel to Šᵉwâ follows (§ 36. 3) and the ă of the preceding syl. being now immediately before the tone-syl. is rounded to â.

*c.* The heavy terminations תֶּם (=*ye* (m.)) and תֶּן (=*ye* (f.)) carry the tone; the ă in the final syl. of the stem is retained unchanged in the closed unaccented syllable; while the ă of the open antepenult is reduced to Šᵉwâ (§ 36. 3. N. 2).

### 61. The Ḳăl Perfect (*Stative*)

[For the full inflection, see Paradigm B.]

#### TABULAR VIEW

|          | 3 m. sg. | 3 f. sg. | 3 c. pl. | 2 m. pl. | 1 c. pl. |
|----------|----------|----------|----------|----------|----------|
| Middle A | קָטַל    | קָטְלָה  | קָטְלוּ  | קְטַלְתֶּם | קָטַלְנוּ |
| Middle E | קָטֵל    | קָטְלָה  | קָטְלוּ  | קְטַלְתֶּם | קָטַלְנוּ |
| Middle O | קָטֹל    | קָטְלָה  | קָטְלוּ  | קְטַלְתֶּם | קָטַלְנוּ |

1. דָּבַק (2:24); שָׁרְצוּ (1:21); שְׁמַעְתֶּם (42:22); שָׁמַעְתִּי (3:10).

2. זָקֵן (18:12); זָקַנְתִּי (18:13); כָּבֵד (12:10); כָּבְדָה (18:20); אֲהֵבוֹ; יָבֵשׁוּ²; אָהַב (37:3), *but* אָהֵב (27:9); כָּבְדָה (44:20).

---

¹ Judg. 20 : 34.                    ² Joel 1 : 12.

3. שָׁכֹלְתִּי (32:11) קָטֹנְתִּי ;(30:8) יָכֹלְתִּי ;'יָכֹלוּ ;(32:26) יָכֹל
(43:14).

Certain verbs expressive of physical or mental states of being are
called *stative* verbs. They show some characteristic forms in inflection.

1. Stative verbs with — under the second radical of the Ḳăl stem
are inflected in the manner described in the preceding section (§ **60.**).

2. Verbs with — (lowered from —) under the second radical, do
not differ from those with — in the inflection of the Perfect, except
that the — appears

    *a.* in the Perfect 3 masc. sing., and

    *b.* when restored in pause (§ **38. 1**), or before the tone.

3. Verbs with — (lowered from —) under the second radical retain the ō whenever the tone would rest upon it, and in pause.

### 62. The Remaining Perfects

[For the full inflection, see Paradigm B.]
**TABULAR VIEW OF IMPORTANT FORMS**

|  | 3 m. sg. | 3 f. sg. | 3 c. pl. | 2 m. pl. | 1 c. pl. |
|---|---|---|---|---|---|
| Nĭfʻăl | נִקְטַל | נִקְטְלָה | נִקְטְלוּ | נִקְטַלְתֶּם | נִקְטַלְנוּ |
| Pŭʻăl | קֻטַּל | קֻטְּלָה | קֻטְּלוּ | קֻטַּלְתֶּם | קֻטַּלְנוּ |
| Hŏfʻăl | הָקְטַל | הָקְטְלָה | הָקְטְלוּ | הָקְטַלְתֶּם | הָקְטַלְנוּ |
| Pĭʻēl | ²קִטֵּל | קִטְּלָה | קִטְּלוּ | קִטַּלְתֶּם | קִטַּלְנוּ |
| Hĭθpăʻēl | הִתְקַטֵּל | הִתְקַטְּלָה | הִתְקַטְּלוּ | הִתְקַטַּלְתֶּם | הִתְקַטַּלְנוּ |
| Hĭfʻîl | הִקְטִיל | הִקְטִילָה | הִקְטִילוּ | הִקְטַלְתֶּם | הִקְטַלְנוּ |

1. *a.* ⁶נִדְבַּרְנוּ ;⁵נִשְׁמַרְתֶּם ;³נִשְׁמָר ;⁴נִסְתְּרָה ;נִפְקְחוּ ;(3:5)

   *b.* ⁸יָלַדְתִּי ;⁷יְלַדְתֶּם ;(6:1) יִלְדוּ ;(24:15) יָלְדָה ;(4:26) יָלַד

---

¹ Ex. 8 : 14.　　　² Or קְטַל.　　　³ 2 Sam. 20 : 10.　　　⁴ Num. 5 : 13.

⁵ Deut. 2 : 4.　　　⁶ Mal. 3 : 13.　　　⁷ Jer. 22 : 26.　　　⁸ Jer. 20 : 14.

c. הָפְקַד¹; הָכְרַת²; הָשְׁלְכוּ³; הָשְׁלַכְתְּ⁴; הָשְׁבַּרְתִּי⁵.

2. a. דֻּבַּר; (44:2) דֻּבְּרָה (39:19); דֻּבְּרוּ (45:15); דֻּבַּרְתֶּם⁶.

b. וְהִתְגַּדִּלְתִּי¹⁰; הִתְקַדִּשׁוּ⁹; הִתְקַדַּשְׁתֶּם⁸; הִתְקַדֶּשׁ⁷.

c. הִמְטִיר; (2:5) הִכְרִיתָה¹¹; הִצְדִּיקוּ¹²; הִרְדַּבַּקְתִּי¹³; הִמְלַכְתָּ¹⁴.

Of the remaining Perfects, it will be noticed that

1. Three follow entirely the inflection of the Ḳăl Perfect, viz.,

    *a.* The Nïf'äl (נִקְטַל *from* נַקְטַל).

    *b.* The Pŭ'äl (קֻטַּל).

    *c.* The Hŏf'äl (הָקְטַל, also sometimes הֻקְטַל).

2. Three present slight variations from the inflection of the Ḳăl, viz.,

    *a.* The Pï'ēl (קִטֵּל *and* קִטַּל, *from* קִטַּל), in which ⸗ appears in the ultima before terminations beginning with a consonant.

    *b.* The Hïθpă'ēl (הִתְקַטֵּל *and* הִתְקַטַּל), in which, also, ă appears, but sometimes ï is retained.

    *c.* The Hïf'îl (הִקְטִיל, anomalous for הִקְטַל, *from* הִקְטַל), in which,

      (1) before the vowel-terminations ⸗ָה and וּ, the anomalous î is retained and *accented;* while

      (2) before terminations beginning with a consonant, ⸗ everywhere appears.

### 63. The Ḳăl Imperfect (Active)
#### TABULAR VIEW

| | | |
|---|---|---|
| 1. *He will kill* | יִקְטֹל, for יַקְטֹל | (with יַ). |
| 2. *She will kill* | תִּקְטֹל, for תַּתְקְטֹל | תַּ, the usual sign of the feminine, here prefixed. |

¹ Lev. 5 : 23.    ² Joel 1 : 9.    ³ Jer. 22 : 28.    ⁴ Isa. 14 : 19.
⁵ Jer. 8 : 21.    ⁶ Ex. 12 : 32.    ⁷ Isa. 30 : 29.    ⁸ Num. 11 : 18.
⁹ Lev. 11 : 44.    ¹⁰ Ezek. 38 : 23.    ¹¹ Lev. 26 : 22.    ¹² Deut. 25 : 1.
¹³ Jer. 13 : 11.    ¹⁴ 1 Kgs. 3 : 7.

3. *Thou* (m.) *wilt kill*    תִּקְטֹל, for תְּתִקְטֹל, תְּ being a pronom. root of 2d pers., *cf.* אַתָּה *thou* (m.).

4. *Thou* (f.) *wilt kill*    תִּקְטְלִי, for תְּקְטֹל (with תְּ as above), and יִ_ (*cf.* הִיא *she*) used as a sign of fem.; *cf.* אַתִּי[1] *thou* (f.).

5. *I shall kill*    אֶקְטֹל, for אַקְטֹל, with אַ; *cf.* אָנֹכִי *I*.

6. *They* (m.) *will kill*    יִקְטְלוּ, for יַקְטֹל (with יַ, see above), and וּ, the usual plur. ending of verbs.

7. *They* (f.) *will kill*    תִּקְטֹלְנָה, for תְּקְטֹל (with תְּ as above), and נָה; *cf.* הֵנָּה *they* (f.).

8. *Ye* (m.) *will kill*    תִּקְטְלוּ, for תְּקְטֹל (with תְּ as above), and וּ, the usual plur. ending of verbs.

9. *Ye* (f.) *will kill*    תִּקְטֹלְנָה, for תְּקְטֹל (with תְּ as above), and נָה; *cf.* אַתֵּנָה *ye* (f.).

10. *We shall kill*    נִקְטֹל, for נַקְטֹל, with נַ, a pronominal root; *cf.* נַחְנוּ *we*.

---

### REMARKS

1. The pronominal elements employed in the inflection of the Imperfect are not so clearly recognized as in the Perfect; they are

  *a. Pre*-fixes: יִ, תְּ, תְּ, תְּ, אַ, יִ, תְּ, תְּ, תְּ, נַ, in all of which — is attenuated to —, but under א is deflected to — (ĕ).

  *b. Af*-fixes: —, —, —, יִ_, —; וּ, נָה, וּ, נָה, —

---
[1] אַתִּי is found in Kᵉθîv seven times for אַתְּ *thou* (f.).

2. *a.* The stem of the Imperfect is קְטֹל, whence comes קָטֹל through the influence of the tone. *Cf.* Arabic *yaḳtul.*

The original form of the Impf. stem was *ḳuṭŭl,* and the same stem forms the basis of the Imperative and Infinitive Construct forms. When the preformative of the Impf. was added, it naturally drew to itself a secondary tone, and so the ŭ of the following syllable was easily lost (*cf. business,* pronounced *biz-ness*). It reappears in certain forms of the Infinitive Construct and Imperative.

*b.* The ō is often written fully (וֹ); but this must be regarded as an error, since it is a tone-long vowel.

*c.* When יִקְטֹל and similar forms are connected by Măḳḳēf with a following word, thus losing the tone, the original ŭ is not lowered to ō, but deflected to ŏ ( ֳ ).

3. The vowel-terminations ִי‎ (seldom יִן‎) and וּ‎ (seldom וּן‎) draw the preceding consonant away from the ultimate vowel, which then necessarily passes into Š⁰wâ (§ **36.** 2. *a*).

4. The termination נָה (seldom ָן‎) does not receive the tone.

### 64. The Ḳăl Imperfect (*Stative*)
[For full inflection, see Paradigm B.]
#### TABULAR VIEW OF IMPORTANT FORMS

| | 3 m. sg. | 2 f. sg. | 3 m. pl. | 3 f. pl. |
|---|---|---|---|---|
| Impf. with ō | יִקְטֹל | תִּקְטְלִי | יִקְטְלוּ | תִּקְטֹלְנָה |
| Impf. with ă | יִקְטַל | תִּקְטְלִי | יִקְטְלוּ | תִּקְטַלְנָה |
| Impf. with ē | יִקְטֵל | תִּקְטְלִי | יִקְטְלוּ | תִּקְטֵלְנָה |

1. יִשְׁבַּת (2:2); יִסְגֹּר (2:21); יִשְׁרְצוּ (1:20); יִתָּפְרוּ (3:7); יִגְבְּרוּ (7:18).

2. יִשְׁכַּב (30:15) *from* שָׁכַב; יִגְדַּל (21:8) *from* גָּדַל; יִגְבְּרוּ (7:18); אֶשְׁכַּל (27:45); יִצְמָח (2:5); יִפַּע (2:8); יִשְׁלַח (3:22); תִּגְעוּ (3:3).

3. יִתֵּן (1:17); תִּתֵּן (3:6); תֵּלֵךְ (3:14); יֵצֵא (4:16).

1. Stative verbs with middle A, with some exceptions, have in the Imperfect the form יִקְטֹל (*orig.* yăk̄-t̬ŭl), the inflection of which is given in § 63.

2. Verbs middle E and verbs middle O, with some verbs middle A, have in the Imperfect a stem with ă instead of ō; this ă is treated like the ō.

**Remark.**—The Imperfect stem קְטַל, instead of קְטֹל, is used also in verbs, whether active or stative, which have a laryngeal for the second or third radical.

3. Some verbs whose first radical is נ, and the verb נָתַן *to give*, have for the Imperfect stem the form קְטֵל, *i. e.*, ē instead of ō or ă. No strong verb has this stem.

**Note 1.**—There were three Perfect stems, קְטַל, קָטֵל, and קָטֹל; and so there are three Imperfect stems, יִקְטֹל, יִקְטַל, and יִקְטֵל, the ă in each case being original, while the ē and ō have come from ĭ and ŭ respectively.

**Note 2.**—It will be seen later that the stem-vowel of the Imperative varies with that of the Imperfect.

### 65. The Remaining Imperfects

[For full inflection, see Paradigm B.]

#### TABULAR VIEW OF IMPORTANT FORMS

|  | 3 m. sg. | 2 f. sg. | 1 c. sg. | 3 f. pl. |
|---|---|---|---|---|
| Nĭfʿăl | יִקָּטֵל | תִּקָּטְלִי | אֶקָּטֵל | תִּקָּטַלְנָה(טַל) |
| Pĭʿēl | יְקַטֵּל | תְּקַטְּלִי | אֲקַטֵּל | תְּקַטֵּלְנָה(טַל) |
| Hĭθpăʿēl | יִתְקַטֵּל | תִּתְקַטְּלִי | אֶתְקַטֵּל | תִּתְקַטֵּלְנָה(טַל) |
| Pŭʿăl | יְקֻטַּל | תְּקֻטְּלִי | אֲקֻטַּל | תְּקֻטַּלְנָה |
| Hŏfʿăl | יָקְטַל | תָּקְטְלִי | אָקְטַל | תָּקְטַלְנָה |
| Hĭfʿîl | יַקְטִיל(יַקְטֵל) | תַּקְטִילִי | אַקְטִיל | תַּקְטֵלְנָה |

1. יִפְרַד (2:10); אֶסְתַּר (4:14); תְּשָׁחֵת (6:11); יִסָּכְרוּ (8:2).

2. יְקַדֵּשׁ (2:3); יְדַבֵּר (8:15); תְּדַבֵּר (31:24).

3. ²תִּשְׁתַּפֵּכְנָה; יִתְלַקְּטוּ (6:6) יִתְעַצֵּב.

4. ⁷תִּשְׁלְכִי; ⁶תָּקְטָר; ⁵יְסֻפַּר; תֻּלַקְּטוּ³; יְכֻפַּר.

5. יַלְבִּשׁ (3:21); יַבְדֵּל (1:4); תַּשְׁבִּיתוּ⁹; תַּשְׁחִיתוּן⁸; יִשְׁכֵּן
(3:24); תַּשְׁלֵךְ (21:15).

1. *a.* The *stem* of the Nĭf'ăl Imperfect differs from that of the
Nĭf'ăl Perfect in two particulars:

(1) the first radical has a vowel,

(2) the original form of the Imperfect was *yănăḳăṭĭl.* Emphasis
upon the preformative caused the elision of the second ă,
with the consequent assimilation of the n to the following
ḳ and its representation by dåǧ. fŏrtē and attenuation of
the preformative ă to ĭ.

**Note.**—The vowel of the ultima, generally —, is sometimes —;
*cf.* the interchange of these vowels in the Pĭ'ēl, and Hĭθpă'ēl.

*b.* In the *inflection* of the Nĭf'ăl Imperfect, there is to be noted,

(1) the use of either — or — before נָה;

(2) the occurrence of — sometimes instead of — under the
pref. א.¹⁰

2. *a.* The *stem* of the Pĭ'ēl Imperfect is identical with that of the
corresponding Perfect, except that the original penultimate — is now
retained.

*b.* In the *inflection* of the Pĭ'ēl Imperfect, there is to be noted,

(1) the use of Š⁽ᵉ⁾wâ under the preformatives, just as also in
the Pŭ'ăl (compound Š⁽ᵉ⁾wâ under the laryngeal א); this
reduction of the preformative vowel in Pĭ'ēl and Pŭ'ăl is
due to strong stress on the following syllable.

(2) the use of either — or — (prevailingly the former) before
נָה.

3. *a.* The *stem* of the Hĭθpă'ēl Imperfect is the same as that of the
corresponding Perfect, except that ה does not appear in the preformative syllable.

¹ Judg. 11 : 3.　　　³ Lam. 4 : 1.　　　³ Isa. 27 : 9.　　　⁴ Isa. 27 : 12.
⁵ Ps. 88 : 12.　　　⁶ Lev. 6 : 15.　　　⁷ Ezek. 16 : 5.　　　⁸ Deut. 4 : 16.
⁹ Ex. 12 : 15.
¹⁰ Always so in the punctuation system of the Babylonian Jews.

*b.* In the *inflection* of the Hîθpă'ēl Imperfect, there is likewise to be noted the use of either ⸗ or ⸗ (prevailingly the former) before נָה.

4. The stem and inflection of the Pŭ'ăl and Hŏf'ăl present no new peculiarities.

5. *a.* The *stem* of the Hîf'îl Imperfect is identical with that of the corresponding Perfect, except that (1) under the preformatives the original ⸗ is retained, and (2) the causative ה is elided, as also in the Hŏf'ăl Imperfect.

    *b.* In the *inflection* of the Hîf'îl Imperfect, there is to be noted,

        (1) the form יַקְטֵל, used as a Jussive (§ 69.), and with Wâw Conversive (§ 70.), the ⸗ of which is regularly lowered from ⸗;

        (2) the retention and accentuation of the stem-vowel ִי⸗ before the vowel-additions ִי⸗, ְ;

        (3) the occurrence of ⸗, rather than ִי⸗, before נָה.

**Note 1.**—The following table will be found serviceable:

| 1. Name of stem, | Ḳăl, | Nîf., | Pî., | Pŭ., | Hîf., | Hŏf., | Hîθpă. |
|---|---|---|---|---|---|---|---|
| 2. Preformative with vowel, | יְ | יִ | יְ | יְ | יַ | יָ | יִת. |
| 3. First radical with vowel, | ק | קָ | קַ | קֻ | ק | ק | קַ |

**Note 2.**—The various elements used as preformatives and afformatives appear from the following table, the asterisks representing radicals:

| 3 m. | *He will* | י*** | *They will* | י***וּ |
| 3 f. | *She will* | ת*** | *They will* | תְ***נָה |
| 2 m. | *Thou wilt* | ת*** | *Ye will* | תְ***וּ |
| 2 f. | *Thou wilt* | תְ***י | *Ye will* | תְ***נָה |
| 1 c. | *I shall* | א*** | *We shall* | נְ*** |

### 66. *The Imperatives*
#### TABULAR VIEW

| | Impf. | Imv. 2 m. sg. | Imv. 2 f. sg. | Imv. 2 m. pl. | Imv. 2 f. pl. |
|---|---|---|---|---|---|
| Ḳăl with ō | יִקְטֹל | קְטֹל | קִטְלִי | קִטְלוּ | קְטֹלְנָה |
| Ḳăl with ă | יִקְטַל | קְטַל | קִטְלִי | קִטְלוּ | קְטַלְנָה |
| Nîf'ăl | יִקְטֵל | הִקָּטֵל | הִקָּטְלִי | הִקָּטְלוּ | הִקָּטֵלְנָה |

| | | | | | |
|---|---|---|---|---|---|
| Pĭʿēl | קַטֵּלְנָה | קַטְּלוּ | קַטְּלִי | קַטֵּל | יְקַטֵּל |
| Hĭfʿîl | הַקְטֵלְנָה | הַקְטִילוּ | הַקְטִילִי | הַקְטֵל | יַקְטִיל |
| Hĭθpăʿēl | הִתְקַטֵּלְנָה | הִתְקַטְּלוּ | הִתְקַטְּלִי | הִתְקַטֵּל | יִתְקַטֵּל |

1. *a.* [4]שְׁכַב (30:15), יִשְׁכַּב[3]; כְּתֹב, יִכְתֹּב[2], כָּתֹב[3]; זְכֹר, יִזְכֹּר[1] (8:1),

    *b.* יַשְׁלִיךְ[5], יַשְׁלֵךְ[6], הַשְׁלֵךְ[7]; תִּשְׁכִּים[8], יַשְׁכֵּם (20:8), הַשְׁכֵּם[9].

    *c.* הַשְׁלֵךְ[7], יַשְׁלִיךְ[5], תִּשָּׁמֵר[10]; תִּשְׁמֵר (24:6), תִּתְחַתֵּן[11], הִתְחַתֵּן[12].

2. *a.* חֶשְׂפִּי[13]; כִּבְשֻׁ(הָ)(ם) (1:28); מִלְאוּ (1:22);

    *b.* הַשְׁלֵךְ[16], הַשְׁלִיכוּ[16] (37:22), הַשְׁלִיכִי[14]; הַקְשֵׁב[15], הַקְשִׁיבָה[16].

1. The *stem* of the Imperative is the same in every case as that of
the Imperfect; it will be noted that, like the Imperfect,

    *a.* The Ḳăl has two forms, one (active) with ō, and one (stative)
with ă.

    *b.* The Hĭfʿîl corresponds in form to the Jussive Imperfect in
ē (§ 69.), rather than to the usual Imperfect, which has î. Both forms
are naturally more quickly spoken than the Indicative.

    *c.* The initial ה which is always absent from a preformative in
the Impf., appears in the Imperative of the Nĭfʿăl, Hĭfʿîl, and Hĭθpăʿēl.

Note.—The pure passives Pŭʿăl and Hŏfʿăl have no Imperative.

2. In the *inflection* of the Imperatives, it will be seen that

    *a.* Before vowel-additions, the vowel of the stem disappears
(except in the Hĭfʿîl); and the short ĭ under the first radical of the
Ḳăl fem. sg., and masc. pl., stands in a closed syllable, the transliteration being ḳĭṭ-lî, ḳĭṭlû.

Note.—Occasional forms like מָלְכִי[17], מָשְׁכוּ[18], and certain
forms with pronominal suffixes (§ 71. 3. *b*) show that the original Imv.

---

[1] Deut. 9 : 7.  [2] Ex. 24 : 4.  [3] Ex. 17 : 14.  [4] 2 Sam. 13 : 5.
[5] Isa. 2 : 20.  [6] Ex. 7 : 10.  [7] Ex. 7 : 9.  [8] Judg. 9 : 33.
[9] Ex. 8 : 16.  [10] Judg. 13 : 13.  [11] Deut. 7 : 3.  [12] 1 Sam. 18 : 22.
[13] Isa. 47 : 2.  [14] Jer. 7 : 29.  [15] Job 33 : 31.  [16] Ps. 5 : 3.
[17] Ezek. 32 : 20.  [18] Judg. 9 : 10, 12 (Ḳᵉrê).

stem was probably vocalized קְטֹל. Hence the ĭ of fem. sg. and masc. pl. is perhaps thinned from ŭ.

*b.* The Hĭf'ĭl Imv. has ē as its stem-vowel in the masc. sg., and fem. pl., but î in the fem. sg. and masc. pl.

**Note 1.**—The stem of the Imperative receives no preformatives, and its afformatives are those of the Imperfect.

**Note 2.**—On the Imperative with הָ‍ (cohortative) see § **69.**

### 67. *The Infinitives*

**TABULAR VIEW**

| Ķăl. | Nĭf'ăl. | Pĭ'ēl. | Pŭ'ăl. | Hĭθpă'ēl. | Hĭf'ĭl. | Hŏf'ăl. |
|---|---|---|---|---|---|---|
| קָטוֹל | { נִקְטֹל / הִקָּטֹל } | { קַטֵּל / קַטֹּל } | קֻטֹּל | הִתְקַטֵּל | הַקְטֵל | הָקְטֵל |
| קְטֹל | הִקָּטֵל | קַטֵּל | | הִתְקַטֵּל | הַקְטִיל | |

1. ‍שָׁמוֹר[1]; הִנָּתֹן[2]; נִכְסֹף (31:30); דַּבֵּר[3]; גָּנֹב (40:15); ‍הַשְׁכֵּם[4]; הַבְדֵּל[5].

2. *a.* מְשֹׁל (1:18); שָׁמֹר (3:24); *but* שָׁכֵב (34:7); הִכָּרֵת[6]; הִתְכַּבֵּד[8]; הַבְדִּיל (1:18); בַּקֵּשׁ[7]; דַּבֵּר (17:22).

*b.* מָשְׁחָה[11]; רָחְצָה[10]; קָרְבָה[9].

Each stem has two Infinitives, called Absolute and Construct; but no example is found of a Pŭ'ăl or Hŏf'ăl Infinitive Construct.

1. The Infinitive *Absolute* has the form of a noun, and is not based upon either the Perfect or Imperfect stem.

*a. In the penult,* an original ă becomes å in the Ķăl and in one form of the Nĭf'ăl, ĭ in the other Nĭf'ăl, and remains unchanged in the Pĭ'ēl, Hĭθpă'ēl and Hĭf'ĭl; while original ŭ appears in the Pŭ'ăl and is deflected to ŏ in the Hŏf'ăl.

---

| | | | |
|---|---|---|---|
| [1] Deut. 5 : 12. | [2] Jer. 32 : 4. | [3] Ex. 4 : 14. | [4] 1 Sam. 17 : 16. |
| [5] Isa. 56 : 3. | [6] Num. 15 : 31. | [7] 1 Sam. 10 : 2. | [8] Nah. 3 : 15. |
| [9] Ex. 36 : 2. | [10] Ex. 30 : 18. | [11] Ex. 29 : 29. | |

*b. In the ultima:*

(1) ô ( = â) in the Ḳăl, Nĭf'ăl, Pŭ'ăl, and sometimes in Pĭ'ēl.

(2) ē in the Hĭf'ĭl, Hŏf'ăl, Hĭθpă'ēl and usually in Pĭ'ēl.

**Remark. 1.**—The Nĭf'ăl Infinitive Absolute has two forms, one (נִקְטֹל) following the analogy of the Perfect; the other (הִקָּטֹל), following the analogy of the stem appearing in the Inf. Construct and Imperative.

**Remark 2.**—The ô in the Inf. Abs., arising always from â, is seldom written fully. Old noun forms in Arabic likewise show long vowels written defectively.

2. *a.* The Infinitive *Construct* has, in each case, the form of the stem found in the Imperfect and Imperative.

**Remark.**—Stative verbs, which have ă in the Imperfect and Imperative, have, nevertheless, ō in the Infinitive Construct. The cases of an Infinitive Construct with ă are very few.

*b.* The Ḳăl Inf. Construct not infrequently takes a form with הָ‍ֿ. This form is found especially with the preposition לְ.

**Note 1.**—The ultimate vowel of the various Infinitives Construct is changeable, while that of the Infinitives Absolute is unchangeable.

**Note 2.**—Only to the Infinitives Construct may prepositions be prefixed, or suffixes added.

### 68. The Participles

**TABULAR VIEW**

| Ḳăl Active. | Ḳăl Stative. | Ḳăl Passive. | Nĭf'ăl. |
|---|---|---|---|
| קֹטֵל | קָטֵל | קָטוּל | נִקְטָל |

|  | Pĭ'ēl. | Pŭ'ăl. | Hĭf'ĭl. | Hŏf'ăl. | Hĭθpă'ēl. |
|---|---|---|---|---|---|
| Impf. | יְקַטֵּל | יְקֻטַּל | יַקְטִיל | יָקְטַל | יִתְקַטֵּל |
| Part. | מְקַטֵּל | מְקֻטָּל | מַקְטִיל | מָקְטָל | מִתְקַטֵּל |

1. *a.* רֹמֶשׂ (1:26);　חֹלֵם (41:1);　הֹלֵךְ (2:14);　עֹבֵד (4:2);　נֹתֵן (9:12).

    *b.* זָקֵן (18:11); כָּבֵד (13:2); שָׁלֵם (33:18); גָּדֵל (26:13).

    *c.* שָׁבוּר[3]; דְּרוּשָׁה[2]; כָּתוּב[1]; בָּרוּךְ (9:26).

2. נִשְׁפָּט[7]; נִפְרַד[6]; נִשְׁבַּר[5]; נִסְתָּר

3. מְדַבֵּר (27:6); מְבַקֵּשׁ (37:16); מִקְדָּשׁ[8]; מִתְהַלֵּךְ (3:8);
מַשְׁלָךְ[9]; מַמְטִיר (7:4); מַשְׁחִית (6:13); מַבְדִּיל (1:6).

1. The Ḳăl stem has two participles; the remaining stems, one each:

    *a.* The Ḳăl *active* is קֹטֵל (sometimes קוֹטֵל)= ḳôṭēl *for* ḳâṭĭl; the ô being obscured from an original â, the ē lowered from ĭ.

    *b.* The Ḳăl *stative* participle has the form of the Perfect 3 masc. sg., קָטֵל (=ḳâṭēl); it is not so uniformly used, however, as is the Ḳăl *active*.

    *c.* In the Ḳăl *passive* participle, viz., קָטוּל (=ḳâṭûl *for* ḳăṭûl); the û is unchangeable, but the â, rounded from ă, is changeable.

2. The Nĭf'ăl Participle is the same as the Nĭf'ăl Perfect, with the vowel of the ultima rounded, since the Participle is a nominal form (§ 36.).

3. The remaining Participles are made by prefixing מ to that form of their respective stems which is used in the Imperfect:—

    *a.* This מ has ⁻ under it in the Pĭ'ēl and Pŭ'ăl, while in the other stems it takes the place of the initial ה of the stem.

    *b.* The ultimate vowel, if not long in the stem, is changed under the tone, the participle being a nominal form.

    **Note 1.**—The מ is probably related to the pronouns מִי and מָה.

    **Note 2.**—For feminine forms of the participle, see § **115.**

### 69. *Special Forms of the Imperfect and Imperative*

1. אֶהֱרָגְךָ (27:41) *I will kill;* אֲגַדֶּלְךָ (12:2) *I will make great;*
אֲדַבְּרָה[10] *I will* (= must) *speak;* נִלְבְּנָה (11:3) *Let us make*

---

¹ Deut. 28 : 61.     ² Isa. 62 : 12.     ³ Lev. 22 : 22.     ⁴ Ps. 19 : 7.
⁵ Isa. 61 : 1.     ⁶ Judg. 4 : 11.     ⁷ Jer. 2 : 35.     ⁸ Ezek. 48 : 11.
⁹ 2 Sam. 20 : 21.     ¹⁰ 2 Sam. 14 : 15.

brick; נִשְׂרְפָה (11:3) Let us burn; נִכְרָתָה (31:44) Let us cut (a covenant); נַזְכִּירָה.[1]

2. יַפְקֵד (41:34); תַּסְתֵּר[3]; יִכְרֵת[2]; [וַיַּקְטִיל. cf. יַקְטִיל]

3. זְכֹר[4] Think; חֲלָצָה[5] Oh save; הַקְשִׁיבָה[6] Attend.

Remark.—אִמָּלְטָה־נָא[7]; שִׁמְעוּ־נָא (13:9); הִפָּרֶד־נָא (19:20).

Some special forms of the Imperfect and Imperative deserve notice:

1. The *Cohortative* Imperfect:

*a.* This is characterized by the ending הָ—ֶ, before which a preceding vowel, unless unchangeable, becomes Šᵉwâ. It is found, with few exceptions, only in the first person singular and plural.

*b.* Its special signification is that of *desire, determination,* and, in the plural, *exhortation.*

2. The *Jussive* Imperfect:

*a.* This is, wherever possible, a shorter form than the regular Imperfect. It is found chiefly in the 2d and 3d persons; and in *strong* verbs only in the Hifʿil stem (viz., with —ֵ instead of י—ִ); but in *all* stems of verbs ל״ה (§ 82.) and ע״וּ (§ 86.). The wâw-conversive form of the Imperfect is also that of the Jussive (*cf.* § 70.).

*b.* Its special signification is that of *wish, command;* with a negative, *dissuasion, prohibition.*

3. The *Cohortative* Imperative; this, like the Cohortative Imperfect, is characterized by the ending הָ—ֶ, and is often more emphatic than the ordinary form. The Hîf. Imv. changes —ֵ to י—ִ before הָ—ֶ.

**Remarks.**—The modal idea in each of these three forms is intensified or enlivened by the particle נָא, which is frequently found in connection with them.

**Note 1.**—The regular Imperfect and Imperative forms may without change convey the ideas characteristic of the forms here discussed.

---

[1] Ct. 1 : 4.  [2] Mal. 2 : 12.  [3] Ps. 27 : 9.  [4] Neh. 5 : 19.
[5] Ps. 6 : 5.  [6] Ps. 5 : 3.  [7] Judg. 13 : 14.

**Note 2.**—The shorter form of the Imperative corresponding to the Jussive is confined to ל"ה verbs, *e. g.*, גַּל for גַּלֵה.

### 70. The Perfect and Imperfect with Wâw Conversive

1. *a.* . . וַיֹּאמֶר (3). . .וְהָאָרֶץ הָיְתָה (2). . . בְּרֵאשִׁית בָּרָא (1:1)

. . וְלַחֹשֶׁךְ קָרָא. . .וַיִּקְרָא (5). . . וַיַּבְדֵּל. . .וַיַּרְא (4). . .וַיְהִי

. . וַיְהִי. . .וַיַּבְדֵּל. . .וַיַּעַשׂ (7). . .וַיֹּאמֶר (6). . .וַיְהִי. . .וַיְהִי

. . וַיְהִי. . .וַיֹּאמֶר (9). . . . .וַיְהִי. . .וַיְהִי. . .וַיִּקְרָא (8)

וַיַּרְא. . . .קָרָא הַמַּיִם וּלְמִקְוֵה. . .וַיִּקְרָא (10)

*b.* . . . .הַשָּׁמַיִם בִּרְקִיעַ מְאֹרֹת יְהִי [אֱלֹהִים וַיֹּאמֶר] (1:14)

. . . .לִמְאוֹרֹת וְהָיוּ. . .לְאֹתֹת וְהָיוּ

(3:22) פֶּן יִשְׁלַח יָדוֹ וְלָקַח גַּם מֵעֵץ הַחַיִּים וְאָכַל וָחַי

לְעוֹלָם:

2. *a.* וַיִּשְׁבֹּת (2:2); וַיַּבְדֵּל (1:4); וַיִּסְגֹּר (2:21); (2:3);

וַיְבָרֶךְ (1:22).

*b.* וְדָבַק (2:24); וְלָקַח (3:22); וְאָכַל (3:22); וְאָמְרָה (24:14);

וְאָכַלְתָּ (3:18).

3. *a.* וַיַּהַרְגֵהוּ (4:8); וַיַּבְדֵּל (1:7); וַיִּרְדְּפֵם (14:15); וַיְבָרֶךְ

וַיַּחְשְׁבֶהָ (15:6); (1:22).

וַיַּבְתֵּר (15:10); וַיִּשְׁקְפוּ (18:16); וַיְדַבֵּר (17:3); וַיִּשְׁבֹּת

(2:2).

**Remark.**—וַיִּלְבַּשׁ, *but* וַיַּלְבִּשֵׁם (3:21).

*b.*[1] וְגָאַלְתִּי (3:20); וְשָׁלַחְתִּי (3:16); וְאָסַפְתָּ (3:13); וְאָמַרְתִּי

וְגָאַלְתִּי (3:21); (6:6).

The use of the Perfect and Imperfect with the so-called Wâw Conversive[2] is one of the most marked peculiarities of the language.

---

[1] These cases are cited from Exodus.

[2] The form is usually called Wâw Consecutive; but this name claims too much for the form; the older term *Conversive*, while not ideal, is less objectionable.

Only what relates to the forms of the conjunction, and to the verbal forms to which the conjunction is joined, will here be noticed.

1. The facts in the case, briefly stated, are as follows:

*a.* In continued narrations of the past, the first verb is in the Perfect, while those that follow, *unless they are separated from the conjunction by intervening words*, are in the Imperfect and connected with the preceding Perfect by means of Wåw Conversive.

*b.* In the narration of actions which are to occur in the future, or which can only be conditionally realized, or which are indefinite so far as their character or occurrence is concerned, the first verb is in the Imperfect (or Participle, or Imperative), while those that follow, *unless they are separated from the conjunction by intervening words*, are in the Perfect and connected with the preceding verb by means of Wåw Conversive.

Note.—This more common usage is very often modified in various ways; but a consideration of these questions belongs to Syntax, and cannot be taken up here.

2. The form of the conjunction, however, is not the same in both cases:

*a.* With the *Imperfect,* the conjunction is וַ, but
    (1) the following consonant regularly has Dåḡēš-fŏrtē;
    (2) the Dåḡēš-fŏrtē may be omitted from a consonant which has only Šᵉwâ under it (§ **14. 2**), and
    (3) before א, in the first person, the Dåḡēš-fŏrtē being omitted, the preceding ־ַ becomes ־ָ.

*b.* With the *Perfect,* the conjunction is the same as the ordinary Wåw Conjunctive, with its various pointings (§ **49.**).

3. With reference to the verbal form employed,
    *a.* In the case of the *Imperfect,* there is used,
        (1) in the first person, a lengthened form exactly similar to that of the Cohortative (§ **69.**)[1]—a usage which is rare and late;

---

[1] *Cf.* וָאֶשְׁלְחָה (32 : 6); וַנַּחֲלֹקָה (41 : 11); וָאֶפְתְּחָה (43 : 21); וָאֶתְּנָה (Num. 8 : 19); *also* Ez. 7 : 27–9 : 6, in which there are seventeen cases.

(2) in the second and third persons, a short form like that of
the Jussive (§ 69.) and found in many weak and bi-
literal verbs and in the Hif'îl of strong verbs.

(3) a form with accent on the penult, and the consequent
vowel changes; but the penult cannot carry the accent
unless it is an open syllable, and the final syllable has a
changeable vowel. This form cannot occur in the strong
verb.

(4) the ordinary verbal form unchanged.

**Remark.**—With Wâw Conversive the Hif'îl, therefore, has ē instead of î; but this î is usually restored, though written defectively,
before suffixes.

*b.* In the case of the *Perfect*, the usual verbal form is employed;
but, *whenever possible*, this form is marked by a change of accent, the
tone passing from the penult to the ultima.

**Note.**—As a matter of fact, the cases in which there is no change
of tone are as numerous as those in which there does occur change.
These cases are grouped by Driver[1] as follows: (1) in those forms of the
Perfect (3 sg., 2 fem. sg., 3 com. pl., 2 masc. pl., 2 fem. pl.) which are al-
ready *Mĭlră'*; (2) when the Perfect is immediately followed by a monosyllable, or dissyllable accented on the penult; (3) when the Perfect
is *in pause;* (4) in the 1 pl. of all conjugations, and in 3 fem. sg. and 3
pl. of the Hif'îl; (5) in the Ḳăl of verbs ל״א and ל״ה; (6) frequently
in those forms of ע״ע and Middle-Vowel Ḳăls and Nîf'ăls which end
in ן and ָה.

### 71. The Verb with Suffixes

[See Paradigm C at end of book.]

1. *a.* [קְטָלַת־ *for* קְטָלָה]; אֲכָלַתְהוּ (37:20); סְמָכְתָּנִי[2];
יְלָדְתָּנִי[5]; [קְטַלְתְּ *for* קְטַלְתִּי־]; מְצָאתָנוּ[4]; שְׁטַפְתָּנִי[3];
צַמַּתָּנִי[8]; [קְטַלְתֶּם *for* קְטַלְתּוּ־]; נְתַתִּיהוּ[7]; הִכְרַעְתָּנִי[6];
זְכַרְתָּנִי (31:28); נְטַשְׁתָּנִי[9]; הֶעֱלִיתָנוּ (40:14).

---

[1] *Use of the Tenses in Hebrew,* § 110.
[2] Isa. 63 : 5.  [3] Ps. 69 : 3.  [4] Num. 20 : 14.  [5] Jer. 15 : 10.
[6] Judg. 11 : 35.  [7] Ezek. 16 : 19.  [8] Zech. 7 : 5.  [9] Num. 20 : 5.

*b.* דְּפָקוּם; גְּמָלוּךָ (50:17) *for* [קְטָלוּ *for* קְטָלוֹ; גְּמָלוּךָ]
(33:13) *for* דְּפָקוּם.

    **Remarks.**—אִשְּׂרוּנִי; שְׁכֵחוּנִי[1]; (30:13);
אֲהֵבוּ (44:20); אֲכַבְּדֶךָ; הִשְׁבִּיעֶךָ[2] (50:6).

*c.* גְּמָלוּךָ (50:17). [קְטָלוּ־הָ; שְׁפָטוּ־ם[3]; יִדְרְשֻׁנְ־הוּ[4];
קְטָלָ־הוּ; נְתָנוּ (31:7) *for* נְתָנָ־ם[5]; נְתָנָ־ם; אֲהֵבְךָ[6];
(32:18). שְׁאֵלְךָ; רִחַמְךָ[7]; שְׁלָחֲךָ[8]; עֲבָדְךָ[7]

אֲכָלָתַם[11]; אֲחָזָתַם[10]; *see above,* 1. *a;* [קְטָלָתֶךָ, קְטָלָתְנוּ]

    **Remark.**—יְדַעְתִּיו (18:19) *for* הֲרָגְנֻהוּ; הֲרַגְנָהוּ (4:25) *for* הֲרָגֻנ;
יְדָעָהּ; יְדָעָה (24:16) *for* יְלָדָתְהוּ; יְלָדַתְהוּ[12] *for* יְלָדָתּוּ; יְדַעְתִּיהוּ;
אֲחֹתָה[13] *for* אֲחָזָתָהּ.

When the object of a verb is a pronoun, it is often expressed by the
union of אֵת and the pronominal suffix.  More often, however, the
pronominal suffix is joined directly to the verbal form.  This occa-
sions certain changes of termination and of stem.  When a suffix is
added to a verbal form, the form becomes subject, so far as the influence of the tone is concerned, to the laws controlling the vocalization of nouns.

    1. In the case of the *Perfect with suffixes*, it is to be noted,

      *a.* In reference to *termination-changes*, that the older endings
are in many cases retained, as

      (1) the older תָ_, for the later הָ_ (3 sg. fem.);

      (2) the older תִי, for the later תְ (2 sg. fem.);

      (3) the older תֻן, for the later תֶם (2 pl. masc.), perhaps
after the analogy of ן in the 3d plural.

    **Remark.**—תָ occurs for תְ (2 m. sg.), often before נִי.

---

[1] Jer. 2 : 32.    [2] Num. 22 : 17.    [3] Deut. 25 : 1.    [4] 1 Chron. 13 : 3.
[5] Josh. 10 : 19.    [6] Deut. 15 : 16.    [7] Deut. 15 : 12.    [8] 1 Sam. 20 : 22.
[9] Deut. 13 : 18.    [10] Ps. 48 : 7.    [11] Hos. 2 : 14.    [12] Ruth 4 : 15.
[13] Jer. 49 : 24.

*b.* In reference to *stem-changes*, that, in the Ḳăl,

(1) the first syllable, being no longer pretonic when a suffix is appended, reduces its original ă in the open syllable to Šᵉwâ; while

(2) the ă of the second syllable, which has been reduced before personal terminations beginning with a vowel, is retained, and, in the open syllable before the tone, rounded to å.

**Remark 1.**—The ⸚ of verbs Middle E appears before suffixes.

**Remark 2.**—The Pĭ'ēl and Hĭθpă'ēl take ⸚ in the last syllable before הָ, כֶם, כֶן, but elsewhere the vowel is rejected; while the ultimate î of the Hĭf'îl suffers no change.

*c.* In reference to the *union of termination and suffix*, that

(1) to a verbal form ending in a vowel, the suffix is attached directly;

(2) to a verbal form ending, in ordinary usage, with a consonant, the suffix is attached by means of a so-called connecting-vowel which is generally å, but before הָ, כֶם, and כֶן, is Šᵉwâ, and before הָ is ē.

(3) to the 3 sg. fem. termination תָ֫, suffixes forming a syllable are attached without a connecting-vowel; other suffixes have a connecting-vowel, viz., ĕ before הָ, but ă before כֶם; the accent, peculiarly, in every case stays on the feminine ending תָ֫.

**Note.**—Certain changes are quite frequent: (1) הוּ⸚ to וֹ; (2) יְהוּ⸚ to יְו⸚; (3) תְּהוּ⸚ to תּוּ⸚; (4) הָ⸚ to הָ⸚; (5) תְהָ⸚ to תָּה⸚. In the *third* and *fifth* of these cases, the dåǧ. is, perhaps, in compensation for the ה. In the fifth, the ה of the present form is merely a vowel-letter. In the *fourth* case, the final vowel was dropped, and the Măppîḳ in ה shows it to be a genuine consonant, rather than a vowel-letter.

2. *a.* תּוֹכִיחֶךָ·²; וַתְּחַשְׁבֵנִי·¹; וּתְקַטְלֶנָה *for* תְּקַטְלוּ׀

---

¹ Job. 19 : 15.       ² Jer. 2 : 19.

b. [וְיִקְטְלֵנִי]; ¹יִשְׁפְּטֵנִי; ²אוֹכִירֵכִי; יִפְגָּשְׁךָ (32:18); ³אֹזְכְּרָךְ;
⁴יִזְכְּרָה

⁶תִּשְׁכָּחֵנִי (40:23); יִשְׁכָּחֵהוּ; ⁵יִלְבָּשֵׁנִי; [וְיִקְטְלֵנִי]

⁸אֲזָמֶּרְךָ; תְּלַמְּדֵם; יִשְׁלָחֵהוּ (3:23); יְקַטְּלֵךָ,[וַיְקַטְּלֵךְ]; [יִקְטְלֵנִי]

⁹אַשְׁמִידֵם (37:20); נַשְׁלִכֵהוּ (3:21); יַלְבִּשֵׁם [וַיַקְטִילֵנִי]

c. ¹²תַּשְׁלִיכֵהוּ; ¹¹תַכְלִימוּהָ; ¹⁰יַסְגִּירוּ־נִי; see examples
under b.

¹³תִּזְכְּרֵנוּ (9:5); אֶדְרְשֶׁנּוּ; [וְיִקְטְלֶנּוּ]

3. a. ¹⁴אֹמְרֵכֶם (3:5); אֲכָלְכֶם (2:17); אֲכָלְךָ; [קְטָלְךָ]; but
בְּבָרְחֲךָ (35:1).

¹⁶עֲבָדֵנוּ; ¹⁵אָמְרָם (2:15); שָׁמְרָהּ (2:15); עֲבָדָהּ; [קְטָלָהּ]

Remarks.—[קְטָלְךָ]; ¹⁷לְבַקֶּשְׁךָ; ¹⁸דִּבֶּרְכֶם; ¹⁹דַּבְּרִי;
²⁰לְבַקְשֵׁנִי.

b. [קְטָלַנִי]; ²¹זְכָרַנִי; ²²שְׁמָרֵנִי; ²³שָׁמְרֵם; ²⁴עֲזָרֵנוּ
²⁷עֲבָדֻהוּ; ²⁶תִּפְשׂוּם; ²⁵עֲזָרוּנִי; [קְטָלוּהָ]
²⁸הַשְׁמִיעֵנִי (23:8); שְׁמָעוּנִי (23:11); שְׁמָעֵנִי; [קְטָלַנִי]
²⁹הַשְׁלִיכֵהוּ

2. In the case of the *Imperfect with suffixes*, it is to be noted,

　a. In reference to *termination-changes*, that נָה (2 and 3 pl.
fem.) always yields to וּ. Note the analogy to the 3d. pers. plur.
in וּ, as also appears in the 2d. pers. plur. masc. (see above).

¹ 1 Sam. 24 : 16.　² Ps. 137 : 6.　³ Ps. 42 : 7.　⁴ 1 Sam. 1 : 19.
⁵ Job 29 : 14.　⁶ Ps. 13 : 2.　⁷ Deut. 5 : 31.　⁸ Ps. 57 : 10.
⁹ Deut. 9 : 14.　¹⁰ 1 Sam. 23 : 11.　¹¹ Ruth 2 : 15.　¹² Ex. 1 : 22.
¹³ Ps. 8 : 5.　¹⁴ Jer. 23 : 38.　¹⁵ Ps. 42 : 11.　¹⁶ Ex. 14 : 5.
¹⁷ 1 Kgs. 18 : 10.　¹⁸ Ex. 12 : 31.　¹⁹ Ex. 19 : 9.　²⁰ 1 Sam. 27 : 1.
²¹ Judg. 16 : 28.　²² Ps. 16 : 1.　²³ Prov. 4 : 21.　²⁴ Josh. 10 : 6.
²⁵ Josh. 10 : 4.　²⁶ 1 Kgs. 20 : 18.　²⁷ 1 Sam. 7 : 3.　²⁸ Ps. 143 : 8.
²⁹ Ex. 4 : 3.

*b.* In reference to *stem-changes*, that before suffixes,

(1) the ŭ (lowered to ō) of Ḳăl forms ending in a consonant usually becomes ⸗, but ŏ before הֶ, כֶם, כֶן, the Šᵉwâ preceding the suffix being vocal;

(2) the ă of Ḳăl forms ending in a consonant is retained and rounded to å;

(3) the final vowel of Pĭˤēl forms ending in a consonant is ordinarily reduced to ⸗, but is deflected to ĕ before הֶ, כֶם, כֶן; while the î of Hĭfˤîl forms remains.

*c.* In reference to the *union of termination and suffix*, that

(1) to verbal forms ending in a vowel the suffix is attached directly; while

(2) to verbal forms ending in a consonant, the suffix is attached by means of a connecting-vowel, which is generally ē, but ⸗ before הֶ, כֶם, כֶן; and ĕ, sometimes å, before הָ;

(3) in pausal and emphatic forms, suffixes are often attached to a verbal form ending in *an*, which under the tone becomes ĕn, of which the נ is generally assimilated.

**Note 1.**—This syllable, ordinarily treated as a union-syllable and called *Nûn Epenthetic* or *Demonstrative*, is found also before suffixes in old Aramaic. It is probably an old form of the verb.

**Note 2.**—In the endings נּוּ⸗ (3 m. sg.) and נָּה⸗ (3 f. sg.), the Dåḡēš-fŏrtē in נ perhaps is in compensation for the ה from הוּ and הָ respectively.

3. In the case of *Infs. and Imvs. with suffixes*, it is to be noted that,

*a.* The Ḳăl *Infinitive* (construct) takes

(1) before הֶ, כֶם, כֶן, generally, the form קָטְל (ŏ); but

(2) before other suffixes the form קֻטְל, the ŏ, in both cases, standing in a closed syllable.

(3) as connecting-vowels, those used in the inflection of nouns.

**Remark 1.**—The Pĭˤēl Infinitive takes ⸗ before הֶ, כֶם, כֶן.

**Remark 2.**—The Infinitive may take either the *verbal* suffix, נִי, or the *nominal* suffix יִ⸗.

*b.* The Ḳăl *Imperative,* taking the connecting-vowel of the Impf.,

(1) in the 2 masc. sg., follows the analogy of the Infinitive;

(2) in the 2 masc. pl., suffers no change;

(3) in the 2 fem. pl., has the form קְטֹלוּ instead of קְטֹלְנָה, just as in the corresponding form of the Imperf. with suffixes.

**Remark 1.**—The Imperative in ă retains and rounds the ă, as does the Imperfect.

**Remark 2.**—In the Hif'il, the form הַקְטִיל is used instead of הַקְטֵל.

**Note.**—The Participles, before suffixes, undergo the same vowel changes as regular nouns of the same formation, and may take either the nominal or the verbal suffixes.

### 72. General View of the Strong Verb

| Mood or Tense. | 1. Ḳăl. | 2. Nif'ăl. | 3. Pi'ēl. | 4. Hiθpă'ēl. | 5. Pŭ'ăl. | 6. Hif'il. | 7. Hŏf'ăl. |
|---|---|---|---|---|---|---|---|
| Perfect (3 m. sg.) | קָטַל[1] | נִקְטַל | קִטֵּל[2] | הִתְקַטֵּל[3] | קֻטַּל | הִקְטִיל | הָקְטַל |
| Imperfect (3 m. sg.) | יִקְטֹל[4] | יִקָּטֵל | יְקַטֵּל | יִתְקַטֵּל | יְקֻטַּל | יַקְטִיל[5] | יָקְטַל |
| Imperative | קְטֹל | הִקָּטֵל | קַטֵּל | הִתְקַטֵּל | —— | הַקְטֵל | —— |
| Infinitive Absolute | קָטוֹל | { נִקְטֹל / קָטֹל הִקָּטֹל } | קַטֵּל | הִתְקַטֵּל | קָטֹל | הַקְטֵל | הָקְטֵל |
| Infinitive Construct | קְטֹל | הִקָּטֵל | קַטֵּל | הִתְקַטֵּל | | הַקְטִיל | |
| Participle Active | קוֹטֵל | | מְקַטֵּל | מִתְקַטֵּל | | מַקְטִיל | |
| Participle Passive | קָטוּל | נִקְטָל | | | מְקֻטָּל | | מָקְטָל |

---

[1] *Cf.* also the Middle E and Middle O forms, קָטֵל, קָטֹל.

[2] *Cf.* also the form with original ◌ַ in the ultima, קִטַּל.

[3] *Cf.* also the form with original ◌ַ in the ultima, הִתְקַטַּל.

[4] *Cf.* also the forms with ◌ַ and ◌ֵ, יִקְטַל, יִקְטֵל.

[5] *Cf.* also the form used as a Jussive, and with Wâw Conversive, יַקְטֵל.

## REMARKS

1. The Ḳăl is the simple verb-stem (§ 58.).

2. The Nĭf'ăl has in every form the letter נ; this letter, however, is assimilated and represented by Dåḡēš-fŏrtē in the Imperfect, Imperative, and Infinitives (§ 58.).

3. The Pĭ'ēl has everywhere (1) the vowel — under the first radical (except in the Perfect), and (2) a Dåḡēš-fŏrtē characteristic in the second radical (§ 58.).

4. The Hĭθpă'ēl is the same as the Pĭ'ēl (except in the Perfect) with the syllable הִתְ prefixed (§ 58. 5).

5. The Pŭ'ăl has everywhere (1) the vowel — under the first radical, and (2) a Dåḡēš-fŏrtē characteristic in the second radical (§ 58. 3).

6. The Hĭf'ĭl has in all forms (except the Perfect) the vowel — under the *preformative* (§ 58. 1).

7. The Hŏf'ăl has in all forms the vowel ŏ (or ŭ) under the *preformative* (§ 58. 3).

## B. THE LARYNGEAL VERB

### 73. Classes of Laryngeal Verbs

1. עָזַב (2:24); הָפַךְ (3:24); אָבַל[1]; חָדַל (18:11); עָצַר (20:18).

2. נִבְהַל[5]; שָׁאַל[4]; בַּעֲרָה[3]; שָׁחַט[2]; רָחַף (1:2).

3. שָׁמַע (3:8); שָׁלַח (3:22); בָּטַח[6]; בָּקַע (7:11); פָּתַח (42:27); גָּבַהּ[7].

Remark.—וַיְבָרֶךְ (1:28); תִּרְמְסֶנָה[8]; קְרַבְתִּי[9].

A Laryngeal Verb is one the root of which contains one or more laryngeal radicals. They fall into three classes, viz.:

1. Pē ('פ) Laryngeal, of which the first radical is a laryngeal (§ 74.).

2. 'Ăyĭn ('ע) Laryngeal, of which the second radical is a laryngeal (§ 75.).

---

[1] Isa. 24 : 7.   [2] Jer. 39 : 6.   [3] Num. 11 : 3.   [4] Judg. 5 : 25.
[5] 1 Sam. 28 : 21.  [6] Ps. 28 : 7.   [7] Isa. 55 : 9.   [8] Isa. 28 : 3.
[9] Isa. 46 : 13.

3. Lāmĕd ('ל) Laryngeal, of which the third radical is a laryngeal (§ 76.).

**Remark.**—Verbs with ר as first or second radical show some of the characteristics of laryngeal verbs, especially in the refusal of ר to take Dåğĕš-fŏrtē.

**Note.**—The terms Pē Laryngeal, etc., are based upon the order of the radicals in the old paradigm-verb, פָּעַל, the first radical being designated by פ, the second by ע, and the third by ל.

### 74. Verbs פ' Laryngeal

[For full inflection, see Paradigm D]

**TABULAR VIEW**

| | Ķăl with ō in Impf. | Ķăl with ă in Impf. | Nif'ăl | Hif'ĭl | Hŏf'ăl |
|---|---|---|---|---|---|
| Perf. | עָטַל | עָטַל | נֶעְטַל | הֶעְטִיל | הָעְטַל |
| Impf. | יַעֲטֹל | יֶעֱטַל | יֵעָטֵל | יַעֲטִיל | יָעֳטַל |
| Imv. | עֲטֹל | עֲטַל | הֵעָטֵל | הַעֲטֵל | —— |
| Inf. abs. | עָטוֹל | עָטוֹל | { נַעְטֹל / הֵעָטֵל } | הַעֲטֵל | הָעְטֵל |
| Inf. const. | עֲטֹל | עֲטַל | הֵעָטֵל | הַעֲטִיל | |
| Part act. | עֹטֵל | עֹטֵל | | מַעֲטִיל | |
| Part. pass. | עָטוּל | עָטוּל | נֶעֱטָל | | מָעֳטַל |

1. [וַיֵּעָטֵל]; וַתֵּרֶא (1:9); אֶחָבֵא (3:10); יֵאָכֵל (6:21); ¹יֵהָפֵךְ.

2. a. [וַיַּעֲטֹל]; יַעֲלֶה (2:6); תַּעֲבֹד (4:12); יַעֲזֹב־ (2:24); יַעֲשׂוּ (3:7).

  b. [יֵעָטֵל]; נֶעֱטַל; הֶעֱטִיל]; יֶחֱזַק (41:56); נֶהְפַּךְ; ²תֶּחְדָּל; יֶחְיֶה (31:32); יִהְיֶה (1:29); but יִהְיֶה־ (47:21); הֶעֱבִיר; ⁴הֶחֱזִיק; יֶאֱסֹף (29:22).

---

¹ Ex. 14 : 5.      ² Ex. 7 : 15.      ³ Ruth 1 : 18.      ⁴ Deut. 22 : 25.

3. *a.* עָשׂוֹת (2:4); עָבֹד (2:5); אָכְלְךָ (2:17); אֲרוּרָה (3:17);

הָרְגוּ (4:25); עֲשֵׂה (6:14); אֱמֹר whence לֵאמֹר (1:22);

אֱכֹל (47:24); אָסֹף.[1]

*b.* נֶחְמָד (2:9); [וְהֶעֱטַל]; אֶעֱשֶׂה (2:18); נַעֲשֶׂה (1:26);

תֶּחְדַּל[2]; נֶהְפַּךְ[3]; יַחְגֹּר[4]; יַחְשְׁבָה (15:6).

*c.* נֶהֶפְכוּ[5]; יַעַבְרוּ (37:28); יַעֲבְדוּךְ (27:29); יְהָרְגֻהוּ (4:8);

*d.* יַאַסְפוּ[8]; וְהַעֲמַדְתָּ[7], but וְהֶעֱמַדְתָּ[6], but (29:22) יֵאָסֵף

Verbs, whose first radical is a laryngeal, exhibit the following peculiarities (§ 42. 1–3):

1. *The laryngeal refuses to be doubled;* hence the Dâḡēš-fŏrtē, representing נ, in the Nîf'al Impf., Imv., and Infs., is rejected, and the
preceding ־ִ becomes ־ֵ (even before ח).

2. *The laryngeal prefers before it the a-class vowels;* hence

*a.* In the Ḳăl Impf. with ō, and in the Ḳăl Impf. of verbs that
are also ל"ה (§ 81.), the original ă of the preformative is retained;
while

*b.* In the Ḳăl Impf. with ־ֵ, in the Nîf'al Perf. and Part., and in
the Hîf'îl Perf., the original preformative vowel is deflected to ĕ, for
the sake of euphony.

**Remark 1.**—A few cases occur of forms like יַעֲטָל or יֶעֱטָל.

**Remark 2.**—In הָיָה and חָיָה the preformative vowel is regularly attenuated to ĭ as in the strong verb.

**Remark 3.**—In the Hîf. Pf. 3d sg. masc. and fem. and 3d pl.,
the ĕ of the preformative is due to the influence of the other six forms
in which ă is the stem-vowel and the preformative vowel undergoes
deflection on its account.

3. *The laryngeal prefers compound to simple Š⁼wâ;* hence

*a.* When the first radical is initial and, according to the inflection of the strong verb, would have a simple Š⁼wâ, it takes instead
־ֲ, or, particularly in the case of א, ־ֱ.

---

[1] Num. 21 : 16.   [2] Ruth 1 : 18.   [3] Ex. 7 : 15.   [4] Lev. 8 : 7.
[5] Ex. 7 : 17.   [6] Ps. 31 : 9.   [7] Num. 3 : 6.   [8] Ex. 4 : 29.

*b.* When the first radical is medial, it may either, according to the inflection of the strong verb, have under it a silent Šᵉwâ or, in order to facilitate the pronunciation, it may receive a compound Šᵉwâ as a helping-vowel, which always corresponds to the preceding vowel; thus, ⁻ᵀ ⁻ᵀ, ⁻ᵀ ⁻ᵀ, ⁻ᵀ ⁻ᵀ (ŏ).

*c.* When, in inflection, a compound Šᵉwâ would come to stand before a simple Šᵉwâ, as when vowel-additions are made to a word, the compound Šᵉwâ gives way to its corresponding short vowel.

*d.* The combination ⁻ᵀ ⁻ᵀ very frequently becomes ⁻ᵀ ⁻ᵀ, when, in inflection, the tone is removed to a greater distance.

**Note.**—The ה and ח of הָיָה and חָיָה have a silent Šᵉwâ according to *b* (above), when medial and vowelless; but a compound Šᵉwâ (⁻ᵀ), when initial and without a full vowel.

### 75. Verbs 'ע Laryngeal

[For full inflection, see Paradigm E]

#### TABULAR VIEW

| | Ḳăl. | Nif'ăl. | Pī'ēl (1). | Pŭ'ăl (1). | Pī'ēl (2). | Pŭ'ăl (2). | Hĭθpă'ēl. |
|---|---|---|---|---|---|---|---|
| Perf. | קָאַל | נִקְאַל | קֵאֵל | קֹאַל | קְחֵל | קָחַל | הִתְקָאֵל |
| Impf. | יִקְאַל | יִקָּאֵל | יְקָאֵל | יְקֹאַל | יְקַחֵל | יְקֻחַל | יִתְקָאֵל |
| Imv. | קְאַל | הִקָּאֵל | קָאֵל | | קַחֵל | | הִתְקָאֵל |
| Inf. abs. | קָאוֹל | קָאֹל נִקְאֹל | | | קַחֵל | | |
| Inf. const. | קְאֹל | הִקָּאֵל קָאֹל | קָאֵל | | קַחֵל | | הִתְקָאֵל |
| Part. act. | קָאֵל | | מְקָאֵל | | מְקַחֵל | | מִתְקָאֵל |
| Part. pass. | קָאוּל נִקְאָל | | | מְקֹאָל | | מְקֻחָל | |

1. *a.* בַּאֵר[1]; גְּאַלְנוּ[2]; מֵאַנְתֶּם[3]; *but also* שָׁאֲלוּ[4]; נֹאַר[5]; נֹאץ[6]; בֵּרַךְ (1:22); וַיְגָרֶשׁ (3:24); גֵּרַשְׁתָּ (4:14); בֶּרֶךְ (28:6); וַיְבָרֶךְ יְבֹרַךְ[7]

---

[1] Deut. 1 : 5.　　[2] Mal. 1 : 7.　　[3] Ex. 16 : 28.　　[4] Ps. 109 : 10.
[5] Lam. 2 : 7.　　[6] Num. 16 : 30.　　[7] 2 Sam. 7 : 29.

*b.* מְרַחֶפֶת (1:2); נֶחָמְתִּי (6:7); שַׁחֵת (6:17); [1]נֻחֲמוּ; [2]רֻחַץ;
[3]הִטַּהֲרוּ; וּבְעַרְתָּ[4]; כְּעַסּוּנִי[5]; יְבַעֵר[6]; מְהַרְתֶּם
יְמַהֵר (18:6); (45:13).

2. *a.* [7]יִבְחַר; תִּגְאַל[8]; יִבְעַר[9]; גָּאַל[10]; שָׁאַל[11]; אַחַר (34:19);
[12]לָהַט.

*b.* [18]טָחֲנִי; שָׁאֲבִי[17]; צַעֲקִי[16]; נֻחֲמוּ[15]; טָעֲנוּ[14]; שָׁחֲטוּ[13];
שָׁאֲלִי[19].

*c.* יְמַהֵר; יְבַעֵר[6]; תִּשָּׁחֵת (6:11); יִגְאַל[22]; יִגְאַל[21]; שָׁאַל[20];
(18:6).

3. נִבְהֲלוּ[23]; כְּעַסּוּנִי[5]; *cf.* also the words cited under 2. *b.*

Verbs, whose second radical is a laryngeal, exhibit the following peculiarities (§ 42. 1–3):

1. *The laryngeal refuses to be doubled;* but

   *a.* While in the case of א (generally), and of ר (always), the preceding vowel is changed (ă to å, ĭ to ē, ŭ to ō),

   *b.* In the case of the stronger laryngeals, viz., ע (prevailingly), ה and ח (almost always), the preceding vowel is retained short, the doubling being implied (§ 42. 1. *b*).

   **Note 1.**—Lowering of ŭ to ō in the Pŭ'ăl takes place frequently in verbs which retain the ĭ or ă of the Pĭ'ēl.

   **Note 2.**—In a few verbs, especially those with א, the vowel is changed in some parts of the inflection, but in other parts retained.

   **Note 3.**—The vowel which is strengthened on account of the rejection of Dåḡēš-förtē is unchangeable.

2. *The laryngeal prefers the a-class vowels;* this is seen

   *a.* In the occurrence of ă, *after* the laryngeal, in the Ḳăl Impf. and Imv., rather than ō, even in Active verbs; and sometimes in the Pĭ'ēl Perf., rather than ē.

---

| | | | |
|---|---|---|---|
| [1] Isa. 40 : 1. | [2] Prov. 30 : 12. | [3] Gen. 35 : 2. | [4] Deut. 13 : 6. |
| [5] Deut. 32 : 21. | [6] 1 Kgs. 14 : 10. | [7] Gen. 13 : 11. | [8] Ruth 4 : 4. |
| [9] Ex. 3 : 3. | [10] Ruth 4 : 6. | [11] Deut. 4 : 32. | [12] Mal. 3 : 19. |
| [13] Ex. 12 : 21. | [14] Gen. 45 : 17. | [15] Isa. 40 : 1. | [16] Jer. 22 : 20. |
| [17] Nah. 3 : 14. | [18] Isa. 47 : 2. | [19] Jer. 48 : 19. | [20] Josh. 15 : 18. |
| [21] Ruth 4 : 4. | [22] Lev. 25 : 30. | [23] Ex. 15 : 15. | |

*b.* In the occurrence of ă, *before* the laryngeal, in the Ķăl Imv. fem. sg. and masc. plur. But it is to be noted that

*c.* In the Ķăl Inf. const., the usual ō remains; and likewise the ultimate ē in the Nĭf'ăl and Pĭ'ēl Imperfects.

Note.—As a matter of fact, the laryngeal exerts less influence on a following than on a preceding vowel.

3. *The laryngeal prefers compound to simple Š°wâ;* this is seen in the almost universal occurrence of ﬞﬞ under the second radical instead of ﬞ.

### 76. *Verbs* לֹ *Laryngeal*

[For full inflection, see Paradigm F]

**TABULAR VIEW**

|  | Ķăl. | Nĭf'ăl. | Pĭ'ēl. | Hĭf'ĭl. | Hĭθpă'ēl. |
|---|---|---|---|---|---|
| Perf. | קָטַח | נִקְטַח | קִטַּח | הִקְטִיחַ | הִתְקַטַּח |
| Impf. | יִקְטַח | יִקָּטַח | יְקַטַּח | יַקְטִיחַ | יִתְקַטַּח |
| Imv. | קְטַח | הִקָּטַח | קַטַּח | הַקְטַח | הִתְקַטַּח |
| Inf. abs. | קָטוֹחַ | נִקְטוֹחַ | קַטֵּחַ | הַקְטֵחַ | —— |
| Inf. const. | קְטֹחַ | הִקָּטַח | קַטֵּחַ | הַקְטִיחַ | הִתְקַטַּח |
| Part. act. | קֹטֵחַ |  | מְקַטֵּחַ | מַקְטִיחַ | מִתְקַטֵּחַ |
| Part. pass. | קָטוּחַ | נִקְטָח |  |  |  |

1. *a.* שְׁלַח¹; יִשְׁלַח (3:22); יִטַּע (2:8); יִפַּח (2:7); יִצְמַח (2:5);

 *b.* וְיֵדַע (12:17); יַנַּע; שְׁלַח³; הִלָּקַח²; יִשָּׁבַע (31:53); וְיֹדַע (41:31);
  יִצְמַח (2:9); שְׁלַח [Inf.] (8:10); שֶׁלַח⁴; וַיִּשְׁלַח (8:7);
  יִשָּׁבַע (50:25); הוֹדִיעַ; הוֹשַׁע⁵; הוֹדַע⁶; וַיִּתְנַגַּח⁷; הִתְוַדַּע (45:1);
  *But cf.:* זָרַע (1:29); יָדַע (3:5); מְזֻבֵּחַ⁸; מִשְׁתַּגֵּעַ⁹; *and*
  שֻׁלַּח¹⁰; פֻּתַּח¹¹; הֻגְּבַהּ¹²; הֻשְׁבַּע¹³; הֻמְלַח¹⁴.

---

¹ Ex. 4 : 4.    ² 1 Sam. 4 : 19.   ³ Ex. 9 : 7.   ⁴ Ex. 4 : 23.
⁵ Jer. 31 : 7.    ⁶ Prov. 9 : 9.   ⁷ Dan. 11 : 40.  ⁸ 1 Kgs. 3 : 3.
⁹ 1 Sam. 21 : 15.  ¹⁰ Deut. 22 : 7.  ¹¹ Isa. 58 : 6.  ¹² Isa. 7 : 11.
¹³ Ex. 13 : 19.   ¹⁴ Ezek. 16 : 4.

c. מַזְרִיעַ (1:11); תַּצְמִיחַ (3:18); ⁴יִזְרַע; ²פָּתוּחַ; ³פָּתֹחַ;

⁹יִשְׁמַע; ⁸יִזְרַע; ⁷לִשְׂמֹחַ; ⁶לִפְתֹּחַ; ⁵נִשְׁלֹוחַ; ⁴שָׁלֹחַ;

¹¹אֲשַׁלֵּחַ; ¹⁰בְּקַע

[See also the cases cited above, in fourth and fifth lines under *b*.]

d. ¹⁶הַמְלַחַתְּ; ¹⁵הִשָּׁבַעַתְּ; ¹⁴שָׁכַחַתְּ; ¹³לָקַחַתְּ; ¹²יָדַעַתְּ.

2. תִּפְקַחְנָה (3:7); שְׁמַעְתִּי (3:10); יָדַעְתִּי (4:9); לָקַחַתְ (3:19).

¹⁷שְׁלָחֲךָ; ¹⁸שַׁלֵּחֲךָ; ¹⁹בְּשַׁלְחֲךָ; נִשְׁלְחָה (26:29).

Verbs whose *third* radical is a laryngeal exhibit, according to § 42. 1–3, the following peculiarities:

1. *The laryngeal prefers the* a*-class vowels;* this is seen

*a.* In the occurrence of ă *before* the laryngeal, in the Ḳăl Impf. and Imv. (where ă was a collateral form), rather than ō, even in Active verbs.

*b.* In the retention of the original stem-vowel ă (§ 59.) in all forms where in the strong verb it becomes ē, except Infs. abs., and Participles.

*c.* In the insertion of a Păθăḥ-furtive (§ 42. 2. *d*) under a final laryngeal when the latter is preceded by a heterogeneous vowel, viz.:

(1) by a naturally long vowel, יִ_, וּ, or וֹ, or

(2) by a vowel essential to the form, as ō in the Ḳăl Inf. construct; or

(3) by the tone-long ē, which is retained *in pause* and also in the Infs. abs. and Parts., because they are really nominal forms.

*d.* In the insertion of a helping-vowel, viz., Păθăḥ, under the laryngeal, in the 2 fem. sg. of the various Perfects.

2. *The laryngeal prefers compound to simple* Šᵉwâ; *but this prefer-ence is indicated only before pronominal suffixes; the simple* Šᵉwâ

---

| | | | |
|---|---|---|---|
| ¹ Ps. 97 : 11. | ² Num. 19 : 15. | ³ Deut. 15 : 8. | ⁴ Num. 22 : 37. |
| ⁵ Esth. 3 : 13. | ⁶ Isa. 45 : 1. | ⁷ Ps. 106 : 5. | ⁸ Deut. 21 : 4. |
| ⁹ 1 Sam. 1 : 13. | ¹⁰ Job 28 : 10. | ¹¹ Ex. 5 : 2. | ¹² 1 Kgs. 2 : 15. |
| ¹³ Ezek. 22 : 12; *cf.* 1 Kgs. 14 : 3. | | ¹⁴ Isa. 17 : 10; *cf.* Jer. 13 : 25. | |
| ¹⁵ Ezek. 27 : 33. | ¹⁶ Ezek. 16 : 4. | ¹⁷ Jer. 28 : 15. | ¹⁸ 1 Sam. 21 : 3. |
| ¹⁹ Deut. 15 : 18. | | | |

being retained under the third radical wherever in ordinary inflection the strong verb would have it.

Note 1.—The Nĭf'ăl Inf. abs. is נִקְטֹח following the analogy of the Perfect stem, rather than that of the Imperfect (§ 67.).

Note 2.—The Pĭ'ēl Inf. abs. and Inf. const. are the same (*cf.* the 'ע laryngeal verb), except that the former, being treated as a noun, changes its ă through ĭ to — and takes Pă𝜃ăḥ-furtive.

Note 3.—Verbs with הּ (*i. e.*, ה with Măppîk) as their third radical are 'ל laryngeal, and are carefully to be distinguished from verbs with the vowel-letter ה (§ 82.).[1]

## C. THE WEAK VERB
### 77. Classes of Weak Verbs

1. נָתַן (1:17); נָטַע (2:8); נָפַל (4:6); נָגֵשׁ (33:7); נָכָה (32:12).

2. אָמַר (1:3); אָכַל (2:16); אָהֵב (27:9); אָחַז (25:26); אָבָה (24:5); אָפָה (40:1).

3. יָשַׁב (4:16), *for* וְשֵׁב; יָצַר (2:8); יָבֵשׁ (8:14); יָלַד (4:18).

4. יָטַב (12:13); יָקַץ (9:24); יָנַק (21:7); יָישַׁר[2]; יָמַן (13:10).

5. עָשָׂה (2:6); בָּנָה (11:5); נָטָה (33:19); גָּלָה (35:7); שָׁקָה (1:11).

6. בָּרָא (1:1); קָרָא (1:5); מָצָא (2:20); מָלֵא (1:28); נָשָׂא (4:7); טָמֵא (34:5).

Those verbs the roots of which contain one or more weak consonants are called Weak Verbs. The consonants in question are such as either easily contract, or quiesce, or suffer elision. The following classes of Weak Verbs are recognized:

1. Pē Nûn (פ״נ), in which the first radical is נ (§ 78.).

2. Pē 'Ălĕf (פ״א), in which the first radical is א, and is in some forms quiescent (§ 79.). There are six such verbs.

3. Pē Wāw (פ״ו), in which the first radical is ו and is sometimes contracted and sometimes elided (§ 80.).

---

[1] The following is a list of these verbs: גָּבַהּ *be high;* כָּמַהּ *long for;* מָהַהּ (in Hi𝜃palpel) *delay;* נָגַהּ *shine;* תָּמַהּ *be astonished.*

[2] Jer. 18 : 4.

4. Pē Yôd (י"פ), in which the first radical is י_ and is contracted (§ 81.).

5. Lāmĕd Hē (ל"ה ), in which the last radical ו or י is often dropped. Many such forms close with the vowel-letter ה, whence the verb gets its name (§ 82.).

6. Lāmĕd 'Ālĕf (ל"א), in which the last radical is א, which frequently quiesces (§ 83.).

**Note 1.**—The Weak Verbs were in all probability once Bi-literal Verbs, and should be treated in Chapter XII. They are kept here, however, for the sake of simplicity of presentation to students just entering upon the study of the language.

**Note 2.**—A single verb sometimes contains more than one weak radical and so combines characteristics of more than one class.

### 78. Verbs Pē Nûn (פ"נ)

[For full inflection, see Paradigm G, p. 201.]

**TABULAR VIEW**

|  | Ķăl. Impf. w. ō. | Ķăl. Impf. w. ă | Nĭf'ăl. | Hĭf'ĭl. | Hŏf'ăl. |
|---|---|---|---|---|---|
| **Perf.** | נָטַל | נָטַל | נִטַּל | הִטִּיל | הֻטַּל |
| **Impf.** | יִטֹּל | יִטַּל | יִנָּטֵל | יַטִּיל | יֻטַּל |
| **Imv.** | נְטֹל | טַל | הִנָּטֵל | הַטֵּל | — |
| **Inf. abs.** | נָטוֹל | נָטוֹל | { נִטֹּל הִנָּטֵל } | הַטֵּל | הֻטֵּל |
| **Inf. const.** | נְטֹל | טֶלֶת | הִנָּטֵל | הַטִּיל | הֻטֵּל |
| **Part. act.** | נֹטֵל | נֹטֵל |  | מַטִּיל |  |
| **Part. pass.** | נָטוּל | נָטוּל | נִטָּל |  | מֻטָּל |

1. *a.* גֶּשֶׁת[1]; גַּעַת[2]; טַעַת[3]; *but cf.* נְסֹעַ יִסַּע (יִסַּע); נְגֹעַ (20 : 6).

*b.* גַּע²; יֵשַׁל; וְשָׁקְהָ־ (27:26); גְּשׁוּ (45:4); יִגַּשׁ¹.³

Remark.—נִפְלוּ⁹; נָתַץ⁸; נִצֹּר⁷; כִּנְפוֹל⁶; לִנְדֹּר⁵; כִּנְבֹל⁴;

2. *a.* נִצָּבִים (6:7); נֶחָמְתִּי (3:3); תִּגְעוּ (2:8); יִטַּע (2:7); יִפַּח (18:2).

*b.* הִגִּיד (3:11); הַשִּׂיא (3:13); וַיִּפֹּל (2:21); יָקֻם (4:15); יִגַּר (22:20).

Remark 1.—*cf.* תִּנָּגְשׁוּ¹⁴; ¹³יִנָּהֲרוּ; ¹²יִנָּאֵף; ¹¹יִנָּאֲמוּ; ¹⁰יִנָּהֵם.

Remark 2.—לָקַ֑חְתָּ¹⁵; קַח (6:21); יִקַּח (2:15); לָקַח (2:22); קַחַת (4:11).

Remark 3.—נָתוֹן; נָתַתִּי (1:29); יִתֵּן (1:17); תֵּן־ (14:21); (41:43); תֵּת (4:12).

Verbs whose first radical is נ exhibit the following peculiarities:

1. The *loss* of נ takes place (§ 40. 1) when initial and with only a Šᵉwâ to sustain it:

*a.* Generally in the Ḳăl Inf. Const. of verbs whose stem-vowel in the Impf. and Imv. is ă; in this case the ending ת is taken on in compensation and the form becomes a Seğolate.

*b.* In the Ḳăl Imv. of verbs which have ă in the Imperfect.

Remark.—The Ḳăl Infinitive and Imperative of verbs with ō in the Imperfect do not often lose the initial נ.

2. The *assimilation* of נ takes place (§ 39. 1) when, having under it a silent Šᵉwâ, it closes a preformative syllable,

*a.* In the Ḳăl Imperfect, and Nifʻăl Perfect and Part.

*b.* Throughout the Hîfʻîl and Hôfʻăl.

Note 1.—The original preformative vowel ŭ appears in the Hôfʻăl, on account of the sharpened syllable (§ 36. 6. *a*).

Note 2.—Care must be taken not to confuse with verbs פ״נ, (1) those verbs פ״ו which assimilate ו (§ 80.) or drop it (in Inf. Const. and Imv. Ḳăl); (2) those so-called ע״ע forms which have a

¹ 2 Sam. 1 : 15.    ² Ex. 3 : 5.    ³ Ps. 144 : 5.    ⁴ Isa. 34 : 4.
⁵ Deut. 23 : 23.    ⁶ 2 Sam. 3 : 34.    ⁷ Ps. 34 : 14.    ⁸ Ps. 58 : 7.
⁹ Hos. 10 : 8.    ¹⁰ Isa. 5 : 29.    ¹¹ Jer. 23 : 31.    ¹² Lev. 20 : 10.
¹³ Jer. 51 : 44.    ¹⁴ Isa. 58 : 3.    ¹⁵ Deut. 31 : 26.

Dåḡēš-fŏrtē (§ 85.); and (3) the Middle Vowel Nif'ăl Impf. which
also has Dåḡēš-fŏrtē.

**Remark 1.**—The ב remains *un*-assimilated in verbs 'ע laryngeal,
and in a few isolated instances besides.

**Remark 2.**—The verb לָקַח *take* treats ל like נ in the Ḳăl and
Hŏf'ăl, but in the Nif'ăl (נִלְקַח) the ל is retained.

**Remark 3.**—The verb נָתַן is peculiar (1) in its Inf. Const. תֵּת (=
תֶּת=תְּנַת), which has as its stem-vowel ĭ, (2) in the appearance
of the same vowel ĭ changed to ē, in the Imv. (תֵּן) and Imperf. (יִתֵּן),
and (3) in the assimilation of the third radical in inflection.

### 79. Verbs Pē 'Ālĕf (פ"א)

[For full inflection, see Paradigm H, p. 202.]

1. וַיֹּאמֶר (1:3); תֹּאכֵל (2:16); נֹאכֵל (3:2); וַתֹּאמֶר (3:2);
אֹכֵל (3:12).

2. תֹּאכֵל (2:16), *but* תֹּאכַל (3:6); נֹאכֵל (3:2), *but* יֹאכַל (3:6);
וַיֹּאמֶר (1:3).

**Remark.**—אֲכָלְךָ (2:17); לֵאמֹר (1:22), *for* לְאֱמֹר; יֵאָכֵל (6:21);
יֵאָמֵר (10:9).

Of the verbs having א for their first radical, there are six (see § 77.)
which show certain peculiarities in the Ḳăl Imperfect:

1. The first radical א loses its consonantal character, and the
vowel of the preformative, orig. ă, is ô (rounded from â, which was
lengthened from ă in compensation for the quiescence of א).[1]

**Note.**—This ·א is retained orthographically, except in the first
sing., where it is dropped after the preformative א (= *I*).

2. The Imperfect stem-vowel is ē (from ĭ) in pause; but elsewhere
generally ă; when the accent recedes, it is ĕ.

**Remark.**—Outside of the Ḳăl Imperfect, these verbs are treated
as verbs 'פ laryngeal (§ 74.).

**Note.**—A few verbs are treated sometimes as א"פ, sometimes as 'פ laryngeal.

---

[1] *Cf.* וַיֶּאֱצַל for וַיַּאֲצַל (Num. 11 : 25).

## 80.  Verbs Pē Wâw (פ״ו)

[For full inflection, see Paradigm I, p. 203.]

### TABULAR VIEW

|            | Ķăl. Impf. w. ē. | Ķăl. Impf. w. ă. | Nif'ăl. | Hif'îl. | Hŏf'ăl. |
|------------|------------------|------------------|---------|---------|---------|
| Perf.      | יָטַל            | יָטַל            | נוֹטַל  | הוֹטִיל | הוּטַל  |
| Impf.      | יֵטַל            | יִיטַל           | יִוָּטֵל | יוֹטִיל | יוּטַל  |
| Imv.       | טַל              | יְטַל            | הִוָּטֵל | הוֹטֵל  | —       |
| Inf. abs.  | יָטוֹל           | יָטוֹל           | —       | הוֹטֵל  | —       |
| Inf. const.| טֶלֶת            | יְטַל            | הִוָּטֵל | הוֹטִיל | הוּטַל  |
| Part. act. | יֹטֵל            | יֹטֵל            |         | מוֹטִיל |         |
| Part. pass.| יָטוּל           | יָטוּל           | נוֹטַל  |         | מוּטַל  |

1. יָדַע (4:1) *for* וְדַע; יָלַד (4:18) *for* וְלַד; יֻלַּד (4:26).

2. *a.* יֵצֵא (4:16); וַתֵּלֶד (4:1); וַיֵּשֶׁב (4:16);
   יֵדַע (4:17); אֵלֵךְ (18:13); תֵּלְדִי (3:16); תֵּשֵׁב (24:55);
   יֵדְעוּ (3:7).
   (4:2) לֶדֶת; דַּע (20:7); שֵׁב (20:15); לֵךְ (12:1); צֵא (8:16);
   דַּעַת (3:22).

   *b.* תִּירְאוּן[3]; יִירַשׁ (21:10); יִּירְאוּ[2]; אִישָׁן[1]; יִישָׁן (2:21).

Remark 1.—[6]לֵדָה; דֵּעָה[5]; דַּעַת (3:22); רֶשֶׁת[4]; לֶדֶת (4:2);
   [10]יְכֹלֶת; יַבֶּשֶׁת (8:7); לִיסֹד[9]; בִּכְבֹשׁ[8]; יִרָא[7].

Remark 2.—לְכָה[11]; שִׁבָה (27:19); רְדָה (45:9); הָבָה (11:3).

Remark 3.—תֵּלֵךְ (12:4); וַיֵּלֶךְ (26:16); לֵךְ; לֶכֶת (11:31);
   (3:15).

3. *a.* [12]הוּסְרוּ; תּוֹרֵשׁ (45:11); יוּתַר (32:25); יוּלַד (4:18);
   בְּהִוָּלֵד (21:5).

*b.* וַיֵּלֶד; הוֹלִדוֹ (5:4); הוֹלִיד (11:27); נוֹלַד (21:3); יִנָּדַע;
(5:3).

*c.* ³.יוּבַל; ²תּוּבַלְנָה; הוּרַד (39:1)

4. ⁸תַּצִּיתוּ; ⁷הִצִּית; תִּצַּת⁶; יִצַּק (28:18); יִצַּע⁵; ⁴יַיְצִיעַ

Verbs whose first radical was originally ו exhibit the following
peculiarities:

1. The original ו passes over into י (§ 44. 1. *a*) whenever it would
be initial, as in the Ḳăl, Pī'ēl and Pŭ'ăl Perfects and Inf. Abs., the
Ḳăl Part., and the strong form of the Ḳăl Inf. Const.; and frequently
also after the prefix הִת (§ 44. 1. *b*).

2. In the Ḳăl Imperfect, Imperative and Inf. Const., two treatments exist, according as the radical ו (or י) is rejected or retained:

    *a.* In those verbs which reject the radical ו,

        (1) the *Imperfect* has for its stem-vowel ē (from ĭ), or (before
        laryngeals) ă, while the preformative takes unchangeable
        ê in compensation for the loss of ו.

        (2) the *Imperative* has the same vowel as the Imperfect;

        (3) the *Infinitive construct*, taking on the ending ת in com-
        pensation (*cf.* verbs פ״ן, § 78. *a*), assumes the form of
        an *a*-class Segolate noun טֶלֶת (*for* טֶלְתְּ, § 89.).

    *b.* In those verbs which retain the radical ו, the *Imperfect* has
for its stem-vowel ă, while the ו, changed to י, unites with the vowel
(ĭ) of the preformative and gives î.

    **Note.**—Only three verbs[9] retain ו (י) in the *Imperative,* and these
are verbs which have no third radical.

    **Remark 1.**—The Inf. Const. has most frequently the form
טֶלֶת (= טֶלְתְּ), before suffixes טֶלְתְּ; several cases, however,
occur of the form טֶלָה; the form יְטֹל is found a few times, while
יְטֶלֶת seldom occurs.

    **Remark 2.**—Seemingly for compensation, the Imperative often
assumes the cohortative ending הָ_ (§ 69.).

---

¹ Ex. 2 : 14.    ² Ps. 45 : 16.    ³ Isa. 18 : 7.    ⁴ Isa. 58 : 5.
⁵ Isa. 14 : 11.    ⁶ Isa. 9 : 17.    ⁷ Jer. 11 : 16.    ⁸ Josh. 8 : 8.
⁹ יָדָה, יָרֵא, יָדַע; *cf.* also the pausal form וּרֻשֶׁה (Deut. 33:23).

**Remark 3.**—The verb הָלַךְ *walk* forms its Ḳăl Imperf., Imv. and Inf. Const. and its Hif. Perf. and Imperf. on the analogy of the Pē Wåw verb.

**Remark 4.**—The verb לָקַח *take* follows the analogy of this class of verbs in its Imperative and Inf. Const. Ḳăl where ל is dropped. In Ḳăl Imperf. it assimilates ל as some Pē Wåw verbs treat ו and as נ is regularly treated in Pē Nûn verbs.

3. The first radical (ו), when medial, remains; but

*a.* It appears as a consonant only when it would be doubled, as in the Nĭf'ăl Imperf., Imv. and Inf. Const. (§ **44.** 5 *c*).

*b.* It unites with the preformative vowel ă, and forms ו (ă+w = ô), in the Nĭf'ăl Perfect and Participle, and throughout the Hĭf'ĭl (§ **44.** 3. *a*).

*c.* It unites with the preformative vowel ŭ, and forms ו throughout the Hŏf'ăl (§ **44.** 3. *e*).

**Note.**—The form יוּכַל (from יָכֹל *be able*) is regarded by some as a regular Hŏf'ăl Imperf.; by others, as a Ḳăl Passive Imperf.

4. In a few verbs פ״י, the י (=ו) is assimilated, just as נ of verbs פ״ן (§ **78.**) was assimilated.

### 81. Verbs Pē Yôd (פ״י)

[For full inflection, see Paradigm I, p. 202.]

#### TABULAR VIEW

|            | Ḳăl.    | Nĭf'ăl. | Hĭf'ĭl.  | Hŏf'ăl. |
|------------|---------|---------|----------|---------|
| Perf.      | יָטֵל    |         | הֵיטִיל   |         |
| Impf.      | יִיטַל   | No      | יֵיטִיל   | No      |
| Imv.       | ——      | forms   | הֵיטֵל    | forms   |
| Inf. abs.  | יָטוֹל   | occur.  | הֵיטֵל    | occur.  |
| Inf. const.| יְטֹל    |         | הֵיטִיל   |         |
| Part.      | יֹטֵל    |         | מֵיטִיל   |         |

1. ‏תֵּינְקוּ‎[1] (34:18); יִיטְבוּ‎ ;וַיִּיקֶץ (9:24) *for* וַיִּיקַץ (12:13); יִיטַב‎ 1.

2. ‏הֵיטִיב‎[2] (4:7); הֵיטִיב ;הֵיטַבְתָּ (21:7); הֵינִיקָה‎ (12:16); הֵיטִיב‎ 2.

‏הֵיטֵב‎ (32:10); וְאֵיטִיבָה ;הֵטִיבִי‎[4]; אֵיטִיב‎[3] (32:13); תֵּינִק‎

‏מֵינֶקֶת‎[7]; מֵיטִיב‎[6]; לְהֵיטִיב‎[5]; (32:13);

Verbs whose first radical was originally ‏י‎ exhibit the following peculiarities:

1. In the Ḳăl Imperfect the radical ‏י‎ unites with the vowel of the preformative (ĭ) and gives î (§ **30**. 2. *a*). No forms of an Imperative occur.

2. In the Hîf'îl the radical ‏י‎ unites with the vowel of the preformative (ă) and gives ê (§ **30**. 4. *b*).

**Note.**—No Nîf'ăl or Hŏf'ăl forms occur.

**82. Verbs ‏ל"ו‎ or ‏ל"י‎, called ‏ל"ה‎**

[For full inflection, see Paradigm K, p. 204 ]

**TABULAR VIEW**

|  | Ḳăl. | Nîf'ăl. | Pī'ēl. | Pŭ'ăl. | Hîf'îl. | Hĭθpă'ēl. |
|---|---|---|---|---|---|---|
| **Perf.** | קָטָה | נִקְטָה | קָטָה | קָטָה | הִקְטָה | הִתְקַטָּה |
| **Impf.** | יִקְטֶה | יִקָּטֶה | יְקַטֶּה | יְקֻטֶּה | יַקְטֶה | יִתְקַטֶּה |
| **Imv.** | קְטֵה | הִקָּטֵה | קַטֵּה | —— | הַקְטֵה | הִתְקַטֵּה |
| **Inf. abs.** | קָטֹה | נִקְטֹה / הִקָּטֵה ; קָטֹה / קַטֵּה | קַטֵּה | —— | הַקְטֵה | —— |
| **Inf. const.** | קְטוֹת | הִקָּטוֹת | קַטּוֹת | קַטּוֹת | הַקְטוֹת | הִתְקַטּוֹת |
| **Part. act.** | קֹטֶה | | מְקַטֶּה | | מַקְטֶה | מִתְקַטֶּה |
| **Part. pass.** | קָטוּי | נִקְטֶה | | מְקֻטֶּה | | |

1. *a.* ‏הָיָה‎ (2:10); הֻשְׁקָה‎ (2:6); כָּלָה‎ (18:33); נִבְנָה‎[8]; הָגְלָה‎[9]

[1] Isa. 66 : 11.    [2] Jer. 1 : 12.    [3] Ex. 2 : 7.    [4] Isa. 23 : 16.
[5] Jer. 4 : 22.    [6] 1 Sam. 16 : 17.    [7] Ex. 2 : 7.    [8] 1 Kgs. 6 : 7.
[9] Esth. 2 : 6.

b. יְהָיֶה (1:29);  יַעֲלֶה (2:6);  אֲכָלֶה (24:45);  אָבְנֶה (30:3);
יָכֶּה.[1]

c. עָשָׂה (1:11);  רֹעֶה (4:2);  מְכַלֶּה[2];  מַכֶּה[3];  מִשְׁתָּאֶה (24:21).

Remark.—עֹשֶׂה[4];  רֹעֶה (4:2);  בָּנֶה.[5]

d. הַכֵּה[9];  הָיֹה (18:18);  נִגְלֹה[7];  קָוֹה[8];  הַרְבֵּה (15:1);  בָּכֹה.[6]

e. עֲשׂוֹת (2:3);  רָאוֹת (2:19);  הַבָּנוֹת[10];  הַחֲיוֹת (6:19);
הִתְהַלְּלוֹת.[11]

f. עֲשֹׂה (6:14);  עֲנֹה[12];  הַחֲיֵה[13];  כַּלֵּה[14];  הַכֵּה[15];  הֵרָאֵה.[16]

Verbs whose third radical is ו are very few, the ו in nearly every
case having passed over into י. Verbs whose third radical is י present the following peculiarities:

1. When the third radical (י) would be final, it appears nowhere
except in the Ḳal passive Participle. Its place is generally supplied
by the vowel-letter ה, and hence these verbs are commonly termed
ל"ה. The following treatments of final י__ occur:

    a. It is wholly rejected, and â, rounded from ă (§ 36. 2), appears
as the vowel of the second radical in all *Perfects*.

    b. It unites with the stem-vowel, and ê, contracted from ăy
(§ 36. 2), appears as the vowel of the second radical in all *Imperfects*.

    c. It unites with the stem-vowel, and ê, contracted from ăy
(§ 36. 2), appears as the vowel of the second radical in all *Participles*,
except the Ḳal passive.

    Remark.—In the construct form of the participle י__ contracts
with the preceding vowel (ă), yielding the form ê (ה__).

    d. It is lacking, and ô (rounded from â) and ē, the usual vowels,
appear as the stem-vowels of the Infs. absolute (the latter (ē) in Hif.
Hŏf., and sometimes in Pĭ'ēl and Nĭf.).

    e. It is lacking, and ô (either rounded from â, or contracted from
ă and w) with the ending ת, appears as the ending of all Infs. Const.

¹ Ex. 21 : 20.          ² Job 9 : 22.          ³ Ex. 2 : 11.          ⁴ Mal. 2 : 17.
⁵ Ps. 147 : 2.          ⁶ 1 Sam. 1 : 10.       ⁷ 1 Sam. 2 : 27.       ⁸ Ps. 40 : 2.
⁹ Deut. 13 : 16.        ¹⁰ Hag. 1 : 2.         ¹¹ 2 Sam. 13 : 2.      ¹² Mic. 6 : 3.
¹³ Josh. 9 : 20.        ¹⁴ Ps. 59 : 14.        ¹⁵ Ezek. 6 : 11.       ¹⁶ 1 Kgs. 18 : 1.

*f.* It unites with the preceding vowel, and ê (written הֶ֫), arising from the contraction of יֶ, appears in all Imvs. (2 masc. sg.).

2. יְרְדוּ (1:26) *for* יִרְדּיוּ; יְכַלּוּ (2:1); יִקְווּ (1:9); הָיוּ (1:14); תִּבְעָיוּן⁴; יִבְכָּיוּן³; יֶאֱתָיוּן²; חָסָיוּ¹; פְּרוּ (1:22); רְבוּ (1:22); יְרַבְּיֻן⁵; יְכַסְיֻ֫מוּ⁶.

3. *a.* הָרְאֵיתָ¹⁰ (45:19); צִוִּיתָ⁹; חָלִיתָ; נִהְיֵיתָ⁸; נִדְמֵיתָ⁷;

   *b.* הִכֵּ֫יתִ¹¹ (4:1); קָנִ֫יתִי (3:14); עָשִׂ֫יתָ (3:5); וִהְיִיתֶם; כִּסֵּ֫יתִי¹⁵; הֶעֱלֵיתָ¹⁴ *and* הֶעֱלִית¹³ *but cf.* הִשְׁתַּחֲוֵ֫ית¹²; צִוִּ֫יתִי¹⁷ *and* כִּסִּ֫יתִי¹⁶; (3:17).

   *c.* תֶּעֱשֶׂ֫ינָה¹⁹; תֶּעֲשֶׂ֫ינָה¹⁸ (19:33); וַתִּשְׁקֶ֫יןָ (41:36); תֶּהְיֶ֫ינָ|, בְּכֶ֫ינָה²⁰.

4. הָיְתָה (1:2); עָשְׂתָה (27:17); רָאֲתָה (38:14); נִרְאֲתָה (9:14); הִשְׁקְתָה (24:46); כָּלְתָה²²; הִפְנְתָה²¹.

2. *Before vowel-additions*, the radical י is usually lacking, together with its preceding vowel; it appears, however, in pausal and emphatic forms.

3. *Before consonant-additions*, the radical י unites with the preceding stem-vowel, always ă, forming the diphthongal *ay*, which appears as

   *a.* ê (יֵ) in the Perfects of the passive stems (rarely it is יֶ).

   *b.* î (יִ), thinned from ê, generally in the Perfects of active stems, though Pî'ēl and Hif'îl stems very frequently have יֵ;

   *c.* ê (יֵ), contracted from *ay*, in Imperfects and Imperatives.

4. The Perfect 3 sg. fem. of all stems lacks the third radical (י) and takes the old feminine ending תְ, to which הָ is added.

**Note.**—This הָ is probably the usual feminine ending, added after the analogy of other verbs.

---

| | | | |
|---|---|---|---|
| ¹ Deut. 32 : 37. | ² Isa. 41 : 5. | ³ Isa. 33 : 7. | ⁴ Isa. 21 : 12. |
| ⁵ Ex. 15 : 5. | ⁶ Deut. 8 : 13. | ⁷ Ezek. 32 : 2. | ⁸ Deut. 27 : 9. |
| ⁹ Isa. 14 : 10. | ¹⁰ Ex. 26 : 30. | ¹¹ Ex. 17 : 5. | ¹² Deut. 4 : 19. |
| ¹³ Ex. 32 : 7. | ¹⁴ Ex. 33 : 1. | ¹⁵ Ezek. 31 : 15. | ¹⁶ Ps. 32 : 5. |
| ¹⁷ Deut. 3 : 21. | ¹⁸ Deut. 1 : 44. | ¹⁹ Lev. 4 : 2. | ²⁰ 2 Sam. 1 : 24. |
| ²¹ Jer. 49 : 24. | ²² Hos. 11 : 6. | | |

5. *a.* ;הַרְבֵּה for הַרְבֵּ for הֶרֶב³ for צַוֵּה ; צַו² for גָּלָה ; גַּל¹ for

הֶרֶף ⁴for הַרְפֵּ for הַרְפֵּה ; הַעֵל ⁵for הַעֲלֵה.

*b.* (1) וַיִּפְתְּ⁶ ; וַיֵּשֶׁב.⁷

(2) וָאֵשְׁתְּ (9:21); וַיֵּבְךְ (27:38); וָאֵשְׁתְּ (24:46).

(3) וַיִּקֶן ; וַיּוּקַר ; וַיִּפֶן⁸ ; יֵרֶב (1:22); וַיִּבֶן (2:22); (33:19).

(4) וַתֵּרֶב (43:34); וַתֵּרֶא (3:6); וַנֵּפֶן¹¹; וַתֵּפֶן¹⁰

(5) וַיֵּשַׁע (4:4); וַתַּחַר (4:1); וַיִּחַר (4:5); וַיַּעַשׂ (1:7); תַּעַשׂ (22:12).

(6) וָאֵרֶא.¹³ ; וַיִּרְא (12:7); תֵּגֶל¹²

(7) וַיֵּכַל (2:2); וַיְצַו (2:16); וַיִּמַן¹⁴; וָאֲצַו¹⁵; וַיִּתְגַּל (9:21).

(8) וַיִּשְׁק (29:10); יֶפְתְּ (9:27); וַיִּפֶן.¹⁶

5. Forms lacking any representation of the third radical are found
as follows:

*a.* Without הָ in the Piʿēl, Hifʿil and Hiθpăʿēl Imperatives;
in Hifʿil forms, a helping ⟋ or ⟋ is often inserted.

*b.* Without הָ in the Imperfect when used as a Jussive, or
with Wâw Conversive (§§ 69. *b*, 70. *d*). In the absence of the הָ,

(1) the verbal form may stand without change; or

(2) it may have the vowel of the preformative modified; or

(3) it may receive the helping-vowel ⟋; or

(4) it may receive the helping-vowel ⟋, and also have the
vowel of the preformative modified;

(5) in laryngeal forms ⟋ is employed as the helping-vowel;

(6) in the Nifʿăl there is no further change;

(7) in the Piʿēl and Hiθpăʿēl there is naturally the absence
of the characteristic Dăḡēš-fŏrtē;

(8) in the Hifʿil the helping vowel ⟋ is frequently employed,
in which case the ⟋ of the preformative is deflected to
ĕ (§ 36. 2).

---

¹ Ps. 119 : 18.      ² Deut. 3 : 28.      ³ Judg. 20 : 38.      ⁴ Deut. 9 : 14.
⁵ Ex. 8 : 1.         ⁶ Job 31 : 27.      ⁷ Num. 21 : 1.       ⁸ Ex. 2 : 12.
⁹ Ruth 2 : 3.       ¹⁰ 1 Kgs. 10 : 13.   ¹¹ Deut. 2 : 1.      ¹² Isa. 47 : 3.
¹³ Ex. 6 : 3.       ¹⁴ Jon. 2 : 1.       ¹⁵ Deut. 3 : 18.     ¹⁶ Judg. 15 : 4.

## 83. Verbs Lâmĕđ ʾÅlĕf (ל"א)

[For full inflection, see Paradigm N. p. 210.]

### TABULAR VIEW

|           | Ḳăl. | Nifʿăl. | Piʿēl. | Hifʿil. | Hiθpăʿēl. |
|-----------|------|---------|--------|---------|-----------|
| Perf.      | קָטָא | נִקְטָא | קִטֵּא | הִקְטִיא | הִתְקַטֵּא |
| Impf.      | יִקְטָא | יִקָּטֵא | יְקַטֵּא | יַקְטִיא | יִתְקַטֵּא |
| Imv.       | קְטָא | הִקָּטֵא | קַטֵּא | הַקְטֵא | הִתְקַטֵּא |
| Inf. abs.  | קָטוֹא | נִקְטֹא | קַטֵּא | הַקְטֵא | — |
| Inf. const.| קְטֹא | הִקָּטֵא | קַטֵּא | הַקְטִיא | הִתְקַטֵּא |
| Part. act. | קֹטֵא | | מְקַטֵּא | מַקְטִיא | מִתְקַטֵּא |
| Part. pass.| קָטוּא | נִקְטָא | | | |

1. בָּרָא (1:1) for בָּרָא; מָצָא (2:20); נִקְרָא¹; קֹרֵא² for קֹרֵא;
תַּדְשֵׁא (1:11).

2. *a.* יִקְרָאֵנִי³ (1:28); וַיִּבְאֶה (2:22); יִמְלְאוּ (25:24); מָלְאוּ
*b.* לְהַבְרִיאֲכֶם⁴; וַיּוֹצִיאֵךְ⁶; יִשָּׂאֵךְ; יִמְצָאֵךְ⁵; נְשָׂאֵךְ⁷.

3. *a.* מְצָאתֶם⁸ (26:32); מְצָאֻנוּ (6:7); בְּרָאתִי (17:19); קָרָאתְ
*b.* שָׂנֵאת¹²; יְרֵאתֶם¹¹ (31:31); יָרֵאתִי¹⁰; מָלֵאתִי⁹; מָלֵאתְ
נַחְבֵּאת¹⁷; בֵּרֵאתְ¹⁶; טֻמֵּאת¹⁵; חָטֵאת¹⁴; נִקְרֵאתִי¹³.
*c.* קֹרֶאן²⁰; (3 *f. pl.*)¹⁹ תִּקְרֶאנָה; (2 *f. pl.*)¹⁸ תִּקְרֶאנָה
תְּמַלֶּאנָה.²¹

**Remark 1.**—צֵאת (24:11) *for* צֵאת; שֵׂאת (36:7) *or* שְׂאֵת
(4:7) *for* שְׂאֵת.

---

¹ Deut. 28 : 10.    ² Isa. 58 : 12.    ³ Ps. 89 : 27.    ⁴ Deut. 1 : 31.
⁵ 1 Kgs. 18 · 12.   ⁶ Deut. 4 : 37.   ⁷ 1 Sam. 2 : 29.   ⁸ Judg. 14 : 12.
⁹ Job 36 : 17.      ¹⁰ Jer. 1 : 11.   ¹¹ Deut. 5 : 5.    ¹² Ps. 5 : 6.
¹³ Esth. 4 : 11.    ¹⁴ Ex. 29 : 36.   ¹⁵ Ezek. 5 : 11.   ¹⁶ Josh. 17 : 15.
¹⁷ 1 Sam. 19 : 2.   ¹⁸ Ruth 1 : 20, 21.  ¹⁹ Ruth 4 : 17.  ²⁰ Ruth 1 : 20.
²¹ Ex. 2 : 16.

Remark 2.—¹בֵּנוּ‎ for ‎בָּאנוּ‎; ‎²נַחְבֵּתֶם‎; ‎צָמֵתִי‎; ‎³תִּשֶּׁנָה‎.⁴

Remark 3.—‎נְטַמְינוּ‎⁵; ‎נָשׂוּי‎⁶; ‎צָמֵת‎⁷ for ‎צָמֵאת‎; ‎דִּכָּאת‎⁸;

‎מְלֵאת‎.⁹

Verbs whose third radical is ‎א‎ exhibit the following peculiarities:

1. *Final* ‎א‎ always quiesces (§ 43. 1); this does not affect any preceding vowel except ă, which, in an open syllable, then becomes å, as in the Ḳăl Perf., Imperf. and Imv.; throughout the Pŭ'ăl and Hŏf'ăl forms, and in the Nĭf'ăl Perfect.

Note.—The Ḳăl Imperf. and Imv. have ă for their stem-vowel, after the analogy of verbs ‎לְ‎′ laryngeal (§ 76.).

2. *Medial* ‎א‎ *is treated as a consonant* (larynge),

    *a.* Before all vowel-additions.

    *b.* Before the Š⁰wâ which precedes the suffixes ‎ךָ‎, ‎כֶם‎, ‎כֶן‎.

3. *Medial* ‎א‎ *quiesces* (*i. e.*, loses its consonantal character) before all consonant-additions, the preceding vowel becoming

    *a.* ⟶, rounded from ă, in the Ḳăl Perfect (active).

    *b.* ⟶, lowered from ĭ, in the Ḳăl Perfect (stative), and in the remaining Perfects.

Note.—This use of ē in the Perfects parallels the usage in ‎לְ″ה‎ verbs (§ 82.).

    *c.* ⟶ (ê), after the analogy of the ‎לְ″ה‎ verb, in the Imperfects and Imperatives.

Remark 1.—In addition to instances indicated under 3 (above), ‎א‎ shows a tendency to become silent in many isolated cases.

Remark 2.—‎א‎, losing its consonantal character, is frequently dropped.

Remark 3.—There are numerous examples of verbs ‎לְ″א‎ with the inflection of verbs ‎לְ″ה‎ (§ 82.), there being an evident confusion, in many cases, of the one class with the other.

¹ 1 Sam. 25 : 8.    ² Josh. 2 : 16.    ³ Judg. 4 : 19.    ⁴ Ruth 1 : 14.
⁵ Job 18 : 3.    ⁶ Ps. 32 : 1.    ⁷ Ruth 2 : 9.    ⁸ Ps. 89 : 11.
⁹ Jer. 29 : 10.

# XII. Bi-literal Verbs

## 84. *Classes of Bi-literal Verbs*

1. קָלוּ (8:8); יִשְׁכּוּ (8:1); יֵרַע (21:12); וַיִּחַל (29:20); חַי (3:22).

2. יָשׁוּף (3:15); יָמוּת (38:11); שָׁב (18:33); תָּשׁוּב (3:19); וַיָּקָם (4:8).

The Semitic vocabulary in general and the Hebrew in particular are predominantly *tri-literal;* i. e., words are, for the most part, made upon the basis of three radical consonants. Hebrew grammars have long taught that all Hebrew words might be explained upon the tri-literal basis; and many still so teach. But it now appears to be true that originally, not only in the Semitic languages as a whole, but also in Hebrew, there were two kinds of words, those organized as *tri-literals*, and those organized as *bi-literals*. But the tendency of the language was toward tri-literality. The bi-literals gradually yielded to this influence and sought in various ways to achieve tri-literality, or its equivalent, for themselves. Some carry the marks of their bi-literal origin more plainly visible than do others. It is probable indeed that all of the Weak Verbs were originally of the bi-literal order; but for the sake of convenience they have been treated here as tri-literals. But there are two classes of verbs which from every point of view are best treated frankly as bi-literals. These are:

1. The ῾Ăyĭn-doubled (עַ״ע) verb, the main characteristic of which is the doubling of the second radical.

Note.—An accurate name for this class awaits discovery. ῾*Ăyĭn* must here be understood as designating the second radical, rather than the middle radical, since these roots have only two consonants.

2. The Middle-Vowel verbs, commonly called ῾Ăyĭn Wâw (עַ״ו) and ῾Ăyĭn Yôd (עַ״י).

Note.—The name "Middle-Vowel verb" is chosen here rather for convenience than for accuracy.

## 85. The ʿĂyĭn-Doubled Verb

[For full inflection, see Paradigm L, p. 206.]

### TABULAR VIEW

|            | Ḳal.                | Nifʿal.              | Hifʿil.        |
|------------|---------------------|----------------------|----------------|
| Perf.      | קַט / קָטֵט          | נָקַט / נָקֵט         | הֵקֵט / הֵקֵט  |
| Impf.      | יָקֹט / יִקַּט       | יִקַּט               | יָקֵט          |
| Imv.       | קֹט                 | הִקַּט               | הָקֵט          |
| Inf. abs.  | קָטוֹט              | הִקֹּט / הִקֵּט       | הָקֵט          |
| Inf. const.| קֹט                 | הִקַּט               | הָקֵט          |
| Part. act. | קֹטֵט               |                      | מֵקֵט          |
| Part. pass.| קָטוֹט              | נָקֹט                |                |

Hŏfʿal: Pf. הוּקַט;   Impf. יוּקַט;   Part. מוּקָט

---

1. a. ²;הָסֵבִּי¹;הֶחֱלָה (18:20); נָסַבּוּ (19:4); יָשֹׁכּוּ (8:1); רְבָה
   נָסַב⁵;יִסֹּב⁴;מְסַבֹּת³.

   b. יָדִם⁶;יִסֹּב⁷;אָכַּת⁸;יִתֹּם (47:15); יִמַּלּוּ⁹;יָקֹד (24:26).

Remark.—יֵסֵב¹⁰;יִתַּם¹¹;וַיִּכַּתּוּ¹²;תַּמֵּר¹³;יְכַּת¹⁴.

2. a. בָּלַל (11:9); חָנַן (33:5); גַּלְלוּ (29:3); צַלְלוּ¹⁵;נָדְדָה¹⁶.

   b. שָׁדוּד¹⁷;שָׁדוּד²⁰;סוֹבֵב¹⁹;חֹצֵץ¹⁸;זוֹלֵל¹⁷.

   c. יְלָבֵב²⁶;הֻשַּׁמֵּם²⁵;לָחְמָם²⁴;לִסְבֹּב²³;לִשְׁדוֹד²²;לִשְׁלָל²⁷.

---

¹ Judg. 20 : 40.      ² Cant. 6 : 5.       ³ Ex. 28 : 11.       ⁴ 1 Kgs. 7 : 15.
⁵ Num. 34 : 4.       ⁶ Ps. 30 : 13.       ⁷ 1 Sam. 5 : 8.      ⁸ Deut. 9 : 21.
⁹ Job 24 : 24.       ¹⁰ Ex. 13 : 18.      ¹¹ 2 Kgs. 22 : 4.     ¹² Deut. 1 : 44.
¹¹ Ex. 23 : 21.      ¹⁴ Isa. 24 : 12.      ¹⁵ Ex. 15 : 10.      ¹⁶ Isa. 10 : 31.
¹⁷ Deut. 21 : 20.    ¹⁸ Prov. 30 : 27.     ¹⁹ 2 Kgs. 6 : 15.    ²⁰ Mic. 2 : 4.
²¹ Judg. 5 : 27.     ²² Isa. 10 : 6.       ²³ Jer. 47 : 4.      ²⁴ Num. 21 : 4.
²⁶ Isa. 47 : 14.     ²⁶ Mic. 6 : 13.       ²⁷ Job 11 : 12.

One group of bi-literal verbs sought to approximate tri-literality by strengthening the consonantal element of the root. As a rule, the second radical was therefore doubled whenever possible. The vowel used before this doubled consonant was the same as that found as characteristic stem-vowel in the corresponding forms of the tri-literal strong verb.

1. *a.* The second radical is regularly doubled, except when final, throughout the Ḳăl, Nǐf'ăl, Hǐf'il and Hŏf'ăl stems.

*b.* Some verbs double the first instead of the second radical in the Ḳăl Imperf. This is the regular form in Aramaic for these verbs; this form of the Imperf. therefore is commonly called the Aramaic Imperf.

**Remark.**—Such forms occur sporadically in the Hǐf'il and Hŏf'ăl.

2. Certain forms of the Ḳăl, Nǐf'ăl, Hǐf'il and Hŏf'ăl become fully tri-literal by writing the second radical twice and vocalizing as in the tri-literal strong verb. These are:

*a.* The Ḳăl Perfect of verbs denoting action or movement in all the forms of the 3d pers.

*b.* The Ḳăl Participles and Infin. Absol. The naturally long vowels of these forms made any other method of strengthening them impossible.

*c.* A few sporadic forms.

3. *a.* גַּלּוֹתִי[1]; סַבּוֹתִי[2]; סַבּוֹתָ[3]; נְקַלּוֹתִי[4]; הֻשַּׁמּוֹת[5]; הֲסִבּוֹת[6]

    *b.* תְּסֻבֶּינָה (37:7); וַתְּחַלֶּינָה (41:54); תְּצֶלֶינָה[7]

    *c.* וְסַבּוֹתֶם[8]; מוּסַבּוֹת[9]; נְקַטּוֹתֶם [וְהֻקְטוֹתֶ].

4. *a.* תְּסֻכֵּנִי[13]; תֻּמִּי[12]; בַּחְקוֹ[11]; יְסֻבֵּנִי[10]; תְּסֻבֶּינָה (37:7); רִבְּכֶם[14].

    *b.* וַיָּמָד[15]; רָנּוּ[16]; רָנִּי[17] (but רֹנִּי)[18].

    *c.* יִסֹּבּוּ[19]; אֶחָל[20].

---

[1] Josh. 5 : 9.    [2] 1 Sam. 22 : 22.    [3] Ex. 40 : 3.    [4] 2 Sam. 6 : 22.
[5] Job 16 : 7.    [6] 1 Kgs. 18 : 37.    [7] 1 Sam. 3 : 11.    [8] Josh. 6 : 3.
[9] Ezek. 41 : 24.    [10] Ps. 49 : 6.    [11] Prov. 8 : 27.    [12] Jer. 27 : 8.
[13] Ps. 139 : 13.    [14] Deut. 7 : 7.    [15] Ruth 3 : 15.    [16] Jer. 31 : 7.
[17] Isa. 54 : 1.    [18] Isa. 12 : 6.    [19] Ezek. 1 : 9.    [20] Ezek. 22 : 26.

d. הֵחֵל (6:1); מֵחֵל'; מֵסֵב'; הָסֵבִּי'; הַשְׁמֹות';

וַתֵּחֶל' (9:20) תִּצְלֶינָה'; וַיָּחֶל תְּחִלֶּינָה (41:54);

3. When terminations beginning with a consonant are attached to forms containing a doubled second radical, a *separating vowel* is inserted to make it possible to retain the doubling of the radical.

a. The forms in the perfect take ô as the separating vowel.

b. The Imperfect takes ê (יֶ) before the termination נָה.

c. The separating vowels regularly carry the tone except before the heavy terminations תֶּם and תֶּן.

Note.—The origin of these separating vowels is not clear, but the probability is that they arose after the analogy of the לה verb forms.

4. The following variations from the form of the *stem-vowel* as it appears in corresponding forms of the tri-literal strong verb are found:

a. The original ŭ regularly appears in the Ḳăl Imperf., Inf., and Imperative, whenever the tone leaves the root-syllable by reason of the addition of affixes or suffixes.

b. The original ŭ is deflected to ŏ in the Ḳăl Imperf. when the tone recedes to the preformative upon the addition of Wăw-conversive; and frequently also in cases covered by 4 a.

c. In the Nĭf'ăl Imperf. and Imv., where ē appears in the strong verb, the original ă is retained unchanged.

d. In the Hĭf'ĭl stem throughout, the attenuated ĭ is not lengthened to î as in the strong verb, but

(1) is lowered to ē when it has the tone;

(2) is retained as ĭ when it loses the tone by reason of the addition of affixes or suffixes, and

(3) is deflected to ĕ when the tone recedes on account of wăw-conversive.

Note.—A naturally long vowel before a doubled consonant is contrary to usage in Hebrew, being rarely, if ever, found.

1 Jer. 25 : 29.          2 Jer. 21 : 4.          3 Cant. 6 : 5.          4 Job 16 : 7.
5 1 Sam. 3 : 11.         6 Judg. 13 : 25.

5. *a.* וַיָּסֹב[1], *but* תְּסֻבֶּינָה (37:7); נָסֵב[2], *but* נְשַׁדֶּנּוּ[3]; נָסֵב[4],

הֻחַל[7]. וַיִּסַבֵּנִי[5]; הָסֵב[6]; *but*

*b.* הָבוֹק תִּבּוֹק[11]; הִבּוֹז תִּבּוֹז[11]; יֵדֹם[10]; יִסֹּב[9]; הֵמַם[8].

*c.* וַהֲשִׁכֹּתִי[15]; יֵהָשַׁמְמָה[14]; הֲקִלֹּתַנִי[13]; מֵחֵל[12]; הֵחֵל (6:1);

**Remark.**—אֶקְלֹ־ (16:5); יֵחַם[16]; יֵחַת[17].

*d.* מוּסַבּוֹת[19]; יוּשַׁד[18]; הוּחַל (4:26).

5. Certain variations occur in the *vowel of the preformative syllable* from the vowel forms in the corresponding places in the strong verb. These are:

*a.* In the regular Ḳăl Imperf., the Nĭf'ăl Perf. and Part., and the Hĭf'îl Imperf. and Imv., the original ă of the preformative syllable is rounded to å when pretonic, but is reduced to Š'wâ when the tone moves farther away.

*b.* In the Nĭf'ăl Imperf., Imv., and Infins. and in the so-called Aramaic Imperf. of the Ḳăl, the ă of the preformative is attenuated to ĭ in the unaccented sharpened syllable and remains without further change.

*c.* In the Hĭf'îl Perf. and Part., the original ă of the preformative is attenuated to ĭ and then lowered to ē when pretonic; but when the tone moves away original ă is reduced to compound Š'wâ (⸗).

**Remark.**—The *intransitive* Ḳăl Imperf. with ă as stem-vowel also has ē in the preformative syllable, but probably here it arises from an original ĭ.

*d.* The preformative ŭ of the Hŏf. stem regularly lengthens to û. This is probably due to the influence of the Middle-Vowel verb (§ 86.).

**Remark.**—Frequently forms appear with ŭ unchanged and the first radical doubled; *e. g.,* הֻמְּכוּ.[20]

---

| | | | |
|---|---|---|---|
| [1] 1 Kgs. 7 : 15. | [2] Num. 34 : 4. | [3] Mic. 2 : 4. | [4] 2 Chr. 14 : 6. |
| [5] Ezek. 47 : 2. | [6] 2 Sam. 5 : 23. | [7] Deut. 2 : 24. | [8] Ps. 68 : 3. |
| [9] 1 Sam. 5 : 8. | [10] Ps. 30 : 13. | [11] Isa. 24 : 3. | [12] Jer. 25 : 29. |
| [13] 2 Sam. 19 : 44. | [14] Job 16 : 7. | [15] Num. 17 : 20. | [16] Deut. 19 : 6. |
| [17] Isa. 7 : 8. | [18] Hos. 10 : 14. | [19] Ezek. 41 : 24. | [20] Job 24 : 24. |

6. *a.* מְחֹקֵק (49:10); יִתְרֹצְצוּ (25:22); ²וְדוֹמַמְתִּי; ¹יְמוֹלֵל;
   ⁴פּוֹרַרְתָּ; ³יִרְצְצוּ

*b.* ⁷הִתְרֹעֲעָה; ⁷הִתְפּוֹרְרָה; ⁶מְחֻלָּל; ⁵עוֹלָל

*c.* ¹²מְכַרְכֵּר; ⁸קִלְקַל; ⁹גִּלְגַּלְתִּי; ¹⁰תְּצַפְצֵף; ¹¹עַרְעֵר;
   הִתְמַהְמְהוּ (43:10).

*d.* ¹⁶רִכְּכָה; יִתְפַּלֵּל (20:7); ¹⁵יְקַלֵּל; ¹⁴הַלְלוּ; ¹³הִלֵּל;
   ¹⁷יְקַלֵּל

7. See forms cited under 3 *a, b, c,* 4 *a, d,* 5 *a, c.*

8. אֲמֹשְׁךָ (27:21), *for*; ¹⁹בְּחֻקּוֹ, *for* לָבֹר; ¹⁸לָבוּר, *for*
   ²²יְרוּץ, *for* יָרֹן; ²¹יְשׁוּד, *for* יֵשֹׁד; ²⁰יִרוֹן, *for* אֲמֹשְׁךָ.

6. The *Intensive Stems* assume special forms in these verbs. These are:

   *a.* The *Pôlēl* stem, as active intensive, with its reflexive *Hiθpôlēl.*

   *b.* The *Pôlăl* stem, as passive of the Pôlēl, with its reflexive Hiθpôlăl.

   *c.* The *Pilpēl* stem appears as an active intensive in a few verbs.

   Note.—These stems serve both for this verb and for the Middle-Vowel verb (§ 86.). In the Pôlēl and Pôlăl forms, the double writing of the 2d radical gives the desired tri-literality; and to express the intensive idea, the vowel of the penult is lengthened (and rounded) in place of another doubling of the 2d radical. In the Pilpēl, the entire bi-literal root is doubled.

   *d.* A few verbs write the 2d radical twice and make intensive stems from this lengthened root exactly as in the tri-literal verb proper. These are forms that developed late.

7. The *tone* generally stays upon the stem-syllable. As a rule, it

¹ Ps. 90 : 6.          ² Ps. 131 : 2.          ³ Judg. 10 : 8.          ⁴ Ps. 74 : 13.
⁵ Lam. 1 : 12.         ⁶ Isa. 53 : 5.          ⁷ Isa. 24 : 19.         ⁸ Eccl. 10 : 10.
⁹ Jer. 51 : 25.        ¹⁰ Isa. 29 : 4.         ¹¹ Jer. 51 : 58.        ¹² 2 Sam. 6 : 14.
¹³ Ps. 10 : 3.         ¹⁴ Ps. 104 : 35.        ¹⁵ Lev. 20 : 9.         ¹⁶ Isa. 1 : 6.
¹⁷ Isa. 65 : 20.       ¹⁸ Eccl. 9 : 1.         ¹⁹ Prov. 8 : 29.        ²⁰ Prov. 29 : 6.
²¹ Ps. 91 : 6.         ²² Isa. 42 : 4.

leaves that syllable only when the separating vowels are used or when pronominal suffixes are added.

8. The forms of this verb sometimes exchange with similar forms of the Middle-Vowel verb (§ 86.).

### 86.  The Middle-Vowel Verb

[For full inflection, see Paradigm M, p. 208.]

**TABULAR VIEW**

|  | Ķăl. Middle û. | Middle î. | Niⁱfăl. | Hiⁱfîl. | Hôfăl. |
|---|---|---|---|---|---|
| **Perf.** | קָל / קֵל | קָל | נָקוֹל | הֵקִיל | הוּקַל |
| **Impf.** | יָקוּל | יָקִיל | יִקּוֹל | יָקִיל | יוּקַל |
| **Imv.** | קוּל | קִיל | הִקּוֹל | הָקֵל |  |
| **Inf. abs.** | קוֹל | קָל | הִקּוֹל / נָקוֹל | הָקֵל |  |
| **Inf. const.** | קוּל | קִיל | הִקּוֹל | הָקִיל | הוּקַל |
| **Part. act.** | קָל | קָל / קֵל |  | מֵקִיל |  |
| **Part. pass.** | קוּל | קִיל / קוּל | נָקוֹל |  | מוּקָל |

1. *a.* שָׁב (18:33); ¹קַמְתָּ; ²שַׁבְתִּי; ³סָרְתֶם; ⁴סָרוּ; ⁵רָמָה; ⁶דָּשׁ; ⁷שָׁבָה.

Remark.—מֵת (42:38); אוֹר (44:3); ⁸בּוֹשׁ; ⁹טוֹב; מֵתוּ (7:22).

*b.* נָבוֹן (41:33); נָכוֹן (41:32); הֵמוֹל (17:10); יִמּוֹל (17:12); ¹²נְפוּגֹתִי; ¹¹נְסוּגֹתִי; ¹⁰נְקֹטֹתֶם; נָפֹצוּ (10:18).

---

| | | | |
|---|---|---|---|
| ¹ 2 Sam. 12 : 21. | ² Zech. 1 : 16. | ³ Mal. 2 : 8. | ⁴ Deut. 9 : 12. |
| ⁵ 1 Sam. 2 : 1. | ⁶ Ruth 1 : 15. | ⁷ 1 Chr. 21 : 20. | ⁸ Jer. 48 : 39. |
| ⁹ Deut. 5 : 30. | ¹⁰ Ezek. 20 : 43. | ¹¹ Isa. 50 : 5. | ¹² Ps. 38 : 9. |

c. יָבוֹא ;(32:9) יֵבוֹשׁ ;יְאוֹר²; יֵאָתוּ¹; נָאוֹת (34:15).

d. הֵבִיא ;(4:4) הֵשִׁיב (14:16); הָאִיר (1:17); אָקִים (17:21);
הֲקִמֹתִי ;לְהָקִים⁴; (9:9) מֵקִים (9:9); יָשִׁיב (50:15); הֲקִמֹתִי
תָּשֵׁב (50:15); הָשֵׁב (38:8); הָקֵם (44:8); הֲשִׁיבֻנוּ
וַהֲקֵמֹתָ⁷; תְּשֻׁבְנָה⁵; וַיָּקֶם⁶; יָבֵא (4:3); (24:8);
וַהֲרֵמֹתָ⁸; הֵבֵאתָ (20:9); וְהֵבֵאתִי (27:12).

e. שׁוּב (31:3); קוּם (13:17); תָּשׁוּב (3:19); יָמוּת (38:11);
שָׁבְנָה¹⁰; קָמְנָה⁹; (42:2) נָמוּת (42:2); סוֹרוּ (19:2);

Remark.—וַיָּרֶץ (18:2); (4:8) תָּקֹץ¹⁴; תָּנֹד¹³; יִשֵּׁב¹²; יִירָם¹¹;
וַתִּשְׁבְּנָה¹⁵; וַיָּנֶם (39:12); וַיָּנֶר (20:1); וַיֵּשֶׁב (26:18).

f. לָלִין (24:23); יָדִין (49:16); אָשִׁית (3:15); יָשִׂים (30:42);
יָבִין¹⁶; בִּינָה¹⁷; בִּין¹⁸.

Remark.—וַיָּשֶׁת (30:40); (2:8) וַיָּשֶׂם ;יָשֵׂם²¹; יָגֵל²⁰; יָבֵן¹⁹;
וַיִּבֶן²².

g. שָׁב²³; זָב²⁴; קָמָה²⁵; קָמִים²⁶; קָאם²⁷; לָאט²⁸.

The Middle-Vowel verb is a bi-literal verb which seeks to approximate tri-literality, mainly by emphasizing the characteristic stem-vowel. Hence

1. Wherever the stem-vowel is characteristic of the form, it becomes naturally long, if the consonantal environment permits.

*a.* The ă of the Ḳăl Perf. becomes â, except before terminations beginning with a consonant.

**Remark.**—Stative verbs have ē or ō in the Ḳăl Perf.

1 Isa. 29 : 22.    2 2 Sam. 2 : 32.    3 2 Kgs. 12 : 9.    4 Num. 7 : 1.
5 Job 20 : 10.    6 Judg. 2 : 16.    7 Ex. 26 : 30.    8 Num. 31 : 28.
9 Isa. 32 : 9.    10 Ruth 1 : 8.    11 Num. 24 : 7.    12 Judg. 7 : 3.
13 Jer. 16 : 5.    14 Prov. 3 : 11.    15 1 Sam. 7 : 14.    16 Ps. 19 : 13.
17 Ps. 5 : 2.    18 Prov. 23 : 1.    19 Jer. 9 : 11.    20 Ps 13 : 6.
21 1 Sam. 22 : 15.    22 1 Sam. 3 : 8.    23 Jer. 30 : 18.    24 Jer. 49 : 9.
25 Mic. 7 : 6.    26 2 Sam. 18 : 31.    27 Hos. 10 : 14.    28 Judg. 4 : 21.

*b.* The original ă of all Nif'al forms is lengthened to â and rounded to ô.

**Note.**—This ô gives way to û in some forms of the Perf., for the sake of euphony.

*c.* The same change to ô takes place in certain verbs having ă as the original stem-vowel of the Ḳăl Imperf.

*d.* The original ă of the Hif'il attenuates to ĭ, which lengthens to î in all forms except the Inf. Abs., the Imv. 2d sing. masc., the Jussive form of the Imperf., the Imperf. with Wâw-conversive, sometimes in the Imperf. before the ending נָה_, and in some exceptional forms.

**Note.**—The î in Hif'il of the tri-literal strong verb is probably due to the influence of this î in the Middle-Vowel verb.

*e.* An original ŭ is lengthened to û in the Ḳăl Imperf. and Infin. Const., and in the Imv. except in the 2d fem. pl., where ŭ is lowered to ō before the affix נָה_.

**Remark.**—In the Jussive form of the Ḳăl Imperf., ŭ is merely lowered to ō; and in the form with Wâw-conversive, ŭ is deflected to ŏ, except where it carries the tone and becomes ō.

*f.* An original ĭ lengthens to î in the Ḳăl Imperf., Imv. and Infin. Const. of the Middle î verb.

**Remark.**—In the Jussive this ĭ becomes ē; and with wâw-conversive ĭ is deflected to ĕ.

*g.* The Ḳăl Active Part. takes â (sometimes with א as vowel-letter), the vowel so characteristic of the penult of this Part. in the tri-literal verb, though in its rounded form ô; here it remains as â. The Ḳăl Infin. Absol. rounds its â into ô, as in the characteristic syllable of the corresponding tri-literal form.

2. *a.* הֲקִימֹת (6:18); ¹הֲקִיצֹתִי; הֲרִמֹתִי (14:22); ³הֲשִׁיבֹנוּ
⁴נְבֹנֹתִי; ⁵נְפוּגֹתִי; ⁶נְסוּגֹתִי (44:8);

*b.* ⁷תְּמוּתֶנָה; ⁷תִּשְׁבֶּינָה; ⁶תְּעוּפֶינָה; ⁵תְּמוּטֶינָה;
¹⁰תְּהִימֶנָה; ⁹תְּבִיאֶינָה

---

¹ Ps. 139 : 18.   ² Isa. 50 : 5.   ³ Ps. 38 : 9.   ⁴ Isa. 10 : 13.
⁵ Isa. 54 : 10.   ⁶ Isa. 60 : 8.   ⁷ Ezek. 16 : 55.   ⁸ Ex. 13 : 19.
⁹ Lev. 7 : 30.   ¹⁰ Mic. 2 : 12.

2. Forms which lengthen the stem-vowel, as indicated above, take certain *separating vowels* before terminations beginning with a consonant. These make it possible to retain the lengthened stem-vowel and, in addition, give a longer form.

*a.* In the Nĭf'äl and Hĭf'ĭl Perfects the separating vowel is ô (וֹ).

*b.* In the Ḳäl Imperf. and rarely in the Hĭf'ĭl Imperf. the separating vowel ê (י_ַ) is used.

*c.* These separating vowels regularly carry the tone, except before the heavy terminations תֶּם_ and תֶּן_.

**Note.**—Just as in the ע"ע verb, the separating vowels are perhaps due to the analogy of the ל"ה verb.

3. *a.* יָמוּת (38:11); יְשׁוּפְךָ (3:15); נָמוּת (42:2); יְשׁוּבוּ (8:3); יָשִׁיב (17:21); אָקִים (50:15); הָשֵׁב (50:15); הָאִיר (1:17); נְסוּגֹתִי; תָשֻׁבְןָה²; נָסֹגוּ¹; נָפֹצוּ (10:18); נְבוּנִים (50:15); נְבוֹנִים⁵ (41:33); נָבוֹן (4:8); וַיָּקָם; נְפוּגֹתִי

*b.* יִמָּלוּ; הִכּוֹן⁶; הִמּוֹל (17:10); יִמּוֹל (17:12); נִמּוֹל (17:26); תְּלוּנוּ⁷ (34:24).

*c.* הָבִיא; הֵשִׁיב (4:4); מֵקִים (14:16); הֵקִים⁸ (9:9); הֲבִיאוֹךְ¹⁰; הֲנִיף; הֲקִמֹתִי (6:18); הֲרִמֹתִי (14:22); הֲסִירָה¹¹.

*d.* See examples cited under 1 c above.

3. The vowel of the preformative syllable, when the latter is open, necessarily undergoes change:

*a.* The original ă rounds to å when pretonic, and is reduced to Šᵉwâ when ante-pretonic, in the Ḳäl Imperf., Nĭf'äl Perf. and Part., Hĭf'ĭl Imperf., Imv., and Infinitives.

*b.* The original ă attenuates to ĭ in the Nĭf'äl Imperf., Imv., and Infinitives, and remains without further change in the sharpened syllable, just as in the tri-literal strong verb in the corresponding forms.

¹ Isa. 42 : 17.    ² Job 20 : 10.    ³ Isa. 50 : 5.    ⁴ Ps. 38 : 9.
⁵ Deut. 1 : 13.    ⁶ Ezek. 38 : 7.    ⁷ Ex. 16 : 7.    ⁸ Josh. 4 : 9.
⁹ Lev. 14 : 12.    ¹⁰ Ezek. 27 : 26.    ¹¹ 2 Chr. 15 : 16.

*c.* The original ă of the Hĭf'îl Perf. and Part. is attenuated to ĭ and lowered to ē when pretonic, but is reduced to Šᵉwâ when ante-pretonic.

*d.* In the preformative of the Ḳăl Imperf., with ă as stem-vowel (1 *c* above) of some *intransitive* verbs original ĭ undergoes the same changes as the attenuated ĭ of the preformative of the Hĭf'îl Perfect.

4. הוּשַׁב (42:28); הוּכַן ;הוּקַן ;יוּמַת [3] ;הוּקַם [2] ;יוּרַם [1] ;הַמּוּשָׁב.

    .מוּסָר [6] ;וַיּוּשַׁב [5] ;(43:12)

5. *a.* אֶתְבּוֹנָן [10] ;יְכוֹנֵן [9] ;כּוֹנַנְתָּ [8] ;כּוֹנֵן [7] ;יְעוֹפֵף (1:20).

   *b.* יִתְכּוֹנָן [13] ;חוֹלָלְתָ [12] ;יִתְבֹּשְׁשׁוּ (2:24) ;כּוֹנְנוּ [11].

   *c.* כָּלְכְּלוּ [15] ;כַּלְכֵּל [14] ;וְכִלְכַּלְתִּי (45:11) ;יְכַלְכֵּל (47:12);

   מְטַלְטֶלְךָ [17] ;תִּתְחַלְחַל [16].

   *d.* לְקַיֵּם [22] ;קִיְּמַנִי [21] ;אֲקַיְּמָה [20] ;קִיְּמוּ [19] ;קַיָּם [18].

4. The Hŏf'ăl stem, having its characteristic vowel in the pre-formative syllable, naturally strengthens that vowel rather than the stem-vowel. Consequently ŭ is lengthened to û (וּ), which is of course without further change. The inflection is otherwise as in the strong verb.

5. The Middle-Vowel verb, having no middle radical to double, forms its intensive stems in a different way.

*a.* The intensive actives, corresponding to the Pĭ'ēl and Hĭθpă'ēl of tri-literal verbs, are known as the *Pôlēl* and *Hĭθpôlēl*.

*b.* The corresponding intensive passive is known as the *Pôlăl*.

**Note.**—For an explanation of the origin of these forms, see § 85.

*c.* Some Middle-Vowel verbs make an intensive stem by simply doubling the bi-literal root as a whole and vocalizing the resulting form like a regular tri-literal Pĭ'ēl, etc. These forms are known as the *Pĭlpēl*, *Pĭlpăl*, and *Hĭθpălpēl*.

---

| | | | |
|---|---|---|---|
| [1] Isa. 30:33. | [2] Ex. 40:17. | [3] Num. 15:35. | [4] Lev. 4:10. |
| [5] Ex. 10:8. | [6] Isa. 17:1. | [7] Ps. 9:8. | [8] Ps. 99:4. |
| [9] Isa. 62:7. | [10] Job 23:15. | [11] Ps. 67:23. | [12] Job 15:7. |
| [13] Prov. 24:3. | [14] Jer. 20:9. | [15] 1 Kgs. 20:27. | [16] Esth. 4:4. |
| [17] Isa. 22:17. | [18] Esth. 9:31. | [19] Esth. 9:27. | [20] Ps. 119:106. |
| [21] Ps. 119:28. | [22] Ruth 4:7. | | |

*d. Pĭʿēl* forms of Middle-Vowel verbs are found only in the later literature.  These were probably made after the analogy of genuine Middle-Wāw verbs, such as צִוָּה, עֹולֵל, עֹות, etc.

6. יִמְלוֹ; (10:18) נָפְצוֹ; (7:22) מֵתוּ; (7:9) בָּאוּ; (8:3) יָשְׁבוֹ .6
;ᵗתְּשׁוּבֶינָה; (6:18) הֲקִמֹתִי; (14:22) הֲרִמֹתִי; (34:24)
.³נְקֹטֹתֶם ;²תְּעוּפֶינָה

7. יָדִין; (49:16) יָשִׂים; (30:42) אָשִׁית; (3:15) לָלִין; (24:23) .7
.⁶גִּילוּ ;⁵בִּין ;⁴בִּינָה

**Remark.**—דִּינוּ;⁷ בִּינֹותִי;⁸ רִיבֹות.⁹

8. בֵּן¹⁰ (from בּוּן; as if from כָּזַז); נָמֵר¹¹ (for נָמֹור, from מֹור;
יֵסַג¹³ (רָמֵם); as if from מָרַר); יֵרֹנְמֹוּ¹² (from רֹום; as if from
(from סוּג).

6. The tendency of the Middle-Vowel verb being to stress the stem-vowel, the tone naturally stays upon this strengthened vowel wherever possible.  It loses the tone only when (*a*) the endings תֶּם and תֶּן are added, which carry the tone; or (*b*) the separating vowels ô or ê are used, which always carry the tone themselves except before תֶּם and תֶּן; or (*c*) in forms with Wāw-conversive, etc., in which the stem-vowel was never strengthened.

7. Middle-ê verbs differ from Middle-û only in the Ḳăl Imperf., Imv. and Inf. Const., and sometimes in the Ḳăl Passive Part., in all of which î appears instead of û.

**Remark.**—A few Middle-ê verbs seem to show a characteristic form of the Ḳăl Perf. with î instead of â.  But these forms are perhaps better considered as *Hĭfʿîls* with the preformative dropped.

8. Since the Middle-Vowel verb and the so-called ʿAyĭn-doubled verb are fundamentally the same, it is natural that the two should often interchange forms.  As a matter of fact, the same root some-

---

| | | | |
|---|---|---|---|
| ¹ Ezek. 16 : 55. | ² Isa. 60 : 8. | ³ Ezek. 20 : 43. | ⁴ Ps. 5 : 2. |
| ⁵ Prov. 23 : 1. | ⁶ Ps. 2 : 11. | ⁷ Jer. 16 : 16. | ⁸ Dan. 9 : 2. |
| ⁹ Job 33 : 13. | ¹⁰ Zech. 4 : 10. | ¹¹ Jer. 48 : 11. | ¹² Ezek. 10 : 15, 17. |
| ¹³ Mic. 2 : 6. | | | |

times develops two sets of forms, one with strengthening of consonants, the other with strengthening of vowels, e. g., בֻּוז and בָּזַז; צוּר and צָרַר, etc. More often, only sporadic forms of a second development appear.

## 87. A Comparative View of the Verb Forms
### 1. THE ḲĂL PERFECT AND IMPERFECT

| | Perfect. | Impf. with ō. | Impf. with ă. | Impf. with ē. |
|---|---|---|---|---|
| | [kătăl] | [yăḳtŭl] | [yăḳtăl] | [yăḳtĭl] |
| Active | קָטַל | יִקְטֹל | יִקְטַל | (יִקְטֵל) |
| Stative | { קָטֵל / קָטֹל } | | | |
| פּ׳ laryng. | עָטַל | יַעֲטֹל [1] | יַעֲטַל [4] | —— |
| עּ׳ laryng. | קָאַל | יִקְאַל [2] | יִקְאַל | —— |
| לּ׳ laryng. | קָטַח | —— | יִקְטַח | —— |
| פּ״ן | נָטַל | יִטֹּל | יִטַּל | יִטֵּל [5] |
| פ״א | אָטַל | —— | יֹאטַל | יֹאטֵל |
| פּ״ו | יָטַל | —— | יִיטַל | יֵיטֵל |
| פּ״י | יָטַל | —— | יִיטַל | —— |
| ע״ע | { קָטַט / קַט } | { יָקֹט / יִקֹּט } | יֵקַט | —— |
| ל״א | קָטָא | —— | יִקְטָא | —— |
| ל״ה | קָטָה | —— | יִקְטֶה | —— |
| ע״ו | קָל (â) | { יָקוּל / יִקֹּל [3] } | יָקֹל (ô) | —— |
| ע״י | קָל (â) | —— | —— | יָקִיל |

---

[1] Or יַעֲטֹל; also יֶעֲטֹל.      [2] Only in verbs פּ״ן and עּ׳ laryng.
[3] Jussive and with Wâw-convers. in pause.
[4] Also יֶעֲטַל.      [5] Only in יִתֵּן.

## 2. THE PĬ‘ĒL AND PŬ‘ĂL PERFECTS AND IMPERFECTS

|  | Pĭ‘ēl Perfect. | Pŭ‘ăl Perfect. | Pĭ‘ēl Impf. | Pŭ‘ăl Impf. |
|---|---|---|---|---|
|  | [ḳăṭṭăl]) | [ḳŭṭṭăl] | [yᵉḳăṭṭăl] | [yᵉḳŭṭṭăl] |
| Strong | קַטֵּל, יַקְטֵּל¹ קָטַל | קֻטַּל | יְקַטֵּל | יְקֻטַּל |
| פ׳ laryng. | עִטֵּל | עֻטַּל | יְעַטֵּל | יְעֻטַּל |
| ע׳ laryng. | קָחֵל, קֵאֵל, קֵאַל | קֹחַל, קֹאַל | יְקָאֵל⁷ | יְקֹאַל⁹ |
| ל׳ laryng. | קִטַּח² | קֻטַּח | יְקַטַּח⁸ | יְקֻטַּח |
| פ״נ | נִטֵּל | נֻטַּל | יְנַטֵּל | יְנֻטַּל |
| פ״ו | יִטֵּל | יֻטַּל | יְיַטֵּל | יְיֻטַּל |
| ל״א | קִטֵּא | קֻטָּא | יְקַטֵּא | יְקֻטָּא |
| ל״ה | קִטָּה | קֻטָּה | יְקַטֶּה | יְקֻטֶּה |
| ע״ע | קִטֵּט | קֻטַּט | יְקַטֵּט | יְקֻטַּט |
| ע״ע | קוֹטֵט³ | קוֹטַט | יְקוֹטֵט | יְקוֹטַט |
| ע״ע | קְטַקֵט⁴ | —— | יְקַטְקֵט | —— |
| ע״ו | קִיֵּל⁵ | —— | יְקַיֵּל | —— |
| ע״ו | קוֹלֵל⁶ | קוֹלַל | יְקוֹלֵל | יְקוֹלַל |
| ע״ו | קִלְקֵל⁴ | —— | יְקַלְקֵל | —— |

## 3. THE HĬF‘ÎL AND HŎF‘ĂL PERFECTS AND IMPERFECTS

|  | Hif‘il Perf. | Hŏf‘ăl Perf. | Hĭf‘il Impf. | Hŏf‘ăl Impf. |
|---|---|---|---|---|
|  | [hăḳṭăl] | [hŭḳṭăl] | [yăḳṭăl] | [yŭḳṭăl] |
| Strong | הִקְטִיל | (ה׳) הָקְטַל¹¹ | יַקְטִיל | יֻקְטַל |
| פ׳ laryng. | הֶעֱטִיל¹⁰ | הָעֳטַל¹² | יַעֲטִיל¹³ | יָעֳטַל |
| ע׳ laryng. | הִקְאִיל | הָקְאַל | יַקְאִיל | יֻקְאַל |
| ל׳ laryng. | הִקְטִיחַ | הָקְטַח | יַקְטִיחַ | יֻקְטַח |

---

¹ Forms with *a* under the second radical are quite frequent.
² In pause קִטָּח.          ³ Pô‘ēl.          ⁴ Pilpēl.          ⁵ Rare.
⁶ Pôlēl.          ⁷ Also יְקַחֵל.          ⁸ In pause יְקַטֵּחַ.          ⁹ Also יְקֹחַל.
¹⁰ Also הֶעֱטִיל.          ¹¹ There are a few forms like הָקְטַל.
¹² Also הָעֳטַל.          ¹³ Also יַעֲטִיל.

| | Hif'il Perf. | Hōf'al Perf. | | Hif'il Imperf. | Hōf'al Imperf. |
|---|---|---|---|---|---|
| | [hăḳṭăl] | [hŭḳṭăl] | | [yăḳṭăl] | [yŭḳṭăl] |
| פ"ן | הִטִּיל | הֻטַּל | | יַטִּיל | יֻטַּל |
| פ"ו | הוֹטִיל | הוּטַל | | יוֹטִיל | יוּטַל |
| פ"י | הֵיטִיל | —— | | יֵיטִיל | —— |
| ל"א | הִקְטִיא | הָקְטָא | | יַקְטִיא | יָקְטָא |
| ל"ה | הִקְטָה | הָקְטָה | | יַקְטֶה | יָקְטֶה |
| ע"ע | הֵקֵט | הוּקַט | | יָקֵט | יוּקַט |
| ע"ו | הֵקִיל | הוּקַל | | יָקִיל | יוּקַל |

## 4. THE NĪF'ĂL AND HĪθPĂ'ĒL PERFECTS AND IMPERFECTS

| | Nĭf'ăl Perf. | Nĭf'ăl Impf. | | Hīθpă. Perf. | Hīθpă. Impf. |
|---|---|---|---|---|---|
| | [năḳṭăl] | [yĭḳḳăṭăl] | | [hĭθḳăṭṭăl] | [yĭθḳăṭṭăl] |
| Strong | נִקְטֵל | יִקָּטֵל¹ | | הִתְקַטֵּל | יִתְקַטֵּל |
| פ' laryng. | נֶעֱטַל² | יֵעָטֵל | | הִתְעַטֵּל | יִתְעַטֵּל |
| ע' laryng. | נִקְאַל | יִקָּאֵל | | הִתְקָאֵל³ | יִתְקָאֵל⁴ |
| ל' laryng. | נִקְטַח | יִקָּטַח | | הִתְקַטַּח | יִתְקַטַּח |
| פ"ן | נִטֵּל | יִנָּטֵל | | הִתְנַטֵּל | יִתְנַטֵּל |
| פ"ו | נוֹטַל | יִוָּטֵל | | הִתְיַטֵּל | יִתְיַטֵּל |
| ל"א | נִקְטָא | יִקָּטֵא | | הִתְקַטֵּא | יִתְקַטֵּא |
| ל"ה | נִקְטָה | יִקָּטֶה | | הִתְקַטָּה | יִתְקַטֶּה |
| ע"ע | נָקַט | יִקַּט | | הִתְקַטֵּט | יִתְקַטֵּט |
| ע"ע | | | | הִתְקוֹטֵט | יִתְקוֹטֵט |
| ע"ו | נָקוֹל | יִקּוֹל | | הִתְקוֹלֵל | יִתְקוֹלֵל |
| ע"ו | | | | הִתְקַלְקֵל | יִתְקַלְקֵל |

¹ Rarely יִקְטֵל.    ² Also נֶעֲטַל.    ³ Also הִתְקַחַל.    ⁴ Also יִתְקַחַל.

## 5.  THE VARIOUS INFINITIVES CONSTRUCT

| | Ḳal. | Nif‘al. | Pi‘el. | Hif‘il. | Hŏf‘al. |
|---|---|---|---|---|---|
| | [ḳᵉṭŭl] | [hĭḳḳāṭăl] | [ḳāṭṭăl] | [hăḳṭăl] | [hŭḳṭăl] |
| Strong | קְטֹל¹ | הִקָּטֵל | קַטֵּל | הַקְטִיל | הָקְטַל |
| פ׳ laryng. | עֲטֹל | הֵעָטֵל | עַטֵּל | הַעֲטִיל | הָעֳטַל |
| ע׳ laryng. | קָאֹל | הִקָּאֵל | { קָאֵל / קַהֵל } | הַקְאִיל | הָקְאַל |
| ל׳ laryng. | קְטֹחַ | הִקָּטֵחַ | קַטֵּחַ | הַקְטִיחַ | הָקְטַח |
| פ״ן | { נְטֹל / טֶלֶת } | הִנָּטֵל | נַטֵּל | הַטִּיל | —— |
| פ״ו | { יְטֹל / טֶלֶת } | הִוָּטֵל | יַטֵּל | הוֹטִיל | הוּטַל |
| פ״י | יְטֹל | —— | —— | הֵיטִיל | —— |
| ל״א | קְטֹא | הִקָּטֵא | קַטֵּא | הַקְטִיא | הָקְטֵא |
| ל״ה | קְטוֹת | הִקָּטוֹת | קַטּוֹת | הַקְטוֹת | הָקְטוֹת |
| ע״ע | קֹט | הִקֵּט | קוֹטֵט | הָקֵט | —— |
| ע״ו | קוּל | הִקּוֹל | קוֹלֵל | הָקִיל | —— |
| ע״י | קִיל | —— | —— | —— | —— |

¹ Rarely קְטַל.

# XIII. Nouns

### 88. The Inflection of Nouns

1. אָמֶר *Saying,* from אמר; דָּבָר *Word,* from דבר; מָוֶת *Death,* from מוּת.

2. אוֹת—אֹתֹת (1:24); רֵאשִׁית (1:1); יַמִּים—יָם (1:22); חַיָּה (1:14); עֵינַיִם (3:6).

3. פָּנִים—פְּנֵי (1:2); דָּגָה—דְּגַת (1:26); רְקִיעַ—רָקִיעַ (1:14); מַלְכִּי־צֶדֶק (14:18); חַיְתוֹ־אֶרֶץ (1:24).

4. אִישׁ—אִישֵׁ (3:16); עַיִן—עֵינֵיכֶם (3:5); יָד—יָדוֹ (3:22); צָפֹנָה (13:14); אַרְצָה (20:1).

The inflection of nouns includes,

1. The formation of the noun-stems from the root, or from other nouns;

2. The addition of affixes for gender and number;

3. The changes of stem and termination in the formation of the construct state;

4. The addition of pronominal suffixes and affixes.

### 89. Nouns with One, Originally Short, Formative Vowel

1. *a.* [קֶטֶל *for* ḳăṭl]; אֶרֶץ *Earth;* עֶרֶב *Evening;* אֶבֶן *Stone;* שֶׁרֶץ *Swarm.*

*b.* [קֵטֶל *for* ḳiṭl]; עֵשֶׂב *Herb;* סֵפֶר *Book;* עֵזֶר *Help;* עֵדֶן *Eden.*

*c.* [קֹטֶל *for* ḳuṭl]; בֹּקֶר *Morning;* חֹשֶׁךְ *Darkness;* אֹמֶר *Saying.*

2. *a.* זֶרַע *Seed;* נֶצַח *Perpetuity;* אֹרַח *Path;* נַעַר *Youth;* תַּחַת *Under.*

*b.* אַף (=אַנְפְּ) (אַנְפִּי=אַפִּי .cf) *Nose;* עֵז (=עֶנְזְ) *Goat.*

*c.* פְּרִי *Fruit;* תֹּהוּ *Desolation;* בֹּהוּ *Waste;* בֶּכֶה *Weeping.*

132

3. דְּבַשׁ *Honey;* מְעַט *A little;* בְּאִשׁ *Stench;* בְּאֵר *Well.*

4. *a.* מַלְכָּה *Queen;* נַעֲרָה *Maiden;* שַׁלְוָה *Rest.*

  *b.* סִתְרָה *Covert;* שִׂמְחָה *Gladness;* אִמְרָה *Saying;* מִנְחָה *Gift.*

  *c.* אָכְלָה *Food;* חָכְמָה *Wisdom.*

1. These nouns, called *Seḡolates,* had, originally, one short vowel (ă, ĭ or ŭ), which, generally, stood with the first radical. A helping-vowel was then inserted under the second radical, and the formative vowel was then changed: ă to ĕ; ĭ to ē; ŭ to ō.

2. When the root contains one or more weak radicals, certain changes occur:

  *a.* In ע׳ or ל׳ laryngeal stems, ă is the helping-vowel, instead of ĕ; and, in ע׳ laryngeal *a*-class stems, the original formative *a* stands unchanged.[1]

  *b.* In ע״ן stems, נ is assimilated, represented in the following consonant by Dâḡēš-fŏrtē, and then rejected from this consonant whenever it is not followed by a vowel.

  *c.* In ל״ה stems occur formations ending in ◌ִי, ◌ֶ and ◌ֶה.

Note.—For so-called ע״ע, ע״ו and ע״י Seḡolates, see § § 100. and 109.

3. In a small number of nouns, the formative vowel stands under the second radical, instead of under the first; in these, ă suffers no change; but ĭ and ŭ, under the tone, become ē and ō; no helping-vowel is needed.

4. Many feminine nouns are formed from Seḡolate stems; the feminine ending being added to the primary form (קְטֵל, קְטָל, קְטֹל); but an original ŭ is generally deflected to ŏ.

Note 1.—The Ḳăl Infinitive Const. (ḳŭṭŭl = ḳᵉṭŭl and ḳŭṭl) is with some suffixes treated like a Seḡolate noun; while the Inf. Const. of verbs פ״ן and פ״ו (שֶׁלֶת = שֶׁלֶת) is a Seḡolate formation.

---

[1] *Cf.,* however, לֶחֶם *bread,* רֶחֶם *womb.*

**Note 2.**—Seğolates in the plural form look like two-vowel nouns. Whether this is a survival of an original two-vowel form in these nouns or is a later development of a one-vowel form by analogy is not clear.

### 90. *Nouns with Two, Originally Short, Formative Vowels*

1. *a.* [קְטָל *for* kătăl]; אָדָם *Man;* חָכָם *Wise;* דְּבָר *Word;* יָשָׁר *Upright;* בָּשָׂר *Flesh;* גָּמָל *Camel;* דָּגָן *Corn;* חָמָס *Violence.*

         שָׂדֶה (=sădăy) *Field;* יָפֶה *Beautiful;* הָרָה *Pregnant.*

*b.* [קְטֵל *for* kătĭl]; זָקֵן *Old man;* כָּבֵד *Heavy;* אָמֵן *Truly;* עָקֵב *Heel;* עָיֵף *Weary;* דָּשֵׁן *Fat;* חָסֵר *Deficient.*

*c.* [קְטֹל *for* kătŭl]; עָגֹל *Round;* עָמֹק *Deep;* נָקֹד *Spotted;* עָרֹם *Naked;* קָטֹן (*cf.* קְטַנִּים) *Small;* אָדֹם *Red.*

*d.* [קְטָל *for* kĭtăl]; לֵבָב *Heart;* צֵלָע *Rib;* חֵמָר *Bitumen.*

2. [קְטָלָה]; צְדָקָה *Righteousness;* אֲדָמָה *Ground;* עֲגָלָה *Chariot;* אֲחֻזָּה *Possession;* [קְטֻלָּה]; בְּהֵמָה *Cattle;* [קְטֵלָה].

A second class includes nouns which are formed by the employment of two, originally short, vowels, ă—ă, ă—ĭ, ă—ŭ, ĭ—ă. These nouns are, for the most part, adjectives or participles:

1. *a.* Original ă—ă, in strong stems, are rounded to å—å; in לִ"ה stems, the second ă is deflected, after the loss of ו or י, to ĕ; in a few cases of לְ"ה stems, the final הָ is lacking.

     *b.* Original ă—ĭ, in strong stems, are changed to å—ē.

     *c.* Original ă—ŭ are changed to å—ō; the latter (ō), however, goes back to ŭ before additions for gender and number, a Dåğēš-fōrtē being inserted in the final consonant.

     *d.* Original ĭ—ă are changed to ē—å.

2. The feminines of these stems are made by the addition of הָ; this addition requiring a change of tone, the vowel of the first radical is reduced to Šᵉwâ.

### 91. Nouns with One Short and One Long Formative Vowel

1. *a.* [קְטוֹל = קָטָל for ḳăṭâl]; גָּדוֹל *Great;* קָדוֹשׁ *Holy;* כָּבוֹד *Honor;* שָׁלוֹם *Peace;* אָדוֹן *Lord;* טָהוֹר *Pure;* מָתוֹק *Sweet.*

*b.* [קְטִיל for ḳăṭîl]; אָסִיר *Captive;* יָמִין *Right hand;* נָשִׂיא *Prince;* מָשִׁיחַ *Anointed;* נָבִיא *Prophet;* פָּקִיד *Overseer;* צָעִיר *Little.*

*c.* [קָטוּל for ḳăṭûl]; אָרוּר *Cursed,* and all Ḳal pass. parts.; עָצוּם *Strong;* עָרוּם *Cunning;* שָׁבוּעַ *Week;* עָבוּר *Grain;* שָׁכוּל *Bereaved.*

*d.* [קְטוֹל or קְטָל for ḳĭṭâl]; כְּתָב *Writing;* קְרָב *War;* עֲבָד *Work;* אֱלָהּ *God;* אֱנוֹשׁ *Man;* חֲמוֹר *Ass;* חֲלוֹם *Dream;* יְאֹר *River.*

*e.* [קְטִיל for ḳĭṭîl or ḳŭṭîl]; נְצִיב *Fool;* בְּדִיל *Tin;* כְּסִיל *Column;* חֲזִיר *Idol;* פְּסִיל *Swine.*

*f.* [קְטוּל for ḳĭṭûl or ḳŭṭûl]; גְּבוּל *Limit;* לְבוּשׁ *Dress;* גְּמוּל *Benefit;* עֱזוּז *Strength;* כְּרוּב *Cherub;* רְכוּשׁ *Property.*

2. גְּדוֹלָה *Great* (f.); נְבִיאָה· *Prophetess;* אֲרוּרָה *Cursed* (f.); אֱמוּנָה *Truth;* חֲגוֹרָה *Girdle;* נְחִילָה *Flute;* בְּתוּלָה *Virgin;*

A third class includes nouns which are formed by the employment of an originally short vowel in the penult, and an originally long vowel in the ultima. These nouns are, for the most part, abstract substantives, neuter adjectives, or passive participles:

1. *a.* Original ă—â become å—ô, the first vowel being rounded to å, the second to ô; this formation is to be distinguished from that with ō, described in § 90. Here belongs the Ḳal Infinitive absolute.

*b.* Original ă—î become å—î; here belong many nouns with a *passive,* and a few with an active signification.

*c.* Original ă—û become å—û; here belong all Ḳăl passive participles.

*d.* Original ĭ—â become ᵉ—â or ᵉ—ô, the first vowel being reduced, the second (â) being sometimes retained, but more frequently rounded to ô.

*e.* Original ĭ—î or ŭ—î become ᵉ—î, the first vowel being reduced.

*f.* Original ĭ—û or ŭ—û become ᵉ—û, the first vowel being reduced.

2. The feminines of these stems are generally made by the addition of הַ‑, the vowel of the first radical becoming Šᵉwâ.

### 92. Nouns with One Long and One Short Formative Vowel

1. [קוֹטָל for ḳâṭăl]; עוֹלָם Eternity; אוֹצָר Treasury; עֹשֶׂה (for 'ôsăy) Making; רֹמֶשֶׂת (for רוֹמֶשֶׂת) Creeping.

2. [קוֹטֵל for ḳâṭĭl]; אוֹיֵב Enemy; חוֹבֵל Pilot; כֹּהֵן Priest; יֹצֵא Going forth; רֹמֵשׂ Creeping; הֹלֵךְ Walking, etc.

3. [קוּטָל for ḳûṭăl]; עוּגָב Flute, organ; שׁוּעָל Fox.

**Remark.**—[קִיטוֹל for ḳîṭâl]; קִיטוֹר Smoke; שִׁיחוֹר Nile; קִימוֹשׂ Nettle.

A fourth class includes nouns with a naturally long vowel in the penultima, and an originally short vowel in the ultima.

1. Original â—ă become ô—å; here belong, besides some substantives, all ל"ה Ḳăl active participles, and also the Ḳăl act. part. fem. (in הַ‑ or הָ‑) of strong forms. The vowels do not change before *af*-fixes of gender and number.

2. Original â—ĭ become ô—ē; here belong a few substantives, and all strong Ḳăl participles; also those feminines of the form קֹטְלָה.

3. Original û—ă become û—å.

**Remark.**—There are a few nouns with an originally long vowel in both penult and ultima; the former, however, is probably long in compensation for an omitted Dåğĕš-fŏrtē (§ 30. 2. *c*).

### 93. Nouns with the Second Radical Reduplicated

1. [קָטָּל for ḳăṭṭăl]; אַיָּל *Hart;* שַׁבָּת *Sabbath;* סַבָּל *Burden;*
יַבָּשָׁה ,יַבֶּשֶׁת *Dry land;* חַטָּאָה *Sin;* אַדֶּרֶת *Magnificence.*

Remark.—גַּנָּב *Thief;* טַבָּח *Cook;* חָרָשׁ *Artificer;* קַנָּא *Jealous.*

2. [קָטֵּל for ḳăṭṭĭl]; מַקֵּל *Shoot, rod;* קַדֵּשׁ *To consecrate.*

3. [קָטֵּל for ḳĭṭṭĭl]; אִלֵּם *Dumb;* עִוֵּר *Blind;* חֵרֵשׁ *Deaf;* עִקֵּשׁ
*Perverse;* פִּקֵּחַ *Clear-sighted;* חִבֵּל *Mast;* אִוֶּלֶת *Folly;*
עִוָּרֵת *Blindness.*

4. *a.* [קַטָּל = ḳăṭṭâl]; see examples under 1. R. above.

   *b.* [קִטָּל = ḳĭṭṭâl *from* ḳăṭṭâl]; אִכָּר *Husbandman;* 1. R. above.

   *c.* [קִטּוֹל = ḳĭṭṭôl]; גִּבּוֹר *Hero;* שִׁכּוֹר *Drunkard;* צִפּוֹר *Spar-*
*row.*

5. [וַקְטִיל]; אַסִּיר *Great;* אַדִּיר אַמִּיץ *Strong;* צַדִּיק *Righteous;* אַסִּיר
*Fettered.*

6. [וַקְטוּל]; עַמּוּד *Pillar;* שַׁכּוּל *Childless;* חַנּוּן *Merciful.*

7. [וַקְטוּל]; לִמּוּד *Learner;* נִחֻמִים *Consolation.*

Remark.—שִׁקּוּץ *Abomination;* גִּלּוּל *Idol;* צִיּוּן *Pillar;* פִּגּוּל
*Unclean Thing.*

A fifth class includes nouns whose second radical is reduplicated.
This doubling intensifies the root-idea, giving it greater force or
greater firmness:

1. Formations like ḳ ă ṭ ṭ â l are frequent, but with no special
significance.

　　Remark.—It is a question whether nouns of this form indicative
of occupation have ă or â (see 4. *a* below); the corresponding Arabic
have â, yet some of these have ă in the Construct state.

2. Formations like ḳ ă ṭ ṭ ē l are rare, except as Pī'ēl Infinitives
Construct.

3. Formations like ḳĭṭṭēl are, mostly, adjectives designating deformities and faults, physical or moral.

4. *a*. Formations like ḳăṭṭâl are, properly, nouns indicative of occupation; but see 1. R. above.

*b*. The form ḳĭṭṭâl is the same as ḳăṭṭâl with the penultimate ă attenuated to ĭ.

*c*. The form ḳĭṭṭôl is the same as ḳĭṭṭâl with â rounded to ô.

5. Formations like ḳăṭṭîl are adjectives expressing a personal quality.

6. Formations like ḳăṭṭûl are descriptive epithets of persons or things.

7. Formations like ḳĭṭṭûl are, for the most part, abstracts, and are often used in the plural.

**Remark.**—This is a favorite formation for terms designating or characterizing idolatrous objects and ideas.

### 94. Nouns with the Third Radical Reduplicated

1. שַׁאֲנָן *Tranquil;* רַעֲנָן *Green;* נָאוֶה (=נַאֲוִי) *Comely;* אֻמְלַל *Faint;* שַׁפְרוּר *Splendor;* חֲכְלִיל *Dark;* נַהֲלָל *Pasture;* נַאֲפוּפִים *Adulteries.*

2. פְּתַלְתֹּל *Full of twists;* הֲפַכְפַּךְ *Full of turns;* אֲדַמְדָּם *Reddish;* שְׁחַרְחֹר *Blackish;* אֲסַפְסֻף *Rabble;* עֲקַלְקַל *Crooked.*

A sixth class, closely related to the fifth class, includes:

1. Noun-formations with the third radical reduplicated, the signification being, in general, the same as when the second radical is doubled.

2. A few words in which the second and third radicals are reduplicated, the signification being that of intensity, or repetition; in the case of adjectives of color, there is a diminutive force.

### 95. Nouns with א and י Prefixed

1. אֶצְבַּע *Finger;* אֶגְרוֹף *Fist;* אֵיתָן *Lasting;* אַכְזָר *Violent.*

2. יִצְהָר *Oil;* יַלְקוּט *Pouch; cf.* the proper names יִצְחָק, יִפְתָּח.

A seventh class includes nouns formed by prefixing א, or י:

1. A few nouns are formed by means of a prosthetic א; this א is merely euphonic and has no significance.

2. Nouns with a prefixed י occur rarely as appellatives; but frequently as proper names, where however they are really verbal forms.

### 96.  Nouns with מ Prefixed

1. מַאֲכֶלֶת [וּמַקְטֵל for מַקְטָל]; מַאֲכָל *Food;* מַמְלָכָה *Kingdom;* מַרְאֶה *Knife;* (מַוְצָא=) מוֹצָא *Exit;* (מִנְתָּן=) מַתָּן *Gift;* (=מַרְאִי) *Appearance.*

2. מִדְבָּר [וּמִקְטֵל for מִקְטָל]; מִשְׁכָּן *Dwelling-place;* *Desert;* מִקְנֶה מִשְׁמֶרֶת *Watch;* מִלְחָמָה *War;* מִשְׁפָּט *Judgment;* (=מִקְנַי) *Property.*

3. מַלְקוֹחַ [וּמַקְטֵל for מַקְטָל]; מַרְבֵּק *Stall;* מַפְתֵּחַ *Key;* מַזְלֵג *Flesh-hook;* (מוֹקֵשׁ=) מַגְּפָה *Smiting;* מַחֲרֵשָׁה *Plough;* מוֹקֵשׁ *Snare.*

4. מִזְבֵּחַ [וּמַקְטֵל for מַקְטָל]; *Altar.*

5. מַאֲכֹלֶת [וּמַקְטֵל for מַקְטָל]; *Fuel.*

6. מַלְקוֹחַ [וּמַקְטֵל, מַקְטוֹל for מִקְטוֹל]; מַחְסוֹר *Want;* מַלְקוֹחַ *Booty;* מִכְשׁוֹל *Stumbling-block;* מִזְמוֹר *Song.*

7. מַמְטִיר [וּמִקְטִיל, מַקְטִיל]; מַבְדִּיל *Dividing;* *Raining.*

8. מַאֲבוּס [וּמַקְטוֹל]; מַלְבּוּשׁ *Garment;* מַנְעוּל *Bolt;* מַאֲבוּס *Granary.*

An eighth class includes nouns formed by prefixing מ, the same element which is used in the formation of participles. So far as concerns the vowels employed the following combinations may be noted:

1. ă—å, the latter of which is rounded from ă. Feminines in ָה and ֶת occur. In פ״ן stems, נ is assimilated; in פ״ו stems, *aw*

becomes ô; in לֵ"ה forms, the second ă becomes ê (probably a contraction of ăy).

2. ĭ—â, the former of which is attenuated, the latter rounded from
an original ă; the usual vowel changes take place in weak stems.

3. ă—ē, the latter of which is lowered from ĭ; the usual vowel
changes take place in weak stems.

4. ĭ—ē, the ĭ of which is the attenuation of ă (cf. 3.).

5. ă—ō, the ō of which is lowered from an original ŭ.

6. ă—ô, ĭ—ô, of which ô is rounded from â, while ĭ is attenuated
from ă.

7. ă—î, used only in the formation of Hîf'îl participles (m.).

8. ă—û, not used to any great extent.

For מ-formations from bi-literal roots, see § 100.

### 97. The Signification of Nouns with מ Prefixed

1. מַשְׁחִית Destroyer; מַשְׂכִּיל A didactic poem (= instructor);
מַעֲרִיץ He who inspires terror; מַפָּל What falls off, chaff;
מִכְסֶה Covering.

2. מִצְעָר מַאֲכָל Food; מַלְקוֹחַ Booty; מַתָּן Gift; מִזְמוֹר Psalm;
That which is small; מֶרְחָק That which is remote.

3. מַאֲכֶלֶת Knife; מַפְתֵּחַ Key; מַלְמֵד Goad.

4. מִשְׁכָּן Dwelling-place; מִדְבָּר Desert; מִזְבֵּחַ Altar.

5. מַגֵּפָה Smiting; מַדְוֶה Sickness; מֵישָׁר Straightness; מִלְחָמָה
War.

The letter מ is from מִי (who) or מָה (what), and is used in the
formation of nouns:

1. To denote the *subject* of an action; cf. its use denoting agency
in Pĭ'ēl, Hîf'îl and Hĭθpă'ēl participles.

2. To denote the *object* of an action, or the *subject* of a quality;
cf. its use in Pŭ'ăl and Hŏf'ăl participles.

3. The *instrument* by which an action is performed.

4. The *place* (or *time*) in which an action is performed.

5. The *action* or *quality* which is contained in the root.

### 98. *Nouns Formed by Prefixing* ת

1. [וּתְקַטָּל for תָּקְטָל]; תָּחְמָם (?); תּוֹשָׁב Tenant; תּוֹכַחַת Reproof; תֵּימָן South; תּוֹדָה Thanks; תּוֹרָה Law.

2. [וּתְקַטָּל for תָּקְטָל]; תִּדְהָר Elm; תִּפְאָרָה Glory; תִּקְוָה Hope.

3. [וּתְקַטֵּל for תָּקְטֵל]; תַּשְׁבֵּץ Checkered cloth; תַּרְדֵּמָה Deep sleep.

4. [וּתְקַטִיל]; תַּלְמִיד Disciple; תַּכְרִיךְ Cloak; תַּכְלִית Completeness.

5. [וּתְקַטוּל]; תַּחֲלָאִים Diseases; תַּנְחוּם Consolation; תַּלְאָבָה Drought; תַּעֲצֻמוֹת Might.

**Remark.**—תַּרְדֵּמָה Deep sleep; תְּשׁוּעָה Deliverance; תִּפְאֶרֶת Glory.

A ninth class of nouns includes those with the prefix ת. This prefix is the same as that used in the Impf. 3 fem. It is used in a neuter sense, and is employed in the formation of abstract nouns, but rarely of concrete nouns. The cases cited above exhibit the various forms assumed by nouns of this class, as well as the vowel changes which take place in formations from weak stems.

**Remark.**—Nouns with ת prefixed have also, in the majority of instances, the feminine ending ָה.

### 99. *Nouns Formed by means of Affixes*

1. כַּרְמֶל Garden; בַּרְזֶל Iron; גִּבְעֹל Cup of a flower; קַרְסֹל Ankle; חַרְטֹם (?) Sacred scribe.

2. *a.* אַחֲרוֹן Last; רִאשׁוֹן First; אֶבְיוֹן Poor; עֶלְיוֹן Most high.

*b.* קִנְיָן Gain; שֻׁלְחָן Table; קָרְבָּן Offering; אַבְדָן Destruction.

c. פִּתְרוֹן *Interpretation;* כִּשְׁרוֹן *Success;* עִוָּרוֹן *Blindness;* גָּאוֹן בִּטָּחוֹן *Confidence;* זִכָּרוֹן *Memorial;* עִצָּבוֹן *Pain;* גָּאוֹן *Majesty.*

A tenth class of nouns includes those with affixes, ל, מ and נ:

1. Nouns formed by the addition of ל and מ are few, and have no special significance; they should perhaps be regarded as quadri-literals and may reflect some foreign influence.

2. Nouns formed by the addition of נ are numerous, including

    *a.* Adjectives formed either from a noun-stem or from a root.

    *b.* Abstract substantives ending in ân.

    *c.* Abstract substantives ending in ôn, rounded from ân.

### 100. Nouns from Bi-Literal Roots

1. *a.* רַב *Great;* רַךְ *Tender;* דַּל *Weak;* מַר *Bitter;* תָּם *Complete;* כַּלָּה *Bride;* מַצָּה *Unleavened bread;* כַּפַּיִם *Hands.*

אֵם *Mother;* תֵּל *Mound;* לֵב *Heart;* שֵׁן *Tooth;* צֵל *Shadow;* מִדָּה *Measurement;* מִלָּה *Word;* בִּצָּה *Swamp;* בִּזָּה *Spoil;* אִמּוֹ *His mother.*

תֹּם *Completeness;* כֹּל *All;* חֹק *Statute;* דֹּב *Bear;* רֹב *Multitude;* תֻּמָּה *Integrity;* חֻקָּה *Statute;* כֻּלָּם *All of them.*

*b.* קָם; רָם; בָּן; Ḳāl act. ptcp. of ע״ו and ע״י verbs.

מֹץ *Chaff;* תּוֹר *Turn;* שׁוֹר *Ox;* שׁוֹק *Leg.*

גֵּר *Stranger;* נֵר *Lamp;* מֵת *Dead;* רֵעַ *Noise.*

מוּת; גּוּר; קוּם; רוּם; Inf. Const. of ע״ו verbs.

גִּילָה, גִּיל *Joy;* רִיב *Strife;* דִּין *Judgment;* בִּינָה *Understanding;* מִין *Sort;* קִינָה *Dirge.*

2. גַּלְגַּל *Wheel;* חַתְחַת *Frightful;* כַּדְכֹּד *Ruby;* קָדְקֹד *Crown of head;* גֻּלְגֹּלֶת *Skull;* בַּקְבּוּק *Flask;* קַלְקַל *Worthless;* תַּעְתֻּעִים *Scorn.*

3. a. מָסָךְ Cover; מֵסַב Circle; מֵרַע Evil; מֵצַר Distress; מְשַׁמָּה Desolation; מָגֵן Shield; מְגִלָּה Roll; מִגְנָה Covering; מְזִמָּה Purpose; מְסִלָּה Highway; מְחִתָּה Terror; מֵסַב Divan; מְסֻכָּה Covering; מְשֻׂכָה Hedge.

b. מָאוֹר Luminary; מָרוֹם Height; מָקוֹם Place; מָגוֹר Terror; מָבוֹא Entrance; מָנוֹחַ Rest; מָנוֹם Flight; מְנוֹרָה Lamp-stand; מְחוֹלָה Dancing; מָצוֹק Pillar; מְגוֹרָה Terror; מָנוּחָה Rest; מְשׁוּבָה Apostasy; מְרוּצָה Running; מְבוּכָה Weeping; מֵקִים Raising; מְרִיבָה Strife; מְדִינָה Province.

c. מוּסָב Surrounding (?); מוּסָךְ Coverer (?); מוּסָר Removed.

d. מְתֹם Soundness; מֹרֶךְ Weakness.

4. a. תְּהִלָּה Praise; תְּחִלָּה Beginning; תְּחִנָּה Favor; תְּפִלָּה Prayer.

b. תְּבוּנָה Understanding; תְּרוּמָה Offering; תְּמוּנָה Likeness; תְּמוּתָה Death; תְּמוּרָה Exchange; תְּבוּסָה Ruin; תְּבוּאָה Product.

5. הֲנָפָה Waving; הֲנָחָה Rest; הֲפוּגָה Cessation; הָאִיר To shine; הָקֵם To raise; הָסֵב To cause to turn.

6. נָכוֹן, נְכוֹנָה Established; נְשַׁמָּה Desolated.

7. יְקוּם Being; יָרִיב Adversary.

8. סֻלָּם Ladder; אוּלָם Porch; עֵירֹם Naked; עָרֹם Naked.

9. תֶּמֶס Melting; תֹּפֶת Contempt.

Under this head are treated those nouns which are formed upon the foundation of two radicals and have not progressed to complete tri-literality by actually writing one of those radicals twice and vocalizing the resultant form as a tri-literal noun, e. g. מִכְלוֹל. There is a relatively wide range of forms in bi-literal nouns.

1. Monosyllabic nouns of various forms:

*a.* Those with one of the original short-vowels as the primary form. The vowels ĭ and ŭ, and occasionally ă, change under the tone to ē, ō and å respectively. When affixes are added, the second radical takes Dågēs̄-fŏrtē and the stem-vowel remains short. These all come from so-called ע"ע roots.

*b.* Those with an unchangeable vowel, which of course is unaffected by the addition of affixes; but â regularly is rounded to ô, except in the Ḳăl act. ptcp. These all come from Middle-Vowel roots.

2. Nouns made by reduplication of the bi-literal stem.

3. Nouns with the prefix מ. These assume several forms:

*a.* Those which in the primary form have the prefix mă with a short stem-vowel. These (1) regularly change both vowels, măḳăl becoming måḳål; măḳĭl becoming måḳēl; and măḳŭl becoming måḳōl; (2) when affixes are added, the second radical of the stem receives Dågēs̄-fŏrtē, the original stem-vowel remains unchanged, and the ă of the preformative syl. is reduced to Š͏̆ewâ (⸗); (3) those having ă as the original stem-vowel generally retain it without change, but the preformative syllable has ē, probably from an original ĭ. This formation occurs only in the so-called ע"ע roots.

*b.* Those which in the primary form have the prefix mă and a naturally long stem-vowel. The preformative ă becomes å in the absolute singular form, but is reduced to Š͏̆ewâ whenever affixes are added. This formation is characteristic of Middle-Vowel roots.

(1) The stem-vowel may be either ô (וֹ), û (וּ), or î (יִ_).

(2) With the stem-vowel î (יִ_), the preformative vowel becomes ē, either by assimilation to the stem-vowel, or after the analogy of the Hîf'îl perfect. This is the form of the Hîf'îl ptcp. of ו"ע and י"ע verbs.

*c.* Those having the prefix mû, with the stem-vowel ă, which is rounded to å. This is the form of the Hŏf'ăl participle of bi-literal verbs.

*d.* A few exceptional forms.

4. Nouns with the prefix ת. These nearly all have the feminine ending and fall into two classes:

a. Those having ĭ as stem-vowel followed by Dåḡēš-fŏrtē in the second radical of the stem. The preformative vowel is reduced to Šᵉwâ upon the addition of the feminine affix.

b. Those having û as stem-vowel, without a following Dåḡēš-fŏrtē, but with the same reduction of the preformative ă to Šᵉwâ upon the addition of the feminine affix.

5. Nouns with the prefix הַ. These are few, aside from the Infinitives of the Hĭf'ĭl, Hŏf'ăl and Nĭf'ăl of bi-literal verbs and are practically all verbal nouns.

6. Nouns with the prefix nă. These are practically confined to the Nĭf'ăl participle and Infin. of bi-literal verbs, in which the ă of the prefix regularly is rounded to å before the tone and is reduced to Šᵉwâ when not pretonic.

7. A few nouns are made with the prefix y (יְ).

8. A few bi-literal nouns with affixes occur, viz. (a) the affix ăm; (b) the affix ŭm. There is room for doubt as to the origin of these nouns.

9. A few isolated formations appear.

### 101. Nouns Having Four or Five Radicals

1. עַקְרָב Scorpion; גִּזְבָּר Treasurer; חֶרְמֵשׁ Sickle; חֲנָמָל Frost; חַלָּמִישׁ Flint; פִּלֶגֶשׁ Concubine; עֲטַלֵּף Bat.

2. אַרְגָּמָן Purple; שַׁעַטְנֵז A kind of cloth; אֲחַשְׁתָּרָן Mule.

1. Nouns with four radicals are comparatively few; they have no special classification or signification.

2. Nouns with five or more radicals are still fewer, and, for the most part, of foreign origin.

### 102. Compound Nouns

1. מְאוּמָה Anything; בְּלִיַּעַל Worthlessness; אֶתְמוֹל Formerly.

2. מַלְכִּי־צֶדֶק King of righteousness; יִשְׁמָעֵאל God hears.

1. Compound words, as common nouns, are few and doubtful.

2. Compound words, as proper names, are very numerous.

### 103. Nouns Formed from Other Nouns

1. שֹׁעֵר *Porter* (*cf.* שַׁעַר *Gate*); כֹּרֵם *Vine-dresser* (*cf.* כֶּרֶם *Vine-yard*).

2. מַעְיָן *Place of the fountain* (*cf.* עַיִן *Fountain*); מַרְגְּלוֹת *Place of feet* (*cf.* רֶגֶל *Foot*).

3. אַחֲרוֹן *Last* (*cf.* אַחַר *After*); עִוָּרוֹן *Blindness* (*cf.* עִוֵּר *Blind*). לִוְיָתָן *Coiled, serpent* (*cf.* לִוְיָה *Wreath*); נְחֻשְׁתָּן *Brazen* (*cf.* נְחֹשֶׁת *Bronze*).

4. *a.* שְׁלִישִׁי *Third* (*cf.* שָׁלֹשׁ); חֲמִישִׁי *Fifth*; etc.

   *b.* עִבְרִי *Moabite*; אֲרַמִּי *Aramœan*; גֵּרְשֻׁנִּי *Gershonite*; מוֹאָבִי *Hebrew.*

   צְפוֹנִי *Northerner*; נָכְרִי *Foreigner*; פְּרָזִי *Villager.*

5. רֵאשִׁית *Beginning*; מַלְכוּת *Kingdom*; אַלְמְנוּת *Widowhood.*

Nouns formed from other nouns, and not directly from the root, are termed denominatives. The most common formations are:

1. Nouns with the form of the Ḳăl active participle, indicating *agency.*

2. Nouns with the prefix מ, indicating the *place* where a thing is found.

3. Adjectives and nouns formed by the affix וֹן or ָן‎ (seldom וּן).

4. Adjectives formed by the affix ִי‎; these are,

   *a.* Ordinals formed from cardinals;

   *b.* Gentilics and patronymics; and a few others.

5. Nouns formed by the affixes ִית‎ and וּת‎, designating abstract ideas.

### 104. The Formation of Noun-Stems

From §§ 88-103. it has been seen that noun-stems are formed,

1. *Directly from the root:*

   *a.* By means of *vowels* given to the root; as in the case of

   (1) nouns with one, originally short, vowel (§§ 89, 100.);

    (2) nouns with one originally long vowel (§ **100.**);

    (3) nouns with two (originally) short vowels (§ **90.**);

    (4) nouns with one (originally) short and one long vowel (§ **91.**);

    (5) nouns with one long and one (originally) short vowel (§ **92.**);

  *b.* By a reduplication of one or more of the consonants of the root; as in the case of

    (1) nouns with the second radical doubled (§ **93.**);

    (2) nouns with the third, or the second and third radicals doubled (§ **94.**);

    (3) nouns with the entire root doubled (§ **100.**);

  *c.* By prefixing vowels and consonants to the root; as in the case of

    (1) nouns with א, ה or י prefixed (§§ **95, 100.**);

    (2) nouns with מ prefixed (§§ **96, 97, 100.**);

    (3) nouns with ת prefixed (§§ **98, 100.**);

  *d.* By affixing vowels and consonants to the root; as in the case of

    (1) nouns with ל, מ or נ affixed, with a vowel (§§ **99, 100.**);

    (2) nouns with four or five radicals (§ **101.**);

    (3) nouns compounded of two distinct words (§ **102.**).

  2. *From other nouns* (and called denominatives), by the various means indicated above (§ **103.**).

### 105.   The Formation of Cases

1. מְתוּ *in* מְתוּשָׁאֵל (4:18); שְׁמוּ *in* שְׁמוּאֵל[1]; פְּנוּ *in* פְּנוּאֵל (32:32).

Remark.—חַיְתוֹ־אָרֶץ (1:24); בְּנוֹ בְעֹר[2]; בְּנוֹ צִפֹּר; מֵעֵינוֹ; מֵימָ[4].

2. *a.* הָאֹהֱלָה (20:1); אַרְצָה הַנֶּגֶב (13:14); יָמָּה (13:14); צָפֹנָה (18:6).

  *b.* שְׁלִשׁוֹ־ם (31:2) *for* šilšâm; חִנָּ־ם (29:15); יוֹמָ־ם[5].

---

[1] 1 Sam. 1:20    [2] Num. 24:3, 15.    [3] Num. 23:18.    [4] Ps. 114:8.
[5] Ex. 13:21.

Very slight evidence of case-endings is found in Hebrew:

1. The only possible case of a nominative ending is the û in the first part of a few proper names; as in the examples cited above, מְתוּ = *man of;* שְׁמוּ = *name of;* פְּנוּ = *face of.* This is open to serious doubt since the words to which û is attached do not function as nominatives in these cases.

**Remark.**—An old ending וֹ=ô, appears in a few forms, but its origin and significance are unknown.

2. The *accusative* had the ending *a* and appears only

    *a.* In the so-called Hē *directive* (הָ‍ָ), which

        (1) is used to denote *direction* or *motion;* but

        (2) is often used in a weaker sense to designate the **place** *where,* and

        (3) in many cases seems to be entirely without force.

    *b.* In the syllables âm and ôm (the latter by the rounding of **â**), which are found in certain adverbs.

3. No *genitive* ending appears in our texts.

### 106. *Affixes for Gender and Number*

1. אוֹר (1:3); טוֹב (1:4); יוֹם (1:5); בֹּקֶר (1:5); רָקִיעַ (1:6).

2. *a.* אִמְרָתִי (4:23); אִשְׁתּוֹ (2:24); מִנְחָתוֹ (4:5). דְּנַת (31:39); גְּנַבְתִּי (1:24); חַיְתוֹ (1:25); (חַיָּה) חַיַּת (1:26); (נְשָׁמָה) נִשְׁמַת (2:7). (דֻּגָה)

    *b.* רֹמֶשֶׂת (1:2); מְרַחֶפֶת (1:26); דְּמוּת (1:1); רֵאשִׁית (1:21). דַּעַת (4:2); לֶדֶת (1:16); מֶמְשֶׁלֶת (3:24); מִתְהַפֶּכֶת (2:9); קַחַת (4:11).

    *c.* אֲדָמָה (2:5); חַיָּה (1:24); בְּהֵמָה (1:24); יַבָּשָׁה (1:9); אִשָּׁה (3:4).

3. אַתְּ (1:14); חֲגֹרֹת (3:7); תּוֹלְדוֹת (2:4).

4. *a.* אֱלֹהִים (1:1); יָמִים (1:22); יָמִים (1:14); מוֹעֲדִים (1:14); שָׁנִים (1:14).

*b.* פְּנֵי (1:2); יֹדְעֵי (3:5); נְשֵׁי (4:23); בְּנֵי (6:4); אַנְשֵׁי (6:4).

5. שְׁנַיִם, *whence* שְׁנֵי (1:16); עֵינַיִם (3:6), *but* עֵינֵי (3:7).

The Hebrew has two genders,—masculine and feminine; and three numbers,—singular, dual and plural.

1. The *masculine singular* has no particular indication.

2. The sign of the *feminine singular* is ת\_. This feminine sign has a threefold treatment:

    *a.* It is retained, with such change of its vowel as may be necessary, whenever the noun of which it is a part is in close connection with what follows; as when it (the feminine-sign, ת) stands

       (1) before a pronominal suffix (§ **108** );

       (2) at the end of a noun in the Construct state (§ **107.**).

    *b.* It appears as ת\_ (with laryngeals ת\_), in the formation and inflection of many nouns, participles and infinitives.

    *c.* ת gives way to ה, which then ceases to be pronounced, but is retained orthographically as a mere symbol of final â rounded from ă. *This form is the more usual indication of the feminine gender.*

3. The *feminine plural* is indicated by the ending וֹת (ôθ *for* âθ), which is unchangeable.

4. The *masculine plural* is indicated by the endings,

    *a.* ים\_ (îm) in the Absolute state (§ **107.**).

    *b.* י\_ (ê) in the Construct state (§ **107.**).

**Note.**—Many masculine nouns have plurals in ôθ, and many feminine nouns have plurals in îm.

5. The *dual*, used chiefly of objects which go in pairs, is indicated by the endings,

    *a.* יִם\_ (ăyĭm) in the Absolute state.

    *b.* י\_ (ê) in the Construct state.

### 107. The Absolute and Construct States

1. אֱלֹהִים (1:1); הַשָּׁמַיִם (1:1); הָאָרֶץ (1:1); הָאוֹר (1:3); רְקִיעַ (1:6).

2. פְּנֵי תְהוֹם (1:2) *faces-of abyss;* רוּחַ אֱלֹהִים (1:2) (the) *spirit-of God;* בִּרְקִיעַ הַשָּׁמַיִם (1:14) *in-(the)-expanse-of the heavens.*

Of two nouns closely related, the second, in Latin or Greek, is in the genitive, *e. g., dominus dominorum.* The same relation is indicated in Hebrew by pronouncing the second noun in close connection with the first. The effort thus to unite the two words in pronunciation as one phrase results invariably in a shortening of the *first* word, because the tone hastens on to the second, but involves also a retention of some old endings which hold their place in the phrase.

1. A noun which is not thus dependent upon a following substantive or pronoun is said to be in the *Absolute state.*

2. A noun which *is* thus dependent on a following substantive or pronoun is said to be in the *Construct state.*

**Note.**—It is the *first* of two nouns, therefore, and not the *second,* which suffers change.

3. עָלָה (3:7), *cf.* מִקְוֶה ;(1:10) *cf.* רֹעֵה ;(4:2), *cf.* רֹעֶה
.²עָלֵה cf. חֵי ;חַי (42:15), *cf.* גֵּיא¹ ;גַּיְא.

4. חַיַּת (1:25) *instead of* חַיָּה ;דְּגַת (1:26) *instead of* דָּגָה.

5. חַיְתוֹ (1:24); גְּנַבְתִּי (31:39); ³בְּנוֹ; ⁴מַעְיְנוֹ; בְּנִי (49:11);
⁶עָזְבִי; ⁵שֹׁכְנִי.

6. פְּנֵי (1:2), *cf.* פָּנִים ;יְמֵי (3:17), *cf.* יָמִים ;דְּמֵי (4:11), *cf.*
עֵינַיִם. *cf.* עֵינֵי ;שְׁנַיִם (1:16), *cf.* שְׁנֵי ;דָּמִים.

**Remark.**—*Abs.,* פְּרִי (1:11), *Const.,* פְּרִי (1:29); *Abs.,* צָבָא,⁷ *Const.,*
צְבָא⁸; *Abs.,* יְרֵא (32:12), *Const.,* יְרָא (22:12); *Abs.,* מֶלֶךְ
(14:17), *Const.,* מֶלֶךְ (14:1); *Abs.,* סֵפֶר,⁹ *Const.,* סֵפֶר (5:1);
*Abs.,* נַעַר (37:2), *Const.,* נַעַר.¹⁰

So far as concerns *endings* or *affixes,* the Construct state differs from the Absolute in the following particulars:

3. Final הַ (i. e., ê = ay) gives place to הֵ (i. e., ê = ay).

**Note.**—Compare with this the fact that in לְ"ה verbs, the Imperfect ends in הֶ (ê), but the Imperative in הֵ (ê).

---

¹ Josh. 15 : 8.          ² Num. 21 : 20.          ³ Num. 23 : 18.          ⁴ Ps. 114 : 8.
⁵ Deut. 33 : 16.          ⁶ Zech. 11 : 17.          ⁷ Num. 1 : 3.          ⁸ Deut. 4 : 19.
⁹ 2 Kgs. 5 : 5.          ¹⁰ 1 Sam. 2 : 13.

4. The original form of the feminine affix ־ַת, preserved by its close connection with what follows, appears instead of the later ־ָה.

5. The endings ô (וֹ) and î (־ִי) appear occasionally in Construct forms, serving as connecting vowels binding the Construct to its genitive.

6. The affix ־ֵי (= ay) appears instead of the ordinary plural and dual endings ־ִים and ־ַיִם.

**Remark 1.**—The feminine plural affix ôθ is the same in Absolute and Construct.

**Remark 2.**—Final vowels, other than those just mentioned, as well as final å when followed by א, and Segolates in the singular (strong and laryngeal) do not suffer change in the Construct state.

**Remark 3.**—The Construct form may best be explained by understanding that it is really a constituent element of a phrase which tends somewhat toward becoming a compound word. The Construct itself, therefore has no primary tone, the tone having passed on to the next word.

### 108. The Pronominal Suffixes

[See Paradigms A. and C.]

#### TABULAR VIEW

|            | Masc. sg. | Masc. plur. | Fem. sg. | Fem. plur. |
|------------|-----------|-------------|----------|------------|
| Absolute   | סוּס      | סוּסִים     | סוּסָה   | סוּסוֹת    |
| Construct  | סוּס      | סוּסֵי      | סוּסַת   | סוּסוֹת    |
| Sing. 1 c. | סוּסִי    | סוּסַי      | סוּסָתִי | סוּסוֹתַי  |
| 2 m.       | סוּסְךָ   | סוּסֶיךָ    | סוּסָתְךָ| סוּסוֹתֶיךָ|
| 2 f.       | סוּסֵךְ   | סוּסַיִךְ   | סוּסָתֵךְ| סוּסוֹתַיִךְ|
| 3 m.       | סוּסוֹ    | סוּסָיו     | סוּסָתוֹ | סוּסוֹתָיו |
| 3 f.       | סוּסָהּ   | סוּסֶיהָ    | סוּסָתָהּ| סוּסוֹתֶיהָ|
| Plur. 1 c. | סוּסֵנוּ  | סוּסֵינוּ   | סוּסָתֵנוּ| סוּסוֹתֵינוּ|
| 2 m.       | סוּסְכֶם  | סוּסֵיכֶם   | סוּסַתְכֶם| סוּסוֹתֵיכֶם|
| 2 f.       | סוּסְכֶן  | סוּסֵיכֶן   | סוּסַתְכֶן| סוּסוֹתֵיכֶן|
| 3 m.       | סוּסָם    | סוּסֵיהֶם   | סוּסָתָם | סוּסוֹתֵיהֶם|
| 3 f.       | סוּסָן    | סוּסֵיהֶן   | סוּסָתָן | סוּסוֹתֵיהֶן|

1. *a.* לְמִינוּ (1:11) *for* ;יָדְ־הוּ ;יָדֹו (3:22) *for* לְמִינֵ־הוּ ;צֹאנוּ
(4:4).

לְמִינָהּ (1:24) *for* ;אִישָׁהּ ;לְמִינֵ־הָ (3:6) *for* ;אִישֵׁ־הָ ;זַרְעָהּ
(3:15).

לִבְּ־ן ;קֹולְ־ן[5] ;יֹומָ־ם[4] ;דַּרְכָּ־ם[3] ;אַרְצָ־ם[2] ;קֹולְ־ם[1],[6]

קְלֹךְ (3:10); גְּהֹנְךָ (3:14); זַרְעֶךָ (3:15); אֲכָלְכֶם (3:5).

*b.* שָׁדֶ־הוּ (23:9); אִישֵׁ־ךְ (3:16); הֵרֹנֵ־ךְ (3:16); צַלְמֵ־נוּ
(1:26).

אָבִיו (2:24); אָחִיךָ (4:9); אָחִיו (4:8); פִּיהָ (4:11).

2. אָמְרָה *but* אָמַרְתִּי (4:23); חָבְרָה *but* חָבַרְתִּי (4:23);
תְּשׁוּקָתֹו (4:7).

The relation existing between a noun and its pronominal suffix is really the Construct relation. The form of the noun, however, is not always identical with that of the Construct, but varies with the position of the tone. In this section only the *endings* of the noun, as affected by the suffix, are treated.

1. Masculine nouns in the singular take,
    *a.* A connecting vowel ă
        (1) in the form of å, before הוּ, הָ, ם and ן, the suffixes of the 3d person;
        (2) in the form of ⟼, before ךָ, כֶם, כֶן.
    *b.* A connecting vowel ĭ
        (1) in the form of ē before הוּ (in ל"ה stems and a few poetical forms), ךָ, נוּ.
        (2) in the form of î before all suffixes in the words אָב *father*, אָח *brother*, פֶּה *mouth*.

**Remark 1.**—Certain changes take place, viz., הוּ_ to וֹ, הָ_ to הָ_, the final vowel of the latter form having been dropped.

**Remark 2.**—Before ךָ, כֶם, כֶן ă is deflected to ĕ in pause.

[1] Num 14:1.　　[2] Deut. 4:38.　　[3] 1 Kgs. 2:4.　　[4] Jer. 15:9.
[5] Ruth 1:9.　　[6] Ex. 35:26.

2. Feminine nouns in the singular preserve before suffixes the earlier form of the feminine affix, which is ־ַת; but the ־ַ when standing in an open syllable is rounded.

**Note.**—The feminine affix is followed by the same connecting vowels as those which occur with masculine nouns (see above, 1. *a*, *b*).

3. *a.* עֲצָמַי (2:23); [1]דְּרָכַי; [2]דְּרָכֶיךָ; [3]פָּנֶיךָ; [4]כְּנָפֶיךָ

   *b.* שְׁנֵיהֶם (2:25); עֵינֵיכֶם (3:5); חֶלְבֵּהֶן [5] (4:4); [5]לְמִינֵהֶם (1:21).

   *c.* חַיֶּיךָ [6] (3:14); אַפֶּיךָ (3:19); פָּנֶיךָ (4:6); פָּנֶיהָ.[6]

   *d.* אַפָּיו (2:7); [7]דְּרָכָיו; פָּנָיו (4:5); [8]כְּנָפָיו.

4. צַלְעֹתָיו (2:21); הֹרֹתָיו (6:9); [9]אֹתָתִי; אֹתוֹתֵינוּ [10]; בְּנֹתַי
   (19:12). בְּנֹתֶיךָ; בְּנֹתֶיךָ [11] (34:9); בְּנוֹתֵינוּ (31:26).

**Remark.**—אֲבֹתָם [12] *and* אֲבוֹתֵיהֶם [13]; *cf.* also שְׁמוֹתָם (25:16); הֹרוֹתָם; אֹתֹתָם [14] (17:7).

3. The masculine plural has before all suffixes the ending ay, which, in the Construct, appears in the form of ê. But certain modifications in the form of this ending take place, due to the character of the following consonants:

   *a.* The form ay (־ַי) appears unchanged
      (1) in the 1 c. sg. ־ַי, the י of the suffix having been absorbed by the final י of the ending.
      (2) in the 2 f. sg. ־ַיִךְ, ךְ being joined by the helping-vowel ־ִ.
   *b.* The form ay (־ַי) is contracted to ê (־ֵי) before all plural suffixes.

   *c.* The form ay (־ַי) is contracted to ־ֶי (ê) before ךָ and ךְ.

   *d.* The original form ay (־ַי) loses י and rounds ă to â before (הֶן changed according to § 44. 4. *c.* to) וֹ, the י being generally retained orthographically.

---

[1] Isa. 58 : 2.　　　[2] Jer. 2 : 33.　　　[3] 1 Sam. 25 : 35.　　　[4] Jer. 2 : 34.
[5] With ־ָ written defectively, instead of ־ֵי.　　　[6] 1 Sam. 1 : 18.
[7] Deut. 10 : 12.　　[8] Deut. 32 : 11.　　[9] Ex. 7 : 3.　　　[10] Ps. 74 : 9.
[11] Ezek. 16 : 20.　　[12] Ex. 4 : 5.　　[13] 1 Chron. 4 : 38.　　[14] Ps. 74 : 4.

4. The feminine plural with suffixes has (1) וֹת, the usual affix of the fem. plur., (2) the masculine plural ending ־ֵי, which is modified in the manner just described (see above, 3. *a–d*); and then (3) the same suffixes as were used with the masc. plur.

Remark.—Very frequently the suffix is attached directly to וֹת; this is done probably in order to obtain a shorter form.

### 109. Stem-Changes in the Inflection of Nouns

1. שָׁלֵם[1] *but* שְׁלֵמָה[2]; מְאֹר[3] *but* מְאֹרֹת[3].; לֵבָב[4] *but* לִבְבוֹת[5];
כְּנָפַיִם[10] *but* כָּנָף[9]; גְּדוֹלִים[8] *and* גְּדוֹלָה[7] *but* גָּדוֹל[6];
גָּחוֹן[11] *but* גְּחֹנְךָ[12]; בָּשָׂר[13] *but* בְּשָׂרִי[14]; שָׂכָר[15] *but* שְׂכָרָה[16].
חֲצֵרֶיהָ[22] *but* חָצֵר[21]; זְקֵנָיו[20] *but* זָקֵן[19]; דְּבָרַי[18] *but* דָּבָר[17].

2. דָּבָר[17] *but* דְּבָרֵי[23]; זָקֵן[19] *but* זִקְנֵי[24]; חָצֵר[21] *but* חֲצֵרֹת[25].
לֵבָב[4] *but* דְּבָר[17] *but* דִּבְרֵיהֶם[26]; זְקֵנֵיכֶם[27]; דָּבָר[17] *but*
לְבַבֵיהֶן[28].

3. זָהָב[33] *but* זְהַב[34].; זָקֵן[31] *but* זְקַן[32]; דָּבָר[29] *but* דְּבַר[30];
רָקִיעַ[35] *but* רְקִיעַ[36].; יָד[37] *but* יַד[38]; דָּם[39] *but* דַּם[40].
בָּשָׂר[43] *but* בְּשַׂרְכֶם[44].; לְבַבְכֶם[42] *but* לֵבָב[41].

**Remark 1.**—לְבָבְךָ[45] *and* בְּשָׂרֶךָ[46], *but* לְבַבְכֶם[42] *and* בְּשַׂרְכֶם[44].

**Remark 2.**—(1) בָּרֵךְ; (2) בְּרָכוֹת (12:2) *from* בְּרָכָה[47], (49:25), (3) בִּרְכַּת (28:4).

**Remark 3.**—כֹּהֵן[48] *but* כֹּהֲנִים[49]; מָצָא[50] *but* מֹצְאַי[51]; שֹׁפֵט[52] *but* שֹׁפְטִים[53].

---

[1] Gen. 15:16.  [2] Deut. 25:15.  [3] Gen. 1:16.  [4] Deut. 28:28.
[5] 1 Chron. 28:9.  [6] Gen. 1:16.  [7] Gen. 15:12.  [8] Gen. 1:21.
[9] Ex. 25:20.  [10] Gen. 1:16.  [11] Lev. 11:42.  [12] Gen. 3:14.
[13] Gen. 2:21.  [14] Gen. 2:23.  [15] Num. 18:31.  [16] Jon. 1:3.
[17] Gen 18:14.  [18] Gen. 24:33.  [19] Gen. 19:4.  [20] Isa. 24:23.
[21] 1 Kgs. 7:8.  [22] Josh. 21:12.  [23] Gen. 24:30.  [24] Gen. 50:7.
[25] 2 Kgs. 21:5.  [26] Gen. 24:52.  [27] Deut. 29:9.  [28] Nah. 2:8.
[29] Gen. 18:4.  [30] Gen. 20:18.  [31] Gen. 19:4.  [32] Gen. 24:2.
[33] Gen. 2:11.  [34] Gen. 2:12.  [35] Gen. 1:6.  [36] Gen. 1:20.
[37] Gen. 38:28.  [38] Gen. 41:35.  [39] Gen. 37:22.  [40] Gen. 9:6.
[41] Deut. 28:28.  [42] Deut. 10:16.  [43] Gen. 2:21.  [44] Gen. 17:13.
[45] Gen. 20:6.  [46] Gen. 40:19.  [47] Ps. 21:7.  [48] Gen. 14:18.
[49] Gen. 47:22.  [50] Ps. 119:162.  [51] Gen. 4:14.  [52] Gen. 18:25.
[53] Deut. 16:18.

The noun-stem, if it contains two changeable vowels (§ 7. 4), is subject to change,

(1) when terminations of gender and number are added;
(2) when the noun stands in the Construct relation with a following word;
(3) when pronominal suffixes are added.

The changes which take place are due to the shifting of the tone:

1. With affixes for gender and number (*Absolute*), viz., הָ_ָ, תִֹ, םִ_, םִ_ַ, and with the light (§ 51. 1. *b*) suffixes, *the tone is shifted one place;* in which case,

*a.* An original ă or ĭ, which had become å or ē[1] before the tone is reduced to Š°wâ;

*b.* An ultimate tone-*long* å or ē is retained, since it stands now directly before the *tone*.

2. With affixes for gender and number in the *Construct,* viz., יֵ_, תֵֹ (also the sing. fem. תַ_), and with the grave suffixes when attached to plural nouns, *the tone is shifted two places;* in which case,

*a.* The penultimate vowel being now in a closed unaccented syllable remains short, but ă is often attenuated to ĭ;

*b.* The ultimate vowel reduces to Š°wâ.

3. In the case of the Construct singular of masculine nouns and with the grave suffixes (כֶם, כֶן) when attached to singular nouns, *the tone is shifted one place;* in which case,

*a.* The penultimate vowel is reduced to Š°wâ.

*b.* An ultimate tone-long (originally short) å or ē gives way to ă.

**Remark 1.**—While an original ă is rounded to å before הָן_ָ, it remains short before כֶם_ָ.

**Remark 2.**—The principles here given apply also to the formation and inflection of feminine nouns.

**Remark 3.**—Ḳăl active participles and nouns of like formation (92.), in whose inflection the final vowel becomes Š°wâ before all affixes (except הָ, כֶם, כֶן), furnish an important exception to the principle stated in 1. *b* above. The difference in treatment is due to the fact that the participial forms have an unchangeable vowel in the penult.

---

[1] The vowel *o*, except in *u*-class Seğolates, is generally unchangeable.

4. *a.* מֶלֶךְ (14:17) *abs.;* מֶלֶךְ (14:1) *Const.;* סֵפֶר¹ *abs.;*
נַעַר² (5:1);

*b.* סִפְרִי⁴; מַלְכִּי³; זַרְעָהּ (3:15); צַלְמוֹ (1:27); צַלְמֵנוּ (1:26);
אָכְלְךָ⁵; יִקְבֶךָ⁶.

*c.* מְלָכִים (14:9); מַלְכוּת⁷; יְלָדִים (33:1); בְּקָרִים⁸.

*d.* מַלְכֵיהָ⁹; עֲצָמַי (2:23); יְלָדִי (30:26); נְדָרֶיךָ¹⁰; קָדָשֶׁיךָ¹¹.

*e.* מַלְכֵי (17:16) נִדְרֵיכֶם¹²; קָדָשֵׁי¹³; קָדְשֵׁיכֶם¹⁴.

*f.* קַרְנַיִם¹⁵ *but* קַרְנֵים¹⁶; מָתְנַיִם¹⁷; צָהֳרַיִם (43:16).

5. *a.* תָּוֶךְ¹⁸, תּוֹךְ (1:2), תּוֹכָהּ (41:48); מוֹת¹⁹, מוֹת (25:11),
בֵּיתִי (12:15), בֵּית (17:12), בַּיִת; מוֹתָיו²⁰, (27:2), מוֹתִי
(15:2), בֵּיתוֹ (12:17).

*b.* אִמּוֹ (3:20), אֵם (21:34); רַבִּים (6:5), רַבָּה (24:25), רַב
חֻקִּים²², (47:22), חֻקָּם (47:22), חֹק; אֻמָּתָם²¹; חֻקָּה²³. (2:24),

6. *a.* שָׂדֶה (2:5) *but* שָׂדֶה (14:7), שָׂדוֹת²⁴, שָׂדַי²⁵; פָּנֶה (*not in*
*use*), פָּנִים (32:31), פְּנֵי (6:13), *but* פְּנֵי (1:2), פְּנֵיהֶם (9:23).

---

4. *Seğolate-stems* (§ 90.) deserve particular attention:

*a.* The form assumed in the absolute, viz., קֶטֶל from קַטְל,
קֹטֶל *from* קֻטְל, קֵטֶל *from* קִטְל, remains unchanged in the Construct singular of words with strong consonants or laryngeals.

*b.* In the singular before *all* suffixes the noun takes the primary
form (§ 90.); ă is sometimes attenuated and ŭ regularly becomes ŏ.

*c.* Before the plural affixes (absolute) a pretonic å appears, and
the primary vowel becomes Š°wâ.

| | | | |
|---|---|---|---|
| ¹ 2 Kgs. 5 : 5. | ³ 1 Sam. 2 : 13. | ³ 2 Sam. 19 : 44. | ⁴ Ex. 32 : 33. |
| ⁵ Lev. 25 : 37. | ⁶ Deut. 15 : 14. | ⁷ Cant. 6 : 8. | ⁸ Ps. 73 : 14. |
| ⁹ Isa. 7 : 16. | ¹⁰ Deut. 12 : 17. | ¹¹ Deut. 12 : 26. | ¹² Deut. 12 : 6. |
| ¹³ Lev. 22 : 15. | ¹⁴ Ezek. 20 : 40. | ¹⁵ Dan. 8 : 6. | ¹⁶ Hab. 3 : 4. |
| ¹⁷ Deut. 33 : 11. | ¹⁸ Judg. 16 : 29. | ¹⁹ Josh. 2 : 13. | ²⁰ Isa. 53 : 9. |
| ²¹ Jer. 16 : 3. | ²² Deut. 4 : 5. | ²³ Ex. 13 : 10. | ²⁴ Neh. 12 : 29. |
| ²⁵ Ruth 1 : 2. | | | |

*d.* In the plural before light suffixes the pretonic å is retained.

*e.* In the plural Const. and before grave suffixes the å disappears, and the primary vowel is retained, though sometimes in attenuated or deflected form.

*f.* In the dual the form is generally that which is found in the plural (see *c*), sometimes that used in the sing. before suffixes (see *b*).

5. *a.* Nouns from bi-literal roots (§ **100.**) of the Middle-Vowel class have monosyllabic forms with ô, ê and î everywhere except in some absol. sing. forms in which ן and י appear as middle consonants. *Cf.* a similar development of diphthongs to consonants in English *bower* from older *būr; dowel* from older *dowl; fire*, often pronounced *fiyur*, from older *fyr*.

*b.* ʿĂyïn Doubled (ע"ע) Seğolate-stems, before affixes of gender and number, and before suffixes, take Dăğĕš-fŏrtē in the second radical, the preceding vowel remaining short.

6. Lămĕđ Hē (ל"ה) nouns ending in ◌ָה lack this before affixes and suffixes beginning with a vowel; the tone-long å of the first radical,

*a.* Is retained when it would be pretonic, but

*b.* Yields to Šᵉwâ in the Construct (sing. or plur.), and when it would be ante-pretonic.

### 110. *Classification of Noun-Stems*

1. תֹּהוּ‎, פְּרִי‎, מָוֶת‎, אֵם‎, נַעַר‎, בֹּקֶר‎, סֵפֶר‎, אֶרֶץ‎.

2. עָרֹם‎, שָׂדֶה‎, לֵבָב‎, כָּבֵד‎, זָקֵן‎, בָּשָׂר‎, אָדָם‎, דָּבָר‎.

3. עֲקָרֹב‎, מִשְׁפָּט‎, אִלֵּם‎, שַׁבָּת‎, עֹשֶׂה‎, אוֹיֵב‎, עוֹלָם‎.

4. מֵקִים‎, מָאוֹר‎, אָרוּר‎, נָבִיא‎, אָסִיר‎, גָּדוֹל‎.

5. רָם‎, דִּין‎, שׁוֹר‎, סוּס‎, עַמּוּד‎, גִּבּוֹר‎, חֲמוֹר‎, כְּתָב‎.

For purposes of inflection, nouns may conveniently be divided into five classes:

1. The *first* class includes the so-called Seğolates, nouns which originally had one changeable vowel (§ **90.**);

2. The *second* class includes nouns which have two changeable

vowels; here belong stems which had originally the vowels ă—ă, ă—ĭ, ă—ŭ, ĭ—ă, etc. (§ 91.).

3. The *third* class includes nouns which have an unchangeable vowel, whether by nature or position, in the penult, and a changeable vowel in the ultima (§ 92.).

4. The *fourth* class includes nouns which have a changeable vowel in the penult, and an unchangeable vowel in the ultima (§ 93.).

5. The *fifth* class may, for convenience, include all nouns of whatever origin, the vowel, or vowels, of which are unchangeable.

### 111. *Nouns of the First Class*

#### 1. STRONG AND LARYNGEAL STEMS.—TABULAR VIEW

|  | mălk (king) | sĭfr (book) | ḳŭdš (holiness) |
|---|---|---|---|
| Sg. abs. | מֶלֶךְ | סֵפֶר | קֹדֶשׁ |
| const. | מֶלֶךְ | סֵפֶר | קֹדֶשׁ |
| 1. suf. | מַלְכִּי | סִפְרִי | קָדְשִׁי |
| gr. suf. | מַלְכְּכֶם | סִפְרְכֶם | קָדְשְׁכֶם |
| Pl. abs. | מְלָכִים | סְפָרִים | קָדָשִׁים |
| const. | מַלְכֵי | סִפְרֵי | קָדְשֵׁי |
| 1. suf. | מְלָכַי | סְפָרַי | קָדָשַׁי |
| gr. suf. | מַלְכֵיכֶם | סִפְרֵיכֶם | קָדְשֵׁיכֶם |
|  | (feet) | (two-fold) | (loins) |
| Du. abs. | רַגְלַיִם | כִּפְלַיִם | מָתְנַיִם |
| const. | רַגְלַי |  | מָתְנַי |

|  | nă'r (a youth) | nĭṣḥ (perpetuity) | pŭ'l (work) |
|---|---|---|---|
| Sg. abs. | נַעַר | נֶצַח | פֹּעַל |
| const. | נַעַר | נֶצַח | פֹּעַל |
| 1. suf. | נַעֲרִי | נִצְחִי | פָּעֳלִי |
| gr. suf. | נַעַרְכֶם | נִצְחֲכֶם | פָּעָלְכֶם |

|          | nă'r<br>(a youth) | niṣḥ<br>(perpetuity) | pŭ'l<br>(work) |
|----------|-------------------|----------------------|----------------|
| Pl. abs. | נְעָרִים | נְצָחִים | פְּעָלִים |
| const.   | נַעֲרֵי | נִצְחֵי | פָּעֳלֵי |
| 1. suf.  | נְעָרַי | נִצְחַי | פָּעֳלַי |
| gr. suf. | נַעֲרֵיכֶם | נִצְחֵיכֶם | פָּעֳלֵיכֶם |
|          | (sandals) |  | (noon) |
| Du. abs. | נְעָלַיִם |  | צָהֳרַיִם |
| const.   | נַעֲלֵי |  |  |

## REMARKS

[For general remarks concerning the inflection of Seğolates see § 109.]

1. Instead of the original pure vowel ⟨ ⟩, there appears everywhere in *u*-class stems the deflected vowel ⟨ ⟩ (ŏ), the latter always representing the former in closed, as distinguished from sharpened, syllables.

2. Instead of simple Šᵉwâ as a reduction of the original ŭ in the pl. abs. and the pl. with light suffixes, a compound Šᵉwâ ⟨ ⟩ is generally found.

3. In the laryngeal stems, ⟨ ⟩ and ⟨ ⟩ before ⟨ ⟩ become ⟨ ⟩ and ⟨ ⟩ (ŏ).

## NOTES[1]

1. In reference to the *a*-class stems, it may be noted that,

*a.* In pause the ă generally becomes å (וָרַע),[2] though sometimes ĕ remains (קֶדֶם)[3];

*b.* In such forms as דְּשֶׁא (1:11), פֶּרֶא (16:12), the א is to be treated as a full consonant.

*c.* In many forms, the original ă, before suffixes and before the dual ending, is attenuated to ĭ (זִבְחִי).[4]

*d.* In a few *a*-class stems, especially 'פ laryngeal, before suffixes, ĕ (⟨ ⟩) stands under the first radical instead of the primary ă (נֶגְדוֹ).[5]

---

[1] Under "Notes" there are given the more important variations from the paradigm-forms.

[2] Gen. 1 : 29.     [3] Gen. 2 : 8.     [4] Ex. 23 : 18.     [5] Gen. 2 : 20.

*e.* In a few plurals, like תִּשְׁעִים ,שִׁבְעִים, pretonic ־ָ does not appear.

*f.* There are a few forms, especially ל' laryngeal, which make a Construct like קֶטַע instead of קְטַע (*cf.* זֶרַע).¹

2. In reference to *i*-class stems it may be noted that,

*a.* In a few cases, ־ֵ (ĕ) stands under the first radical instead of the original ־ֶ (עֶזְרִי,² עֶגְלֵי).³

3. In reference to *u*-class stems it may be noted that,

*a.* The ō is sometimes retained before suffixes (תָּאֳרוֹ).⁴

*b.* The writing ־ֳ (ŏ) is sometimes found as a substitute for ־ֻ (°) (קֳדָשִׁים).⁵

4. Segolates with the vowel under the second radical,

*a.* In some cases have the usual inflection (שָׁכְבָהּ *from* שֶׁכֶב),⁶

*b.* In others treat this vowel as unchangeable (זְאֵבִי).⁷

*c.* In still others preserve it by an artificial doubling of the final consonant before affixes (מְעַטִּים).⁸

### 2. לַ"ה ,עַ"י ,עַ"ו AND עַ"ע STEMS.—TABULAR VIEW

|  |  |  |  |  |  |  |
|---|---|---|---|---|---|---|
| Sg. abs. | מָוֶת | זַיִת | פְּרִי | יָם | אֵם | חֹק |
| const. | מוֹת | זֵית | פְּרִי | יָם ,יָם | אֵם | חָק־ |
| 1. suf. | מוֹתִי | זֵיתִי | פְּרִיִי | יָמִי | אִמִּי | חֻקִּי |
| gr. suf. | מוֹתְכֶם | זֵיתְכֶם | פֶּרְיְכֶם | יַמְּכֶם | אִמְּכֶם | חֻקְּכֶם |
| Pl. abs. | מוֹתִים | זֵיתִים | צְבָיִים | יַמִּים | אֻמּוֹת | חֻקִּים |
| const. | מוֹתֵי | זֵיתֵי |  | יַמֵּי | אֻמּוֹת | חֻקֵּי |
| 1. suf. | מוֹתַי | זֵיתַי |  | יַמַּי | אִמּוֹתַי | חֻקַּי |
| gr. suf. | מוֹתֵיכֶם | זֵיתֵיכֶם |  | יַמֵּיכֶם | אִמּוֹתֵיכֶם | חֻקֵּיכֶם |
| Du. abs. |  | עֵינַיִם | לְחָיַיִם | כַּפַּיִם |  | שְׁנַיִם |
| const. |  | עֵינֵי | לְחָיֵי | כַּפֵּי |  | שְׁנֵי |

¹ Num. 11 : 7.　　² Ex. 18 : 4.　　³ 1 Kgs. 12 : 28.　　⁴ Isa. 52 : 14.
⁵ Ex. 30 : 36.　　⁶ Gen. 19 : 33.　　⁷ Zeph. 3 : 3.　　⁸ Ps. 109 : 8.

### REMARKS

1. The absolute forms of Middle-Vowel stems are perhaps developments from diphthongal forms which were the basis of both Absolute and Construct forms; $mau\theta$ or $maw\theta$, e. g., becoming $m\hat{o}\theta$ and $m\mathring{a}w\breve{e}\theta$; $bayt$ or $bai\theta$ becoming both $b\acute{a}yi\theta$ and $b\hat{e}\theta$; cf. the analogous case of the Middle-Vowel Pïʹēl forms.

2. In פְּרִי, the ־ֱ is a reduction of the original ־ֵ, while î = ïy, the third radical with a helping vowel; the ï of פ in פִּרְיִי is an attenuation of the original ־ֵ, while the ־ֱ of פֶּרְיְכֶם is a deflection of ă.

3. In ע״ע stems, the original vowel, ă, ĭ, ŭ, is generally changed in the abs. sg.; but before affixes the second radical is doubled and the original vowel retained, though ŏ is rarely found for ŭ.

### NOTES

1. In reference to Middle-Vowel stems, it may be noted that,

a. Full tri-literal forms sometimes occur in the plural (חֲיָלִים),[1] and before suffixes and Hē directive (בֵּיתָה).[2]

b. Stems ע״א, (e. g., רֹאשׁ = רַאְשׁ,[3] צֹאן = צַאְן)[4] are a-class Seğolates, the ă, lengthened to â, becoming ô; these also will be included in the fifth class.

2. In reference to ל״ה stems, it may be noted that,

a. Forms like פְּרִי become, in pause, פֶּרִי,[5] the ĕ being a deflection of the original ă.

b. Inflected forms like אֲרָיוֹת,[9] שְׁלָוִים,[8] שַׁלְוֹת,[7] שַׁלְוִי,[6] צְבָאִים[10] for צְבָיִים, occur; cf. also forms like בְּכֶה,[11] תֹהוּ[12]; these are some of the irregular forms assumed by ל״ה stems.

3. In reference to ע״ע stems, it may be noted that,

a. While הַר[13] stands even in Abs., יָם[14] stands even in Const.

b. Forms like חַי have Const. like חֵי.[15]

c. ־ַ is often attenuated to ־ִ (פִּתֶּן[16] for פַּתֶּן).

---

1 1 Kgs. 15 : 20.     3 Ex. 28 : 26.      5 Gen. 3 : 15.      4 Gen. 4 : 2.
5 Eccl. 2 : 5.        6 Ps. 30 : 7.       7 Jer. 22 : 21.     8 Num. 11 : 31.
9 Judg. 14 : 5.       10 1 Chron. 12 : 8  11 Ezra 10 : 1.     12 Gen. 1 : 2.
13 Jer. 50 : 6.       14 Gen. 14 : 3.     15 Gen. 42 : 15.    16 Ruth 2 : 14.

*d.* Many fully tri-literal forms are in use.

*e.* ע"ן forms like אַף (= 'ănp) are inflected like ע"ע forms (אַפּיו).[1]

### 112. Nouns of the Second Class
#### TABULAR VIEW

|  | dă-văr (word) | ḥă-χăm (wise) | ză-ḳīn (old) | ḥă-ṣīr (court) | să-dăy (field) | 'ă-mŭḳ (deep) |
|---|---|---|---|---|---|---|
| Sg. abs. | דָּבָר | חָכָם | זָקֵן | חָצֵר | שָׂדֶה | עָמֹק |
| const. | דְּבַר | חֲכַם | זְקַן | חֲצַר | שְׂדֵה | עֲמֹק |
| 1. suf. | דְּבָרִי | חֲכָמִי | זְקֵנִי | חֲצֵרִי | שָׂדִי | |
| gr. suf. | דְּבַרְכֶם | חֲכַמְכֶם | זְקַנְכֶם | חֲצֵרְכֶם | שָׂדְכֶם | |
| Pl. abs. | דְּבָרִים | חֲכָמִים | זְקֵנִים | חֲצֵרִים | שָׂדִים] וְשָׂדִים | עֲמָקִים |
| const. | דִּבְרֵי | חַכְמֵי | זִקְנֵי | חַצְרֵי | שְׂדֵי | עֲמְקֵי |
| 1. suf. | דְּבָרֵי | חֲכָמַי | זְקֵנַי | חֲצֵרַי | שָׂדַי | |
| gr. suf. | דִּבְרֵיכֶם | חַכְמֵיכֶם | זִקְנֵיכֶם | חַצְרֵיכֶם | | |

|  | (wings) | (loins) | (thighs) |
|---|---|---|---|
|  | כְּנָפַיִם | חֲלָצַיִם | יְרֵכַיִם |
| Du. abs. | | | |
| const. | כַּנְפֵי | | |

#### REMARKS

1. This class includes all nouns with two, orig. short, vowels.

2. While the original penultimate ă, in Const. pl. and before grave suffixes, is generally attenuated to ĭ, it is retained unchanged under laryngeals.

3. In ḳă-ṭĭl forms, there appears in the Const. sg., ă instead of ĭ, because the latter cannot stand in a closed accented syllable;[2] in the sg. with grave suffixes, this ĭ is deflected to ĕ.

4. The הָ and הֶ in the Abs. and Const. of ל"ה stems is for ăy; this ăy is entirely lacking before affixes of gender and number, and before suffixes.

---

[1] Gen. 2 : 7.

[2] This principle is known as Philippi's law, after the scholar who first formulated it.

5. Many words artificially double the last consonant before all
affixes; the preceding vowel is then necessarily sharpened. Here
may be included,

    *a.* Adjectives in ō, עָגֹל ,נָקֹד ,אָדֹם, etc.

    *b.* Nouns in å, גָּמָל, the adjective form קָטָן, etc.

### NOTES

1. The אָ‑ of ל״א stems stands unchanged even in the Construct.

2. Some words of this class assume in the Construct state a Segolate
form, *e. g.*, כָּתֵף[1] from כָּתֵף, יֶרֶךְ[2] from יָרֵךְ; some of these
words have also the regular form in the Const., *e. g.*, כָּבֵד, both
כְּבַד[3] and כְּבֵד[4].

3. In some verbal adjectives the ē, lowered from ĭ, is retained even
in the Construct state, *e. g.*, יָשֵׁן[7], שָׂמֵחַ[6], חָפֵץ[5].

### 113. *Nouns of the Third Class*
#### TABULAR VIEW

| | 'ō-lǎm (eternity) | mĭš-pǎṭ (judgment) | 'ō-yĭv (enemy) | 'Il-lĭm (blind) | ḥō-zǎy (prophet) | 'ō-fǎn (wheel) |
|---|---|---|---|---|---|---|
| Sg. abs. | עוֹלָם | מִשְׁפָּט | אֹיֵב | אִלֵּם | חֹזֶה | אוֹפָן |
| const. | עוֹלַם | מִשְׁפַּט | אֹיֵב | | חֹזֶה | אוֹפַן |
| 1. suf. | עוֹלָמִי | מִשְׁפָּטִי | אֹיְבִי | | חֹזִי | אוֹפַנִּי |
| gr. suf. | עוֹלַמְכֶם | מִשְׁפַּטְכֶם | אֹיִבְכֶם | | חֹזְכֶם | |
| Pl. abs. | עוֹלָמִים | מִשְׁפָּטִים | אֹיְבִים | אִלְּמִים | חֹזִים | אוֹפַנִּים |
| const. | עוֹלְמֵי | מִשְׁפְּטֵי | אֹיְבֵי | | חֹזֵי | |
| 1. suf. | עוֹלָמַי | מִשְׁפָּטַי | אֹיְבַי | | חֹזַי | |
| gr. suf. | עוֹלְמֵיכֶם | מִשְׁפְּטֵיכֶם | אֹיְבֵיכֶם | | חֹזֵיכֶם | |
| | | (tongs) | (balances) | | | |
| Du. abs. | | מֶלְקָחַיִם | מֹאזְנַיִם | | | |
| const. | | | מֹאזְנֵי | | | |

---

## REMARKS

1. This class includes nouns with an unchangeable vowel in the penult; this may be a naturally long vowel, or a short vowel in a closed syllable.

2. The following formations are included: קוֹטָל, קוֹטֵל, קוּטָל, קְטֵל, קְטָל, קַטֵל, קַטָל; many nouns with the third, or the second and third radicals reduplicated; some nouns with א, ה and י prefixed; תַּקְטָל, מַקְטֵל, מִקְטָל, מִקְטֵל, מַקְטָל, מַקְטֵל, תִּקְטֵל, תִּקְטָל; many nouns formed by affixes; some nouns with four radicals.

The existence of the form ḳôṭăl from ḳâṭăl is questioned by many scholars, who trace such words to a ḳăuṭăl form. But many proper names and the ḳăl active participle seem to make this form secure.

3. Original ă in the sg. Const., and in the sg. with grave suffixes remains unchanged; it is reduced in the pl. Const., and in the pl. with grave suffixes.

4. An original ĭ in the sg. before ךָ, כֶם, כֶן is usually unchanged, but sometimes is deflected to ĕ; *before all other suffixes and before affixes it is reduced.*

5. The Ḳăl act. participle of verbs לְ"ה has the same ending (ה_ֶ), as was seen in certain nouns of the second class, like שָׂדֶה; but its first vowel is unchangeable.

6. Many nouns of this class treat the ultimate changeable vowel in the manner described in § 112. R. 5, *i. e.*, artificially double the following consonant, and sharpen the vowel:

*a.* אוֹפָן (§ 92.); שׁוֹשָׁן (§ 99.); מִשְׂגָּב (§ 96.); and others.

*b.* רַעֲנָן, שַׁאֲנָן (§ 94.); אֲדַמְדַּם (§ 94. 2); and others.

*c.* בַּרְזֶל, כַּרְמֶל (§ 99. 1. *a*); גַּלְגַּל (§ 100. 1); and others.

*d.* עַקְרָב, חַרְטֹם, קַרְדֹּם (§ 101. 1); and others.

## 114. *Nouns of the Fourth and Fifth Classes*

### TABULAR VIEW

| | gā-đôl (*great*) | pā-ḳîđ (*overseer*) | ʻā-nîy (*poor*) | sûs (*horse*) | tăl-mîđ (*disciple*) | kĭ-θāv (*writing*) |
|---|---|---|---|---|---|---|
| **Sg.** | | | | | | |
| **abs.** | גָּדוֹל | פָּקִיד | עָנִי | סוּס | תַּלְמִיד | כְּתָב |
| **const.** | גְּדוֹל | פְּקִיד | עֲנִי | סוּס | תַּלְמִיד | כְּתָב |
| **1. suf.** | | פְּקִידִי | | סוּסִי | תַּלְמִידִי | כְּתָבִי |
| **gr. suf.** | | פְּקִידְכֶם | | סוּסְכֶם | תַּלְמִידְכֶם | כְּתָבְכֶם |
| **Pl.** | | | | | | |
| **abs.** | גְּדוֹלִים | פְּקִידִים | עֲנִיִּים | סוּסִים | תַּלְמִידִים | כְּתָבִים |
| **const.** | גְּדוֹלֵי | פְּקִידֵי | עֲנִיֵּי | סוּסֵי | תַּלְמִידֵי | כְּתָבֵי |
| **1. suf.** | | פְּקִידַי | | סוּסַי | תַּלְמִידַי | כְּתָבַי |
| **gr. suf.** | | פְּקִידֵיכֶם | עֲנִיֵּיכֶם | סוּסֵיכֶם | תַּלְמִידֵיכֶם | כְּתָבֵיכֶם |

### REMARKS ON NOUNS OF THE FOURTH CLASS

1. The fourth class includes nouns which have a changeable vowel in the penult and an unchangeable vowel in the ultima. Here belong many adjectives like קָטוֹל and קָטִיל (§ **91.** 1. *a, b*); passive participles like קָטוּל (§ **91.** 1. *c*); formations in which a ◌ַ, originally in a closed syllable, has become ◌ָ in an open syllable; and a few nouns ending in ôn with a pretonic ◌ָ (**99.** 2. *e*).

2. In a few ל״ה stems with the form קָטִיל (§ **91.** 1. *b*) the radical י, when final, in the absence of an affix, is absorbed in the formative vowel î; but when affixes of any kind are attached, it appears in the form of Dåğēš-fŏrtē; עֲנִיִּים.

### REMARKS ON NOUNS OF THE FIFTH CLASS

1. This class includes those nouns which do not suffer change of any kind in inflection.

2. Here belong monosyllabic nouns like סוּס, דִּין, שׁוֹר, with an unchangeable vowel; participles like קָם and מֵת; formations like

קְטָל, קְטוֹל, קְטִיל, קָטִיל, קָטוֹל (§ 91. *d–f*) which have an unchangeable vowel, with a Šᵉwâ reduced from an original ĭ or ŭ; formations
like מַקְטוֹל, מַקְטִיל, מָקְטוּל (§ 96. 6–8); formations like
תַּקְטוֹל, תִּקְטִיל (§ 98. 4, 5); some formations with the affix
ôn (§ 99. 2); and a few denominatives (§ 103.).

### 115. Feminine Nouns

#### I. FEMININES OF THE FIRST CLASS

#### TABULAR VIEW

| | măl-kăθ (queen) | ḥĭr-păθ (reproach) | ḥŭr-băθ (ruin) | ḥŭḳ-ḳăθ (statute) | gᵉvărt (mistress) |
|---|---|---|---|---|---|
| Sg. abs. | מַלְכָּה | חֶרְפָּה | חָרְבָּה | חֻקָּה | גְּבֶרֶת |
| const. | מַלְכַּת | חֶרְפַּת | חָרְבַּת | חֻקַּת | גְּבֶרֶת |
| 1. suf. | מַלְכָּתִי | חֶרְפָּתִי | חָרְבָּתִי | חֻקָּתִי | גְּבִרְתִּי |
| gr. suf. | מַלְכַּתְכֶם | חֶרְפַּתְכֶם | חָרְבַּתְכֶם | חֻקַּתְכֶם | גְּבִרְתְּכֶם |
| Pl. abs. | מְלָכוֹת | חֲרָפוֹת | חֳרָבוֹת | חֻקּוֹת | [גְּבָרוֹת] |
| const. | מַלְכוֹת | חֶרְפוֹת | חָרְבוֹת | חֻקּוֹת | |
| Du. abs. | | רִקְמָתַיִם (embroidery) | | | מְצִלְתַּיִם (cymbals) |

#### REMARKS

1. The feminine ending is added to the ground form, ĕ and ŏ appearing in *i*-class and *u*-class stems in closed syllables; the older
form תְ appears in the Const. and before suffixes.

2. The pretonic â is found in the feminine declension as well as in
the masculine.

3. Examples of weak feminine Segolates and monosyllabic nouns
with feminine ending are (1) נַעֲרָה, (2) טָהֳרָה, (3) עוֹלָה,
מִדָּה (9), חַיָּה (8), אַלְיָה (7), סוּפָה (6), בִּינָה (5), צֵידָה (4)

(10) זִמָּה, (11) חֻקָּה, of which those numbered 3–6, 8–11 suffer **no**
change of stem, following the inflection of חֻקָּה given above.

4. Just as מֶלֶךְ is derived from מַלְךְ, so גְּבֶרֶת is derived
from גְּבַר by the addition of ת_, and the deflection of ă to ĕ.
Before suffixes the original — is attenuated to ĭ.

## 2. FEMININES OF THE SECOND CLASS

### TABULAR VIEW

| | ṣă-dă-ḳăθ (righteousness) | ză-'ă-ḳăθ (cry) | šă-năθ (year) | 'ă-ṭă-răθ (crown) | gᵉzī-lăθ (violence) |
|---|---|---|---|---|---|
| Sg. abs. | צְדָקָה | זְעָקָה | שָׁנָה | עֲטָרָה | גְּזֵלָה |
| const. | צִדְקַת | זַעֲקַת | שְׁנַת | עֲטֶרֶת | גְּזֵלַת |
| 1. suf. | צִדְקָתִי | זַעֲקָתִי | שְׁנָתִי | יְבָמָה | (sister-in-law) |
| gr. suf. | צִדְקַתְכֶם | זַעֲקַתְכֶם | שְׁנַתְכֶם | | |
| Pl. abs. | צְדָקוֹת | | שָׁנוֹת | עֲטָרוֹת | |
| const. | צִדְקוֹת | | שְׁנוֹת | עַטְרוֹת | |
| | | | (lips) | | |
| Du. abs. | | | שְׂפָתַיִם | | |
| const. | | | שִׂפְתֵי | | |

## REMARKS

1. The same stem-changes take place before the ending ה_ as
before the plural endings (§ 109.).

2. In the Const. sg. and pl., as well as before suffixes, the original
ă of the first syl., while retained with laryngeals, is generally attenuated to ĭ.

3. The Šᵉwâ before the endings ת_ (Const. sg.) and וֹת (Const.
pl.) is silent, except in laryngeal nouns where it serves as a helping-
vowel.

4. Before the fem. ending the final ־י of ל"ה forms is lacking;
in this case the ă of the first syl. is rounded or reduced according to
the position of the accent.

5. Several nouns with the form קְטָלָה in the Abs. have קְטֶלֶת in the Const.; these in the singular as well as those which have the form קְטֶלֶת in the Abs., attenuate the original ă to ĭ before suffixes.

6. Nouns of the form קְטֵלָה frequently retain the ‎ ֵ ‎ in the Construct.

## NOTES

1. Forms like kă-ṭĭl become kă-ṭăl when the fem. ending is added.

2. Forms like גֵּרָה, זִבָה, מֵתָה, from bi-literal roots in which the stem-vowel is naturally long, retain it in the Const.

### 3. FEMININES OF THE THIRD AND FOURTH CLASSES

#### TABULAR VIEW

| | yô-năkt (sprout) | gŭl-gŭlt (skull) | kô-ṭĭ-lăθ (killing f.) | geḏô-lăθ (great f.) | teḥīl-lăθ (praise) | menû-ḥăθ (rest) |
|---|---|---|---|---|---|---|
| Sg. abs. | יוֹנֶקֶת | גֻּלְגֹּלֶת | קוֹטְלָה | גְּדֹלָה | תְּהִלָּה | מְנוּחָה |
| const. | יוֹנֶקֶת | גֻּלְגֹּלֶת | קוֹטְלַת | גְּדֹלַת | תְּהִלַּת | מְנוּחַת |
| 1. suf. | יוֹנַקְתִּי | גֻּלְגָּלְתִּי | קוֹטַלְתִּי | | תְּהִלָּתִי | מְנוּחָתִי |
| gr. suf. | יוֹנַקְתְּכֶם | גֻּלְגָּלְתְּכֶם | | | תְּהִלַּתְכֶם | |
| Pl. abs. | [יוֹנְקוֹת] | גֻּלְגָּלוֹת | קוֹטְלוֹת | גְּדֹלוֹת | תְּהִלּוֹת | מְנוּחוֹת |
| const. | יוֹנְקוֹת | גֻּלְגָּלוֹת | | גְּדֹלוֹת | תְּהִלוֹת | |

## REMARKS

1. Feminines in ‎ תָ ‎ of the third class arise in the same manner as those described in § 115. 1. R. 4, the ground-form generally having ă in the ultima, though sometimes ŭ.

2. As before, the original ă (or ŏ deflected from ŭ) appears before suffixes.

3. The feminine participle most frequently assumes the form קֹטֶלֶת, though קֹטְלָה is common; the form יֹלֶדְתְּ (Gen. 16:11) is of interest.

4. Feminines of the fourth class present no points of difficulty.

## 116. Irregular Nouns

1. אָב *Father;* Const. אֲבִי; with suf., אָבִי (*my father*), אָבִיךָ,
אֲבִיכֶם; plur., אָבוֹת; Const., אֲבוֹת or אָבִיו ,אָבִיהָ ,אֲבִיהוּ.

2. אָח *Brother;* Const., אֲחִי; with suf., אָחִי (*my brother*), אָחִיךָ,
אֲחִיכֶם; plur., אַחִים; Const., אֲחֵי; with suf., אַחַי, אָחִיךָ,
אֲחֵיכֶם, etc.

3. אֶחָד (for אַחַד, with D. f. implied) *One;* Const., אַחַד (used
also before מִן); fem., אַחַת (= אַחְדַת), in pause, אֶחָת;
plur., אֲחָדִים *Some, the same.*

4. אָחוֹת *Sister;* Const., אֲחוֹת; with suf., אֲחוֹתִי; plur. with suf.,
אֲחִיתָיו; also אַחְוֹתֵיכֶם ,אַחְיוֹתַי from אָחָה.

5. אִישׁ *Man;* plur., אֲנָשִׁים (three times אִישִׁים); Const., אַנְשֵׁי.

6. אָמָה *Maid-servant;* with suf., אֲמָתְךָ; plur., אֲמָהוֹת; Const.,
אַמְהוֹת.

7. אִשָּׁה *Woman;* Const., אֵשֶׁת = 'išt; with suf., אִשְׁתִּי, אִשְׁתְּךָ;
plur., נָשִׁים; Const., נְשֵׁי; with suf., נָשָׁיו, נְשֵׁיהֶם.

8. בַּיִת *House;* Const., בֵּית; plur., בָּתִּים; Const., בָּתֵּי; with suf.,
בָּתֵּיהֶם.

9. בֵּן *Son;* Const., בֶּן־, בִּן־ ,בְּנִי־ (Gen. 49:11), בְּנוֹ (Num. 23:18);
with suf., בְּנִי, בִּנְךָ; plur., בָּנִים; Const., בְּנֵי; with suf.,
בָּנַי, בָּנֶיךָ, בְּנֵיהֶם.

10. בַּת (for בַּנְתְּ, fem. of בֵּן) *Daughter;* with suf., בִּתִּי (=בִּנְתִּי
=בַּנְתִּי); plur., בָּנוֹת (*cf.* בָּנִים *sons*); Const., בְּנוֹת.

11. חָם *Father-in-law;* with suf., חָמִיךָ; חָמוֹת *Mother-in-law;*
*cf.* אָח, אָחִיךָ ,אָחוֹת.

12. יוֹם *Day;* plur., יָמִים; Const., יְמֵי and יְמוֹת; dual, יוֹמַיִם.

13. כְּלִי *Vessel;* plur., כֵּלִים; Const., כְּלֵי; with suf., כֶּלִי, כְּלֵיהֶם.

14. מַיִם (plur.) *Water;* Const., מֵי, מֵימֵי; with suf., מֵימָיו, מֵימֵיהֶם.

15. עִיר *City;* plur., עָרִים; Const., עָרֵי.

16. פֶּה *Mouth;* Const., פִּי (*cf.* אֲחִי, אֲבִי); with suf., פִּיךָ, פִּי, פִּיו or פִּיהוּ; plur., פִּיּוֹת.

17. רֹאשׁ (רֵאשׁ=רָאשׁ *for*) *Head;* plur., רָאשִׁים (רְאָשִׁים *for*); Const., רָאשֵׁי; with suf., רֹאשֵׁנוּ.

18. שָׁמַיִם (plur.) *Heavens;* Const., שְׁמֵי.

## 117. Numerals
### GENERAL VIEW

| | With the Masculine. | | With the Feminine. | |
| --- | --- | --- | --- | --- |
| | *Absolute.* | *Construct.* | *Absolute.* | *Construct.* |
| *1* | אֶחָד | אַחַד | אַחַת | אַחַת |
| *2* | שְׁנַיִם | שְׁנֵי | שְׁתַּיִם | שְׁתֵּי |
| *3* | שְׁלֹשָׁה | שְׁלֹשֶׁת | שָׁלֹשׁ | שְׁלֹשׁ |
| *4* | אַרְבָּעָה | אַרְבַּעַת | אַרְבַּע | אַרְבַּע |
| *5* | חֲמִשָּׁה | חֲמֵשֶׁת | חָמֵשׁ | חֲמֵשׁ |
| *6* | שִׁשָּׁה | שֵׁשֶׁת | שֵׁשׁ | שֵׁשׁ |
| *7* | שִׁבְעָה | שִׁבְעַת | שֶׁבַע | שְׁבַע |
| *8* | שְׁמֹנָה | שְׁמֹנַת | שְׁמֹנֶה | |
| *9* | תִּשְׁעָה | תִּשְׁעַת | תֵּשַׁע | תְּשַׁע |
| *10* | עֲשָׂרָה | עֲשֶׂרֶת | עֶשֶׂר | עֲשַׂר |

| | With the Masc. | With the Fem. |
| --- | --- | --- |
| *11* | אַחַד עָשָׂר<br>עַשְׁתֵּי עָשָׂר | אַחַת עֶשְׂרֵה<br>עַשְׁתֵּי עֶשְׂרֵה |

| | | |
|---|---|---|
| 12 | שְׁנֵים עָשָׂר | שְׁתֵּים עֶשְׂרֵה |
|    | שְׁנֵי עָשָׂר | שְׁתֵּי עֶשְׂרֵה |
| 13 | שְׁלֹשָׁה עָשָׂר | שְׁלֹשׁ עֶשְׂרֵה |

| | |
|---|---|
| 100 מֵאָה fem.; Const., | 4,000 אַרְבַּעַת אֲלָפִים |
| מֵאוֹת ;.pl מֵאַת | רְבָבָה, but in later books, |
| 200 מָאתַיִם dual (for (מְאָתַיִם | 10,000 רִבּוֹ, רִבּוֹא; plural, (רִבּוֹת contracted רִבֹּאוֹת) |
| 300 שְׁלֹשׁ מֵאוֹת | 20,000 רִבֹּתַיִם (dual) also שְׁתֵּי רִבּוֹת |
| 400 אַרְבַּע מֵאוֹת | |
| 1,000 אֶלֶף; plural, אֲלָפִים | 30,000 שְׁלֹשׁ רִבֹּאוֹת |
| 2,000 אַלְפַּיִם (dual) | 40,000 אַרְבַּע רִבֹּאוֹת |
| 3,000 שְׁלֹשֶׁת אֲלָפִים | 60,000 שֵׁשׁ־רִבֹּאוֹת |

## REMARKS

1. The numeral אֶחָד *one* is an *adjective*, standing after and agreeing with its noun.

2. The numeral שְׁנַיִם (fem. שְׁתַּיִם, pronounced štă-yĭm) is a *noun*, used either in the appositional or Construct relation with the word which it enumerates, and agreeing with it.

3. The numerals from *three* to *ten* are abstract feminine substantives, used in appositional construction with the noun which they enumerate. The *feminine* form is used with masculine nouns; the masculine is a shorter form used with feminines.

4. The numerals from *eleven* to *nineteen* are formed by uniting עָשָׂר *ten* (or the feminine form עֶשְׂרֵה) with the units; here it may be noted:

*a.* In *eleven,* אַחַד and אַחַת have a form like that of the Construct.

*b.* עַשְׁתֵּי, in the second form of *eleven,* is to be connected with an Assyrian word *išten* (=one).

*c.* In *twelve*, שְׁנֵים is a contraction of שְׁנַיִם, and שְׁנֵי a
shortened form of שְׁנֵים, the contraction and shortening being due
to the close connection of the words; these forms cannot be called
Constructs.

*d.* The feminines from *thirteen* upward have a shortened, but
not a real Construct, form.

5. The numerals *thirty* to *ninety* are formed by adding the masc.
plur. ending ים_ to the units, but *twenty* (עֶשְׂרִים) is the plural
of *ten* (עֶשֶׂר).

6. The units are added to the tens by means of וְ; in the earlier
books preceding the tens, in later books following them.

7. The units take the noun in the plural; the tens, when before
it, take the noun in the singular, when after it, in the plural.

8. The numerals *eleven* to *nineteen* take the noun in the plural,
except in the case of a few very common nouns like *day*, *man*, etc.

9. The ordinal *first* is רִאשׁוֹן (*cf.* רֹאשׁ, *head*).

10. The ordinals from *two* to *ten* are formed from the corresponding cardinals by means of the termination י_, another י_ being inserted between the second and third consonants. Note that רְבִיעִי
lacks the initial א.

11. Above *ten*, cardinals are used for ordinals.

12. The feminines of the ordinals are used to express fractional
parts.

# XIV. Separate Particles

## 118. Adverbs

1. a. אֵי *Where?;* אָז *There;* לֹא *Not;* שָׁם *There;* אַל *Not.*

b. זֶה *Here;* הֵנָּה *Hither;* שָׁלֹשׁ *Thrice;* שֶׁבַע *Seven times.*

c. מְאֹד *Very;* חוּץ *Abroad;* לְבַד *Alone;* מִבַּיִת *Within.*

d. הַרְבֵּה *Much;* הֵיטֵב *Well;* הַשְׁכֵּם *Early;* מַהֵר *Speedily.*

e. אָמֵן *Firmly;* טוֹב *Well;* רִאשׁוֹנָה *Formerly;* נִפְלָאוֹת *Wonderfully.*

f. מִן with מַעֲלָה (=מִלְמַעְלָה) *Upward;* (מַה־יָדוּעַ=) מַדּוּעַ *Why?;* and לְ) לָמָה *Wherefore?*

2. a. הֵן *Here is;* הֵנָּם ,הֶנְּכֶם ,הִנֶּנּוּ ,הִנְּךָ ,הִנְנִי, etc.

b. יֵשׁ *There is;* יֶשְׁכֶם ,יֶשְׁנוֹ ,יֶשְׁךָ.

c. אַיִן *There is not;* אֵינְכֶם ,אֵינֶנּוּ ,אֵינְךָ ,אֵינֶנִּי, etc.

d. אַיֵּה *Where is?;* אַיָּם ,אַיּוֹ ,אַיֶּכָּה.

e. עוֹד *Still is;* עוֹדָם ,עוֹדֶנּוּ ,עוֹדֶנָּה ,עוֹדֶנּוּ ,עוֹדְךָ ,עוֹדֶנִּי.

1. Adverbs, and words used adverbially, may be briefly classified as follows:

   a. Those which may be called primitive.
   b. Pronouns and numerals used in an adverbial sense.
   c. Nouns, either alone or with a preposition.
   d. Infinitives absolute, especially of Hif'il and Pi'ēl stems.
   e. Adjectives of all formations, especially in the feminine.
   f. Words formed by the composition of two or more distinct words.

2. Certain adverbial particles, involving a verbal idea and thus

173

often dispensing with the copula, take suffixes. The suffixes attached are, in most cases, the verbal suffixes. The so-called Nûn Demonstrative (§ **71.** 2. *c.* (3) and N. 1) is of frequent occurrence.

### 119. Prepositions

1. אַחַר *After;* בֵּין *Between;* בְּעַד *About;* וְּלָתִי *Besides;* יַעַן *On account of;* מוּל *Over against;* נֶגֶד *Before;* עַד *During, until;* עַל *Upon;* עִם *With;* תַּחַת *Under, in place of.*

2. מִתַּחַת *From under;* לְמִן *Since;* אֶל־בֵּין *Till between;* לִפְנֵי *Before;* לְפִי *According to;* לְמַעַן *For the sake of;* בִּבְלִי *Without;* מִבְּלִי *For lack of, without;* בְּעוֹד *During;* כְּדֵי *According to measure of.*

3. *a.* אַחַר *After,* more often אַחֲרֵי; with suf., אַחֲרֵי,אַחֲרָיו, etc.

    *b.* אֶל־ *Unto,* poet., אֱלֵי; with suf., אֵלַי,אֵלֶיךָ,אֲלֵיכֶם, אֲלֵיכֶן, etc.

    *c.* בֵּין *Between;* with sg. suf., בֵּינִי,בֵּינְךָ,בֵּינוֹ, (בֵּינָיו K⁼ri); with plur. suf., בֵּינֵיכֶם,בֵּינוֹתֵינוּ,בֵּינוֹתָם, also בֵּינֵינוּ.

    *d.* סָבִיב *Around;* with suf., סְבִיבָיו,סְבִיבֶיךָ,סְבִיבִין, also with fem. סְבִיבֹתָיו,סְבִיבֹתִי,סְבִיבֹתֵיהֶם, etc.

    *e.* עַד *Unto,* poet., עֲדֵי; with suf., עָדַי,עָדֶיךָ,עָדָיו.

    *f.* עַל *Upon,* poet., עֲלֵי; with suf., עָלַי,עָלֶיךָ,עָלָיו,עָלֶיהָ, עֲלֵיהֶם,עֲלֵיכֶם.

    *g.* תַּחַת *Under;* with suf., תַּחְתִּי,תַּחְתָּיו,תַּחְתֵּיהֶם,תַּחְתָּם; *cf.* also the form with Nûn Demonstrative תַּחְתֶּנָּה.

1. Prepositions were originally, in most cases, nouns; they were generally Constructs, governing the following noun as if it were a genitive.

**Note.**—Many words in common use as prepositions still retain their original force as substantives.

2. Prepositional phrases, composed of two prepositions or of a preposition and a noun, or of a preposition and an adverb, occur frequently.

3. Many prepositions, especially those denoting space and time, are in reality plural nouns; some of them, when standing alone, have the form of the plural Construct, ending in יִ‬ָ‬; before pronominal suffixes, most of them assume this form.

Note.—For the inseparable prepositions, see §§ 47. 1–5; 51. 3–5.

### 120.  Conjunctions

1. וְ *And;* אוֹ *Or;* אַף *Also;* אִם *When, if, or.*

2. כִּי *That, because, for, when.*

3. אַל *That not;* פֶּן *That not, lest;* בְּטֶרֶם *Before that;* אֲשֶׁר.

4. עֵקֶב אֲשֶׁר, תַּחַת כִּי, תַּחַת אֲשֶׁר, עַל־כִּי, עַל־אֲשֶׁר
   כַּאֲשֶׁר *In order that;* לְמַעַן אֲשֶׁר, עֵקֶב כִּי, *Because, since;*
   *According as.*

Conjunctions may be classified as to their origin as follows:

1. Certain words used *only* as conjunctions, the origin of which is, in most cases, doubtful.

2. Certain words which were originally pronouns.

3. Certain words which were originally substantives, or composed of a substantive and a preposition.

4. Prepositions which, by the addition of אֲשֶׁר or כִּי, become themselves a part of a compound conjunction.

Note 1.—In general it may be said that any preposition may be followed by אֲשֶׁר or כִּי, and be used as a conjunction.

Note 2.—In many cases the אֲשֶׁר or כִּי is omitted, and the preposition standing alone used as a conjunction.

### 121.  Interjections

1. אֲהָהּ, אָח *Ah!* הֶאָח *Ho! aha!* הַם *Hush!* אִי *Alas!*

2. אוֹי, הוֹי *Woe!* הֵן, הִנֵּה *Behold!* רְאֵה *Lo!* הָבָה *Come on!*
   לְכָה *Come on!* חָלִילָה *Far be it!* בִּי *I beseech!* נָא *Pray!*

Interjections may be divided into two classes:

1. Those which were originally interjections, "natural sounds called forth by some impression or sensation."

2. Those which were originally substantives or verbal forms, which have become interjections by usage.

# PARADIGMS

*Paradigm A.  The Personal*

| Nominative of the Pronoun or Separate Pronoun. | Genitive of the Pronoun, or *Suffix of the Noun (possessive Pron.)*. | |
|---|---|---|
| | With Nouns Singular. | With Nouns Plur. and Dual. |
| *Sing.* <br> 1. *com.* אָנֹכִי, in pause <br> אֲנִי; אָנֹכִי, in pause <br> אָנִי *I.* | ִי__ *my* (prop. Gen. *mei*). | ַי__ *my.* |
| 2. <br> *m.* (אַתְּ) אַתָּה in pause אָתָּה <br> *f.* אַתְּ (אַתִּי). } *thou.* | ךָ ךְ ךֶ__, in pause ךָ__ <br> ךְ, ךְ__, (ךְ__) } *thy (tui).* | יךָ__ <br> יךְ__ } *thy.* |
| 3. <br> *m.* הוּא *he.* <br> *f.* הִיא *she.* | (ה)וֹ, וֹ__, וּ וֹהוּ, הוּ *his (ejus* and *suus).* <br> הָ; הָ__; הָ__ *her.* | יו__, ַיו__, יְהוּ__, *his.* <br> יהָ__ *her.* |
| *Plur.* <br> 1. *com.* (נַחְנוּ) אֲנַחְנוּ, <br> (אֲנוּ) *we.* | נוּ; נוּ__; (נוּ__) *our.* | ֵינוּ *our.* |
| 2. <br> *m.* אַתֶּם <br> *f.* אַתֵּנָה, אַתֵּן } *ye.* | כֶם; כֶם__ <br> כֶן; כֶן__ } *your.* | יכֶם__ <br> יכֶן__ } *your.* |
| 3. <br> *m.* הֵם, הֵמָּה <br> *f.* הֵן, הֵנָּה } *they.* | הֶם; ם__; מוֹ__ <br> הֶן, הֶן, ן__ } *their.* | יהֶם__; ֵימוֹ__ <br> יהֶן__ } *their.* |

*Pronoun and Pronominal Suffixes*

Accusative of the Pronoun, or *Suffix of the Verb.*

| By itself. | With Nûn demonstrative. |
|---|---|
| נִי ;נִ֫י_ ;נִי_ *me.* | _נִ֫י, _נִי_ |
| ךָ; ךָ_, in p. ךָ_, ךְ_ ; ךָ_, (_נְךָ) <br> ךְ; ךְ_; ךְ_, ךְ_ } *thee.* — not found. | |
| הוּ, וֹ; הוּ_ (הָ), וֹ; הוּ, הוּ_ *him.* | (נוֹ), _נוּ, _נְהוּ |
| הָ; הָ_; הָ_ *her.* | _נָּה |
| נוּ; נוּ_; נוּ_ *us.* | _נוּ(?) |
| כֶם; כֶם_ <br> כֶן; כֶן_ } *you.* | These forms |
| (הֶם), ם; ם_, ם_; ם_, ם_; <br> מוֹ_, מוֹ_. } *them.* <br> (הֶן), ן; ן_, ן_; ן_ *them.* | do not occur. |

*Paradigm B.  The*

| Ḳal. | | Hiθpǎ'ēl. | Hŏf'ǎl. | Hif'îl. |
| Middle O. | Middle E. | | | |
| --- | --- | --- | --- | --- |
| קָטַל | קָטֵל | הִתְקַטֵּל | הָקְטַל | הִקְטִיל |
| קָטְלָה | קָטְלָה | הִתְקַטְּלָה | הָקְטְלָה | הִקְטִילָה |
| קָטַלְתָּ | קָטַלְתָּ | הִתְקַטַּלְתָּ | הָקְטַלְתָּ | הִקְטַלְתָּ |
| קָטַלְתְּ | etc. | הִתְקַטַּלְתְּ | הָקְטַלְתְּ | הִקְטַלְתְּ |
| קָטַלְתִּי | | הִתְקַטַּלְתִּי | הָקְטַלְתִּי | הִקְטַלְתִּי |
| קָטְלוּ | | הִתְקַטְּלוּ | הָקְטְלוּ | הִקְטִילוּ |
| קְטַלְתֶּם | | הִתְקַטַּלְתֶּם | הָקְטַלְתֶּם | הִקְטַלְתֶּם |
| קְטַלְתֶּן | | הִתְקַטַּלְתֶּן | הָקְטַלְתֶּן | הִקְטַלְתֶּן |
| קָטַלְנוּ | | הִתְקַטַּלְנוּ | הָקְטַלְנוּ | הִקְטַלְנוּ |
| יִקְטֹל  etc. | יִקְטַל | יִתְקַטֵּל | יָקְטַל | יַקְטִיל |
| | תִּקְטַל | תִּתְקַטֵּל | תָּקְטַל | תַּקְטִיל |
| | תִּקְטַל | תִּתְקַטֵּל | תָּקְטַל | תַּקְטִיל |
| | תִּקְטְלִי | תִּתְקַטְּלִי | תָּקְטְלִי | תַּקְטִילִי |
| | אִקְטַל | אֶתְקַטֵּל | אָקְטַל | אַקְטִיל |
| | יִקְטְלוּ | יִתְקַטְּלוּ | יָקְטְלוּ | יַקְטִילוּ |
| | תִּקְטֹלְנָה | תִּתְקַטֵּלְנָה | תָּקְטֵלְנָה | תַּקְטֵלְנָה |
| | תִּקְטְלוּ | תִּתְקַטְּלוּ | תָּקְטְלוּ | תַּקְטִילוּ |
| | תִּקְטֹלְנָה | תִּתְקַטֵּלְנָה | תָּקְטֵלְנָה | תַּקְטֵלְנָה |
| | נִקְטַל | נִתְקַטֵּל | נָקְטַל | נַקְטִיל |
| | קְטַל | הִתְקַטֵּל | | הַקְטֵל |
| | קִטְלִי | הִתְקַטְּלִי | wanting | הַקְטִילִי |
| | קִטְלוּ | הִתְקַטְּלוּ | | הַקְטִילוּ |
| | קְטֹלְנָה | הִתְקַטֵּלְנָה | | הַקְטֵלְנָה |
| | קְטוֹל | (הִתְקַטֹּל) | הָקְטֵל | הַקְטֵל |
| | קְטֹל (קְטַל) | הִתְקַטֵּל | | הַקְטִיל |
| | קֹטֵל | מִתְקַטֵּל | מָקְטָל | מַקְטִיל |

*Strong Verb*

| Pŭ‘ăl. | Pi‘ēl. | Nif‘ăl. | Ḳăl. | | |
|---|---|---|---|---|---|
| קֻטַּל | קִטֵּל | נִקְטַל | קָטַל | Sg. 3 m. | |
| קֻטְּלָה | קִטְּלָה | נִקְטְלָה | קָטְלָה | 3 f. | |
| קֻטַּלְתָּ | קִטַּלְתָּ | נִקְטַלְתָּ | קָטַלְתָּ | 2 m. | |
| קֻטַּלְתְּ | קִטַּלְתְּ | נִקְטַלְתְּ | קָטַלְתְּ | 2 f. | Perfect. |
| קֻטַּלְתִּי | קִטַּלְתִּי | נִקְטַלְתִּי | קָטַלְתִּי | 1 c. | |
| קֻטְּלוּ | קִטְּלוּ | נִקְטְלוּ | קָטְלוּ | Pl. 3 c. | |
| קֻטַּלְתֶּם | קִטַּלְתֶּם | נִקְטַלְתֶּם | קְטַלְתֶּם | 2 m. | |
| קֻטַּלְתֶּן | קִטַּלְתֶּן | נִקְטַלְתֶּן | קְטַלְתֶּן | 2 f. | |
| קֻטַּלְנוּ | קִטַּלְנוּ | נִקְטַלְנוּ | קָטַלְנוּ | 1 c. | |
| יְקֻטַּל | יְקַטֵּל | יִקָּטֵל | יִקְטֹל | Sg. 3 m. | |
| תְּקֻטַּל | תְּקַטֵּל | תִּקָּטֵל | תִּקְטֹל | 3 f. | |
| תְּקֻטַּל | תְּקַטֵּל | תִּקָּטֵל | תִּקְטֹל | 2 m. | |
| תְּקֻטְּלִי | תְּקַטְּלִי | תִּקָּטְלִי | תִּקְטְלִי | 2 f. | |
| אֲקֻטַּל | אֲקַטֵּל | אֶקָּטֵל | אֶקְטֹל | 1 c. | Imperfect. |
| יְקֻטְּלוּ | יְקַטְּלוּ | יִקָּטְלוּ | יִקְטְלוּ | Pl. 3 m. | |
| תְּקֻטַּלְנָה | תְּקַטֵּלְנָה | תִּקָּטַלְנָה | תִּקְטֹלְנָה | 3 f. | |
| תְּקֻטְּלוּ | תְּקַטְּלוּ | תִּקָּטְלוּ | תִּקְטְלוּ | 2 m. | |
| תְּקֻטַּלְנָה | תְּקַטֵּלְנָה | תִּקָּטַלְנָה | תִּקְטֹלְנָה | 2 f. | |
| נְקֻטַּל | נְקַטֵּל | נִקָּטֵל | נִקְטֹל | 1 c. | |
| | קַטֵּל | הִקָּטֵל | קְטֹל | Sg. 2 m. | |
| | קַטְּלִי | הִקָּטְלִי | קִטְלִי | 2 f. | Imperative. |
| wanting | קַטְּלוּ | הִקָּטְלוּ | קִטְלוּ | Pl. 2 m. | |
| | קַטֵּלְנָה | הִקָּטַלְנָה | קְטֹלְנָה | 2 f. | |
| קֻטֹּל קַטֵּל | קַטֹּל; נִקְטֹל | הִקָּטֹל | קָטוֹל | abs. | Infin. |
| | קַטֵּל | הִקָּטֵל | קְטֹל | Const. | |
| | מְקַטֵּל | | קֹטֵל | act. | Part. |
| מְקֻטָּל | | נִקְטָל | קָטוּל | pass. | |

*Paradigm C.   Strong Verb*

| 3 pl. f. | 3 pl. m. | 2 pl. m. | 1 pl. c. | 3 sg. f. |
|---|---|---|---|---|
| קְטָלֶן | קְטָלָם |  | קְטָלָנוּ | קְטָלָה |
|  | קְטָלַתַם | — | קְטָלַתְנוּ | קְטָלַתָּה |
|  | קְטַלְתָּם | — | קְטַלְתָּנוּ | קְטַלְתָּה |
|  | קְטַלְתִּים | — | קְטַלְתִּינוּ | קְטַלְתִּיךָ |
| קְטַלְתִּין | קְטַלְתִּים | קְטַלְתִּיכֶם | — | קְטַלְתִּיהָ |
| קְטָלוּן | קְטָלוּם / קְטַלְתוּם | — | קְטָלוּנוּ / קְטַלְתוּנוּ | קְטָלוּהָ |
|  | קְטַלְנוּם | קְטַלְנוּכֶם | — | קְטַלְנוּהָ |
| קְטֶלֶן | קְטֶלֶם | קְטֶלְכֶם | קְטֶלָנוּ | קְטֶלָה |
|  | יִקְטְלֵם | יִקְטְלְכֶם | יִקְטְלֵנוּ | יִקְטְלֶהָ / יִקְטְלָה |
| — |  |  | יִקְטְלֵנוּ | יִקְטְלֶנָּה |
|  | יִקְטְלוּם / תִּקְטְלוּם | יִקְטְלוּכֶם | יִקְטְלוּנוּ / תִּקְטְלוּנוּ | יִקְטְלוּהָ / תִּקְטְלוּהָ |
| — | קָטְלֵם | — | קָטְלֵנוּ | קָטְלֶהָ / קָטְלָה |
| קָטְלָן | קָטְלָם | קָטְלְכֶם / קָטְלְכֶם | קָטְלֵנוּ | קָטְלָה |

*with Suffixes*

| 3 sg. m. | 2 sg. f. | 2 sg. m. | 1 sg. c. | |
|---|---|---|---|---|
| קְטָלָהוּ }{ קְטָלוֹ | קְטָלֵךְ | קְטָלֵךְ | קְטָלַנִי | **Ḳäl** 3 m. |
| קְטָלַתְהוּ }{ קְטָלַתּוּ | קְטָלָתֶךְ | קְטָלָתֶךָ | קְטָלַתְנִי | 3 f. |
| קְטַלְתֶּהוּ }{ קְטַלְתּוּ | — | — | קְטַלְתַּנִי | 2 m. |
| קְטַלְתִּיהוּ | — | — | קְטַלְתִּינִי | 2 f. |
| קְטַלְתִּיו }{ קְטַלְתִּיהוּ | קְטַלְתִּיךְ | קְטַלְתִּיךָ | — | 1 c. |
| קְטָלוּהוּ | קְטָלוּךְ | קְטָלוּךָ | קְטָלוּנִי | Pl. 3 c. |
| קְטַלְתּוּהוּ | — | — | קְטַלְתּוּנִי | 2 m. |
| קְטַלְנוּהוּ | קְטַלְנוּךְ | קְטַלְנוּךָ | — | 1 c. |
| קְטֵלוֹ | קְטֵלֵךְ | קְטֵלֶךָ | קְטֵלַנִי | Sg. 3 m. Middle E |
| יִקְטְלֵהוּ | יִקְטְלֵךְ | יִקְטְלֶךָ | יִקְטְלֵנִי | Sg. 3 m. With Nûn |
| יִקְטְלֶנּוּ | — | יִקְטְלֶךָּ | יִקְטְלֶנִּי | Epenthet. |
| יִקְטְלוּהוּ | יִקְטְלוּךְ | יִקְטְלוּךָ | יִקְטְלוּנִי | Pl. 3 m. |
| תִּקְטְלוּהוּ | — | — | תִּקְטְלוּנִי | 2 f. |
| קָטְלֵהוּ | — | — | קָטְלֵנִי | Sg. 2 m. |
| קָטְלוֹ | קָטְלֵךְ | קָטְלְךָ }{ קָטְלֶךָ | קָטְלִי }{ קָטְלֵנִי | Construct |

Perfect. · Perf. · Imperfect. · Impv. · Inf.

| Hŏf'ăl | Hif'îl | Nif'ăl | Ḳăl | | |
|---|---|---|---|---|---|
| הָעֳטַל | הֶעֱטִיל | נֶעֱטַל | עָטַל | *Sg.* 3 *m.* | |
| הָעֳטְלָה | הֶעֱטִילָה | נֶעֶטְלָה | עָטְלָה | 3 *f.* | |
| הָעֳטַלְתָּ | הֶעֱטַלְתָּ | נֶעֱטַלְתָּ | עָטַלְתָּ | 2 *m.* | |
| הָעֳטַלְתְּ | הֶעֱטַלְתְּ | נֶעֱטַלְתְּ | עָטַלְתְּ | 2 *f.* | Perfect. |
| הָעֳטַלְתִּי | הֶעֱטַלְתִּי | נֶעֱטַלְתִּי | עָטַלְתִּי | 1 *c.* | |
| הָעֳטְלוּ | הֶעֱטִילוּ | נֶעֶטְלוּ | עָטְלוּ | *Pl.* 3 *c.* | |
| הָעֳטַלְתֶּם | הֶעֱטַלְתֶּם | נֶעֶטַלְתֶּם | עֲטַלְתֶּם | 2 *m.* | |
| הָעֳטַלְתֶּן | הֶעֱטַלְתֶּן | נֶעֱטַלְתֶּן | עֲטַלְתֶּן | 2 *f.* | |
| הָעֳטַלְנוּ | הֶעֱטַלְנוּ | נֶעֱטַלְנוּ | עָטַלְנוּ | 1 *c.* | |
| יָעֳטַל | יַעֲטִיל | יֵעָטֵל | יֶעְטַל   יַעֲטֹל | *Sg.* 3 *m.* | |
| תָּעֳטַל | תַּעֲטִיל | תֵּעָטֵל | תֶּעְטַל   תַּעֲטֹל | 3 *f.* | |
| תָּעֳטַל | תַּעֲטִיל | תֵּעָטֵל | תֶּעְטַל   תַּעֲטֹל | 2 *m.* | |
| תָּעֳטְלִי | תַּעֲטִילִי | תֵּעָטְלִי | תַּעֲטְלִי | 2 *f.* | |
| אָעֳטַל | אַעֲטִיל | אֵעָטֵל | אֶעְטַל   אַעֲטֹל | 1 *c.* | Imperfect. |
| יָעֳטְלוּ | יַעֲטִילוּ | יֵעָטְלוּ | יַעֲטְלוּ | *Pl.* 3 *m.* | |
| תָּעֳטַלְנָה | תַּעֲטֵלְנָה | תֵּעָטַלְנָה | תַּעֲטֹלְנָה תֶּעְטַלְנָה | 3 *f.* | |
| תָּעֳטְלוּ | תַּעֲטִילוּ | תֵּעָטְלוּ | תַּעֲטְלוּ | 2 *m.* | |
| תָּעֳטַלְנָה | תַּעֲטֵלְנָה | תֵּעָטַלְנָה | תַּעֲטֹלְנָה תֶּעְטַלְנָה | 2 *f.* | |
| נָעֳטַל | נַעֲטִיל | נֵעָטֵל | נֶעְטַל   נַעֲטֹל | 1 *c.* | |
| | הַעֲטֵל | הֵעָטֵל | עֲטֹל   עֲטֹל | *Sg.* 2 *m.* | |
| | הַעֲטִילִי | הֵעָטְלִי | עִטְלִי   עֲטְלִי | 2 *f.* | Imperative. |
| wanting | הַעֲטִילוּ | הֵעָטְלוּ | עִטְלוּ   עֲטְלוּ | *Pl.* 2 *m.* | |
| | הַעֲטֵלְנָה | הֵעָטַלְנָה | עֲטֹלְנָה עֲטֹלְנָה | 2 *f.* | |
| הָעֳטֵל | הַעֲטֵל | { נַעֲטוֹל<br>{ הֵעָטֵל | עָטוֹל | *abs.* | Infin. |
| | הַעֲטִיל | הֵעָטֵל | עֲטֹל | *Const.* | |
| | מַעֲטִיל | | עֹטֵל | *act.* | Part. |
| מָעֳטַל | | נֶעֱטַל | עָטוּל | *pass.* | |

| Hiṯpăʿēl. | Pŭʿăl. | Pĭʿēl. | Nĭfʿăl. | Ḳăl. | | |
|---|---|---|---|---|---|---|
| הִתְקָאֵל | קֻאַל | קֵאַל, קִאַל | נִקְאַל | קָאַל | Sg. 3 m. | |
| הִתְקָאֲלָה | קֻאֲלָה | קֵאֲלָה | נִקְאֲלָה | קָאֲלָה | 3 f. | |
| הִתְקָאַלְתָּ | קֻאַלְתָּ | קֵאַלְתָּ | נִקְאַלְתָּ | קָאַלְתָּ | 2 m. | |
| הִתְקָאַלְתְּ | קֻאַלְתְּ | קֵאַלְתְּ | נִקְאַלְתְּ | קָאַלְתְּ | 2 f. | Perfect. |
| הִתְקָאַלְתִּי | קֻאַלְתִּי | קֵאַלְתִּי | נִקְאַלְתִּי | קָאַלְתִּי | 1 c. | |
| הִתְקָאֲלוּ | קֻאֲלוּ | קֵאֲלוּ | נִקְאֲלוּ | קָאֲלוּ | Pl. 3 c. | |
| הִתְקָאַלְתֶּם | קֻאַלְתֶּם | קֵאַלְתֶּם | נִקְאַלְתֶּם | קְאַלְתֶּם | 2 m. | |
| הִתְקָאַלְתֶּן | קֻאַלְתֶּן | קֵאַלְתֶּן | נִקְאַלְתֶּן | קְאַלְתֶּן | 2 f. | |
| הִתְקָאַלְנוּ | קֻאַלְנוּ | קֵאַלְנוּ | נִקְאַלְנוּ | קָאַלְנוּ | 1 c. | |
| יִתְקָאֵל | יְקֻאַל | יְקָאֵל | יִקָּאֵל | יִקְאַל | Sg. 3 m. | |
| תִּתְקָאֵל | תְּקֻאַל | תְּקָאֵל | תִּקָּאֵל | תִּקְאַל | 3 f. | |
| תִּתְקָאֵל | תְּקֻאַל | תְּקָאֵל | תִּקָּאֵל | תִּקְאַל | 2 m. | |
| תִּתְקָאֲלִי | תְּקֻאֲלִי | תְּקָאֲלִי | תִּקָּאֲלִי | תִּקְאֲלִי | 2 f. | |
| אֶתְקָאֵל | אֲקֻאַל | אֲקָאֵל | אֶקָּאֵל | אֶקְאַל | 1 c. | |
| יִתְקָאֲלוּ | יְקֻאֲלוּ | יְקָאֲלוּ | יִקָּאֲלוּ | יִקְאֲלוּ | Pl. 3 m. | Imperfect. |
| תִּתְקָאֵלְנָה | תְּקֻאַלְנָה | תְּקָאֵלְנָה | תִּקָּאַלְנָה | תִּקְאַלְנָה | 3 f. | |
| תִּתְקָאֲלוּ | תְּקֻאֲלוּ | תְּקָאֲלוּ | תִּקָּאֲלוּ | תִּקְאֲלוּ | 2 m. | |
| תִּתְקָאֵלְנָה | תְּקֻאַלְנָה | תְּקָאֵלְנָה | תִּקָּאַלְנָה | תִּקְאַלְנָה | 2 f. | |
| נִתְקָאֵל | נְקֻאַל | נְקָאֵל | נִקָּאֵל | נִקְאַל | 1 c. | |
| הִתְקָאֵל | | קָאֵל | הִקָּאֵל | קְאַל | Sg. 2 m. | |
| הִתְקָאֲלִי | | קָאֲלִי | הִקָּאֲלִי | קַאֲלִי | 2 f. | Imperative. |
| הִתְקָאֲלוּ | wanting | קָאֲלוּ | הִקָּאֲלוּ | קַאֲלוּ | Pl. 2 m. | |
| הִתְקָאֵלְנָה | | קָאֵלְנָה | הִקָּאַלְנָה | קְאַלְנָה | 2 f. | |
| —— | — | קָאֵל | נִקְאוֹל | קָאוֹל | abs. | Infin. |
| הִתְקָאֵל | — | קָאֵל | הִקָּאֵל | קְאַל | Const. | |
| מִתְקָאֵל | מְקֻאָל | מְקָאֵל | | קֹאֵל | act. | Part. |
| | מְקֻאָל | | נִקְאָל | קָאוּל | pass. | |

| Hithpăʿēl. | Hifʿil. | Pīʿēl. | Nifʿăl. | Ḳăl. | |
|---|---|---|---|---|---|
| הִתְקַטַּח | הִקְטִיחַ | קִטַּח | נִקְטַח | קָטַח | Sg. 3 m. |
| הִתְקַטְּחָה | הִקְטִיחָה | קִטְּחָה | נִקְטְחָה | קָטְחָה | 3 f. |
| הִתְקַטַּחְתָּ | הִקְטַחְתָּ | קִטַּחְתָּ | נִקְטַחְתָּ | קָטַחְתָּ | 2 m. |
| הִתְקַטַּחַתְּ | הִקְטַחַתְּ | קִטַּחַתְּ | נִקְטַחַתְּ | קָטַחַתְּ | 2 f. |
| הִתְקַטַּחְתִּי | הִקְטַחְתִּי | קִטַּחְתִּי | נִקְטַחְתִּי | קָטַחְתִּי | 1 c. |
| הִתְקַטְּחוּ | הִקְטִיחוּ | קִטְּחוּ | נִקְטְחוּ | קָטְחוּ | Pl. 3 c. |
| הִתְקַטַּחְתֶּם | הִקְטַחְתֶּם | קִטַּחְתֶּם | נִקְטַחְתֶּם | קְטַחְתֶּם | 2 m. |
| הִתְקַטַּחְתֶּן | הִקְטַחְתֶּן | קִטַּחְתֶּן | נִקְטַחְתֶּן | קְטַחְתֶּן | 2 f. |
| הִתְקַטַּחְנוּ | הִקְטַחְנוּ | קִטַּחְנוּ | נִקְטַחְנוּ | קָטַחְנוּ | 1 c. |
| יִתְקַטַּח | יַקְטִיחַ | יְקַטַּח | יִקָּטַח | יִקְטַח | Sg. 3 m. |
| תִּתְקַטַּח | תַּקְטִיחַ | תְּקַטַּח | תִּקָּטַח | תִּקְטַח | 3 f. |
| תִּתְקַטַּח | תַּקְטִיחַ | תְּקַטַּח | תִּקָּטַח | תִּקְטַח | 2 m. |
| תִּתְקַטְּחִי | תַּקְטִיחִי | תְּקַטְּחִי | תִּקָּטְחִי | תִּקְטְחִי | 2 f. |
| אֶתְקַטַּח | אַקְטִיחַ | אֲקַטַּח | אֶקָּטַח | אֶקְטַח | 1 c. |
| יִתְקַטְּחוּ | יַקְטִיחוּ | יְקַטְּחוּ | יִקָּטְחוּ | יִקְטְחוּ | Pl. 3 m. |
| תִּתְקַטַּחְנָה | תַּקְטַחְנָה | תְּקַטַּחְנָה | תִּקָּטַחְנָה | תִּקְטַחְנָה | 3 f. |
| תִּתְקַטְּחוּ | תַּקְטִיחוּ | תְּקַטְּחוּ | תִּקָּטְחוּ | תִּקְטְחוּ | 2 m. |
| תִּתְקַטַּחְנָה | תַּקְטַחְנָה | תְּקַטַּחְנָה | תִּקָּטַחְנָה | תִּקְטַחְנָה | 2 f. |
| נִתְקַטַּח | נַקְטִיחַ | נְקַטַּח | נִקָּטַח | נִקְטַח | 1 c. |
| הִתְקַטַּח | הַקְטַח | קַטַּח | הִקָּטַח | קְטַח | Sg. 2 m. |
| הִתְקַטְּחִי | הַקְטִיחִי | קַטְּחִי | הִקָּטְחִי | קִטְחִי | 2 f. |
| הִתְקַטְּחוּ | הַקְטִיחוּ | קַטְּחוּ | הִקָּטְחוּ | קִטְחוּ | Pl. 2 m. |
| הִתְקַטַּחְנָה | הַקְטַחְנָה | קַטַּחְנָה | הִקָּטַחְנָה | קְטַחְנָה | 2 f. |
| ———— | הַקְטֵחַ | קַטֵּחַ | נִקְטֹחַ | קָטוֹחַ | abs. |
| הִתְקַטֵּחַ | הַקְטִיחַ | קַטֵּחַ | הִקָּטֵחַ | קְטֹחַ | Const. |
| מִתְקַטֵּחַ | מַקְטִיחַ | מְקַטֵּחַ |  | קֹטֵחַ | act. |
|  |  |  | נִקְטָח | קָטוּחַ | pass. |

| Hŏf'ăl. | Hif'îl. | Nif'ăl. | Ḳăl. | | |
|---|---|---|---|---|---|
| הֻטַּל | הִטִּיל | נִטַּל | נָטַל | Sg. 3 m. | Perfect. |
| הֻטְּלָה | הִטִּילָה | נִטְּלָה | etc. | 3 f. | |
| הֻטַּלְתָּ | הִטַּלְתָּ | נִטַּלְתָּ | | 2 m. | |
| הֻטַּלְתְּ | הִטַּלְתְּ | נִטַּלְתְּ | | 2 f. | |
| הֻטַּלְתִּי | הִטַּלְתִּי | נִטַּלְתִּי | regular | 1 c. | |
| הֻטְּלוּ | הִטִּילוּ | נִטְּלוּ | | Pl. 3 c. | |
| הֻטַּלְתֶּם | הִטַּלְתֶּם | נִטַּלְתֶּם | | 2 m. | |
| הֻטַּלְתֶּן | הִטַּלְתֶּן | נִטַּלְתֶּן | | 2 f. | |
| הֻטַּלְנוּ | הִטַּלְנוּ | נִטַּלְנוּ | | 1 c. | |
| יֻטַּל | יַטִּיל | יִנָּטֵל | יִטַּל   יִטֹּל | Sg. 3 m. | Imperfect. |
| תֻּטַּל | תַּטִּיל | תִּנָּטֵל | תִּטַּל   תִּטֹּל | 3 f. | |
| תֻּטַּל | תַּטִּיל | תִּנָּטֵל | תִּטַּל   תִּטֹּל | 2 m. | |
| תֻּטְּלִי | תַּטִּילִי | תִּנָּטְלִי | תִּטְּלִי | 2 f. | |
| אֻטַּל | אַטִּיל | אֶנָּטֵל | אֶטַּל   אֶטֹּל | 1 c. | |
| יֻטְּלוּ | יַטִּילוּ | יִנָּטְלוּ | יִטְּלוּ | Pl. 3 m. | |
| תֻּטַּלְנָה | תַּטֵּלְנָה | תִּנָּטַלְנָה | תִּטַּלְנָה תִּטֹּלְנָה | 3 f. | |
| תֻּטְּלוּ | תַּטִּילוּ | תִּנָּטְלוּ | תִּטְּלוּ | 2 m. | |
| תֻּטַּלְנָה | תַּטֵּלְנָה | תִּנָּטַלְנָה | תִּטַּלְנָה תִּטֹּלְנָה | 2 f. | |
| נֻטַּל | נַטִּיל | נִנָּטֵל | נִטַּל   נִטֹּל | 1 c. | |
| | הַטֵּל | הִנָּטֵל | טַל   נְטֹל | Sg. 2 m. | Imperative. |
| | הַטִּילִי | הִנָּטְלִי | טְלִי   נִטְלִי | 2 f. | |
| wanting | הַטִּילוּ | הִנָּטְלוּ | טְלוּ   נִטְלוּ | Pl. 2 m. | |
| | הַטֵּלְנָה | הִנָּטַלְנָה | טֹלְנָה נְטֹלְנָה | 2 f. | |
| הֻטֵּל | הַטֵּל | הִנָּטֵל {<br>נִטּוֹל} | נָטוֹל | abs. | Infin. |
| הֻטֵּל | הַטִּיל | הִנָּטֵל | טֶלֶת   נְטֹל | Const. | |
| | מַטִּיל | | נֹטֵל | act. | Part. |
| מֻטָּל | | נִטָּל | נָטוּל | pass. | |

*Paradigm H.*   *Verb Pē ʾÁlĕf* (פ״א)׃   *Verb Pē Yôđ* (פ״י)׃   *Para-*

| Nif'al. | Kal. | Hif'il (prop. פ״ו). | Kal (prop. פ״ו). |
|---|---|---|---|
| Same as the verb Pē Laryngeal. | אָטַל | הֵיטִיל | יָטַל |
|  | Same as the verb Pē Laryngeal | הֵיטִילָה | etc. |
|  |  | הֵיטַלְתְּ |  |
|  |  | הֵיטַלְתְּ |  |
|  |  | הֵיטַלְתִּי | regular |
|  |  | הֵיטִילוּ |  |
|  |  | הֵיטַלְתֶּם |  |
|  |  | הֵיטַלְתֶּן |  |
|  |  | הֵיטַלְנוּ |  |
| יֵאָטַל (יֵאָטֵל) | יֵיטִיל | יִיטַל |
| תֵּאָטַל | תֵּיטִיל | תִּיטַל |
| תֵּאָטַל | תֵּיטִיל | תִּיטַל |
| תֵּאָטְלִי | תֵּיטִילִי | תִּיטְלִי |
| אֹטַל | אֵיטִיל | אִיטַל |
| יֵאָטְלוּ | יֵיטִילוּ | יִיטְלוּ |
| תֵּאָטַלְנָה | תֵּיטֵלְנָה | תִּיטַלְנָה |
| תֵּאָטְלוּ | תֵּיטִילוּ | תִּיטְלוּ |
| תֵּאָטַלְנָה | תֵּיטֵלְנָה | תִּיטַלְנָה |
| נֵאָטַל | נֵיטִיל | נִיטַל |
| אָטֵל | הֵיטֵל | יְטַל |
| אָטְלִי | הֵיטִילִי | יְטְלִי |
| אָטְלוּ | הֵיטִילוּ | יְטְלוּ |
| אָטַלְנָה | הֵיטֵלְנָה | יְטַלְנָה |
| אָטוֹל | הֵיטֵל | יָטוֹל |
| אֵטֵל, אֶטֵל | הֵיטִיל | יְטֹל |
| אֹטֵל | מֵיטִיל | יֹטֵל |
| אָטוֹל |  | יָטוֹל |

*digm I. Verb Pē Wåw* (פ״ו)

| Hŏf‘ăl. | Hif‘il. | Nif‘ăl. | Ḳăl. | | |
|---|---|---|---|---|---|
| הוּטַל | הוֹטִיל | נוֹטַל | יָטַל | Sg. 3 m. | Perfect. |
| הוּטְלָה | הוֹטִילָה | נוֹטְלָה | etc. | 3 f. | |
| הוּטַלְתָּ | הוֹטַלְתָּ | נוֹטַלְתָּ | | 2 m. | |
| הוּטַלְתְּ | הוֹטַלְתְּ | נוֹטַלְתְּ | | 2 f. | |
| הוּטַלְתִּי | הוֹטַלְתִּי | נוֹטַלְתִּי | regular | 1 c. | |
| הוּטְלוּ | הוֹטִילוּ | נוֹטְלוּ | | Pl. 3 c. | |
| הוּטַלְתֶּם | הוֹטַלְתֶּם | נוֹטַלְתֶּם | | 2 m. | |
| הוּטַלְתֶּן | הוֹטַלְתֶּן | נוֹטַלְתֶּן | | 2 f. | |
| הוּטַלְנוּ | הוֹטַלְנוּ | נוֹטַלְנוּ | | 1 c. | |
| יוּטַל | יוֹטִיל | יוּטַל | יֵטַל  יֵיטַל | Sg. 3 m. | Imperfect. |
| תּוּטַל | תּוֹטִיל | etc. | תֵּטֵל  תֵּיטֵל | 3 f. | |
| תּוּטַל | תּוֹטִיל | | תֵּטֵל  תֵּיטֵל | 2 m. | |
| תּוּטְלִי | תּוֹטִילִי | | תֵּטְלִי  תֵּיטְלִי | 2 f. | |
| אוּטַל | אוֹטִיל | regular | אֵטַל  אִיטַל | 1 c. | |
| יוּטְלוּ | יוֹטִילוּ | | יֵטְלוּ  יֵיטְלוּ | Pl. 3 m. | |
| תּוּטַלְנָה | תּוֹטֵלְנָה | | תֵּיטַלְנָה תֵּטַלְנָה | 3 f. | |
| תּוּטְלוּ | תּוֹטִילוּ | | תֵּטְלוּ  תֵּיטְלוּ | 2 m. | |
| תּוּטַלְנָה | תּוֹטֵלְנָה | | תֵּיטַלְנָה תֵּטַלְנָה | 2 f. | |
| נוּטַל | נוֹטִיל | | נֵטַל  נִיטַל | 1 c. | |
| wanting | הוֹטֵל | הִוָּטֵל | טֵל, טַל | Sg. 2 m. | Imperative. |
| | הוֹטִילִי | הִוָּטְלִי | טְלִי | 2 f. | |
| | הוֹטִילוּ | הִוָּטְלוּ | טְלוּ | Pl. 2 m. | |
| | הוֹטֵלְנָה | הִוָּטֵלְנָה | טֵלְנָה | 2 f. | |
| — | הוֹטֵל | — | יָטוֹל  יָטֹל | abs. | Infin. |
| — | הוֹטִיל | הִוָּטֵל | טֶלֶת, טֶלֶת ,יָטֹל | const. | |
| | מוֹטִיל | | יֹטֵל | act. | Part. |
| מוּטָל | | נוֹטָל | יָטוּל | pass. | |

*Paradigm K. Verb*

| Hiθpăʻēl. | Höfʻăl. | Hifʻil. | Püʻăl. |
|---|---|---|---|
| הִתְקַטְּה | הׇקְטְה | הׇקְטְה | קֻטְּה |
| הִתְקַטְּתָה | הׇקְטְתָה | הׇקְטְתָה | קֻטְּתָה |
| הִתְקַטֵּיתָ | הׇקְטֵיתָ | הׇקְטֵיתָ (‎ֵ‎יתָ‎) | קֻטֵּיתָ |
| הִתְקַטֵּית | הׇקְטֵית | הׇקְטֵית (‎ֵ‎ית‎) | קֻטֵּית |
| הִתְקַטֵּיתִי | הׇקְטֵיתִי | הׇקְטֵיתִי (‎ֵ‎יתִי‎) | קֻטֵּיתִי |
| הִתְקַטְּוּ | הׇקְטְוּ | הׇקְטְוּ | קֻטְּוּ |
| הִתְקַטֵּיתֶם | הׇקְטֵיתֶם | הׇקְטֵיתֶם (‎ֵ‎יתֶם‎) | קֻטֵּיתֶם |
| הִתְקַטֵּיתֶן | הׇקְטֵיתֶן | הׇקְטֵיתֶן | קֻטֵּיתֶן |
| הִתְקַטֵּינוּ | הׇקְטֵינוּ | הׇקְטֵינוּ | קֻטֵּינוּ |
| יִתְקַטְּה | יׇקְטְה | יׇקְטְה | יְקֻטְּה |
| תִּתְקַטְּה | תׇּקְטְה | תׇּקְטְה | תְּקֻטְּה |
| תִּתְקַטְּה | תׇּקְטְה | תׇּקְטְה | תְּקֻטְּה |
| תִּתְקַטְּי | תׇּקְטְי | תׇּקְטְי | תְּקֻטְּי |
| אֶתְקַטְּה | אׇקְטְה | אׇקְטְה | אֲקֻטְּה |
| יִתְקַטְּוּ | יׇקְטְוּ | יׇקְטְוּ | יְקֻטְּוּ |
| תִּתְקַטֵּינָה | תׇּקְטֵינָה | תׇּקְטֵינָה | תְּקֻטֵּינָה |
| תִּתְקַטְּוּ | תׇּקְטְוּ | תׇּקְטְוּ | תְּקֻטְּוּ |
| תִּתְקַטֵּינָה | תׇּקְטֵינָה | תׇּקְטֵינָה | תְּקֻטֵּינָה |
| נִתְקַטְּה | נׇקְטְה | נׇקְטְה | נְקֻטְּה |
| הִתְקַטְּה, הִתְקַטֵּט | | הׇקְטֵה | |
| הִתְקַטֵּי | | הׇקְטֵי | |
| הִתְקַטְּוּ | wanting | הׇקְטֵוּ | wanting |
| הִתְקַטֵּינָה | | הׇקְטֵינָה | |
| —— | הׇקְטֵה | הׇקְטֵה | |
| הִתְקַטּוֹת | הׇקְטוֹת | הׇקְטוֹת | קֻטּוֹת |
| מִתְקַטְּה | מׇקְטְה | מׇקְטֵה | מְקֻטְּה |
| | מׇקְטְה | | מְקֻטְּה |

# Lắmĕd Hē (ל״ה)

| Pi'ēl. | Nif'āl. | Ḳāl. | | |
|---|---|---|---|---|
| קִטָּה | נִקְטָה | קָטָה | Sg. 3 m. | |
| קִטְּתָה | נִקְטְתָה | קָטְתָה | 3 f. | |
| קִטִּיתָ | נִקְטֵיתָ (־ֵיתָ) | קָטִיתָ | 2 m. | |
| קִטִּית | נִקְטֵית | קָטִית | 2 f. | |
| קִטִּיתִי, קִטֵּיתִי | נִקְטֵיתִי | קָטִיתִי | 1 c. | Perfect. |
| קִטּוּ | נִקְטוּ | קָטוּ | Pl. 3 c. | |
| קִטִּיתֶם | נִקְטֵיתֶם | קְטִיתֶם | 2 m. | |
| קִטִּיתֶן | נִקְטֵיתֶן | קְטִיתֶן | 2 f. | |
| קִטִּינוּ | נִקְטֵינוּ | קָטִינוּ | 1 c. | |
| יְקַטֶּה | יִקָּטֶה | יִקְטֶה | Sg. 3 m. | |
| תְּקַטֶּה | תִּקָּטֶה | תִּקְטֶה | 3 f. | |
| תְּקַטֶּה | תִּקָּטֶה | תִּקְטֶה | 2 m. | |
| תְּקַטִּי | תִּקָּטִי | תִּקְטִי | 2 f. | |
| אֲקַטֶּה | אֶקָּטֶה | אֶקְטֶה | 1 c. | Imperfect. |
| יְקַטּוּ | יִקָּטוּ | יִקְטוּ | Pl. 3 m. | |
| תְּקַטֶּינָה | תִּקָּטֶינָה | תִּקְטֶינָה | 3 f. | |
| תְּקַטּוּ | תִּקָּטוּ | תִּקְטוּ | 2 m. | |
| תְּקַטֶּינָה | תִּקָּטֶינָה | תִּקְטֶינָה | 2 f. | |
| נְקַטֶּה | נִקָּטֶה | נִקְטֶה | 1 c. | |
| קַטֵּה, קַט | הִקָּטֵה | קְטֵה | Sg. 2 m. | |
| קַטִּי | הִקָּטִי | קְטִי | 2 f. | |
| קַטּוּ | הִקָּטוּ | קְטוּ | Pl. 2 m. | Imperative. |
| קַטֶּינָה | הִקָּטֶינָה | קְטֶינָה | 2 f. | |
| קַטֹּה, קַטֵּה | נִקְטֹה, הִקָּטֵה | קָטֹה | abs. | Infin. |
| קַטּוֹת | הִקָּטוֹת | קְטוֹת | const. | |
| מְקַטֶּה | | קֹטֶה | act. | Part. |
| | נִקְטֶה | קָטוּי | pass. | |

*Paradigm L.  Verb*

| Hîθpôʿēl. | Pôʿăl. | Pôʿēl. | Hŏfʿăl. |
|---|---|---|---|
| הִתְקוֹטֵט | קוֹטַט | קוֹטֵט | הוּקַט |
| הִתְקוֹטְטָה | קוֹטְטָה | קוֹטְטָה | הוּקְטָה |
| הִתְקוֹטַטְתָּ | קוֹטַטְתָּ | קוֹטַטְתָּ | הוּקַטְתָּ |
| הִתְקוֹטַטְתְּ | קוֹטַטְתְּ | קוֹטַטְתְּ | הוּקַטְתְּ |
| הִתְקוֹטַטְתִּי | קוֹטַטְתִּי | קוֹטַטְתִּי | הוּקַטְתִּי |
| הִתְקוֹטְטוּ | קוֹטְטוּ | קוֹטְטוּ | הוּקְטוּ |
| הִתְקוֹטַטְתֶּם | קוֹטַטְתֶּם | קוֹטַטְתֶּם | הוּקַטְתֶּם |
| הִתְקוֹטַטְתֶּן | קוֹטַטְתֶּן | קוֹטַטְתֶּן | הוּקַטְתֶּן |
| הִתְקוֹטַטְנוּ | קוֹטַטְנוּ | קוֹטַטְנוּ | הוּקַטְנוּ |
| יִתְקוֹטֵט | יְקוֹטַט | יְקוֹטֵט | יוּקַט, יְקַט |
| תִּתְקוֹטֵט | תְּקוֹטַט | תְּקוֹטֵט | תּוּקַט |
| תִּתְקוֹטֵט | תְּקוֹטַט | תְּקוֹטֵט | תּוּקַט |
| תִּתְקוֹטְטִי | תְּקוֹטְטִי | תְּקוֹטְטִי | תּוּקְטִי |
| אֶתְקוֹטֵט | אֲקוֹטַט | אֲקוֹטֵט | אוּקַט |
| יִתְקוֹטְטוּ | יְקוֹטְטוּ | יְקוֹטְטוּ | יוּקְטוּ |
| תִּתְקוֹטַטְנָה | תְּקוֹטַטְנָה | תְּקוֹטַטְנָה | תּוּקַטֵּינָה |
| תִּתְקוֹטְטוּ | תְּקוֹטְטוּ | תְּקוֹטְטוּ | תּוּקְטוּ |
| תִּתְקוֹטַטְנָה | תְּקוֹטַטְנָה | תְּקוֹטַטְנָה | תּוּקַטֵּינָה |
| נִתְקוֹטֵט | נְקוֹטַט | נְקוֹטֵט | נוּקַט |
| הִתְקוֹטֵט | | קוֹטֵט | |
| הִתְקוֹטֲטִי | *wanting* | קוֹטֲטִי | *wanting* |
| הִתְקוֹטֲטוּ | | קוֹטֲטוּ | |
| הִתְקוֹטֵטְנָה | | קוֹטֵטְנָה | |
| הִתְקוֹטֵט | | קוֹטֵט | — |
| — | קוֹטֵט | קוֹטֵט | הוּקַט, הָשְׁמָה |
| מִתְקוֹטֵט | | מְקוֹטֵט | |
| | מְקוֹטָט | | מוּקָט |

### 'Ăyin Doubled (ע"ע)

| Hif‘il. | Nif‘al. | Ḳăl. | | | |
|---|---|---|---|---|---|
| הֵקֵט, הֵקַט | נָקַט, נָקֵט | קַט, קָטַט | | Sg. 3 m. | Perfect. |
| הֵקַטָּה | נָקַטָּה | קַטָּה, קָטְטָה | | 3 f. | |
| הֲקַטּוֹתָ | נְקַטּוֹתָ | קַטּוֹתָ | | 2 m. | |
| הֲקַטּוֹת | נְקַטּוֹת | קַטּוֹת | | 2 f. | |
| הֲקַטּוֹתִי | נְקַטּוֹתִי | קַטּוֹתִי | | 1 c. | |
| הֵקַטּוּ, הֵקַטּוּ | נָקַטּוּ | קַטּוּ, קָטְטוּ | | Pl. 3 c. | |
| הֲקַטּוֹתֶם | נְקַטּוֹתֶם | קַטּוֹתֶם | | 2 m. | |
| הֲקַטּוֹתֶן | נְקַטּוֹתֶן | קַטּוֹתֶן | | 2 f. | |
| הֲקַטּוֹנוּ | נְקַטּוֹנוּ | קַטּוֹנוּ | | 1 c. | |
| יָקֵט, יַקֵט | יִקַט | יָקֹט | יִקַּט, יֵקַל | Sg. 3 m. | Imperfect. |
| תָּקֵט | תִּקַט | תָּקֹט | תִּקַּט | 3 f. | |
| תָּקֵט | תִּקַט | תָּקֹט | תִּקַּט | 2 m. | |
| תָּקֵטִּי | תִּקַטִּי | תָּקֹטִי | תִּקַּטִי | 2 f. | |
| אָקֵט | אִקַט | אָקֹט | אִקַּט | 1 c. | |
| יָקֵטּוּ, יַקֵטּוּ | יִקַטּוּ | יָקֹטּוּ | יִקַּטּוּ | Pl. 3 m. | |
| תְּקַטֵּינָה | תִּקַטֵּינָה | תָּקֹטְנָה תִּקַּטְנָה | | 3 f. | |
| תָּקֵטּוּ | תִּקַטּוּ | תָּקֹטּוּ | תִּקַּטּוּ | 2 m. | |
| תִּקְטֵּינָה | תִּקַטֵּינָה | תָּקֹטְנָה תִּקַּטְנָה | | 2 f. | |
| נָקֵט | נִקַט | נָקֹט | נִקַּט | 1 c. | |
| הָקֵט | הִקַט | קֹט | | Sg. 2 m. | Imperative. |
| הָקֵטִּי | הִקַטִּי | קֹטִּי | | 2 f. | |
| הָקֵטּוּ | הִקַטּוּ | קֹטּוּ | | Pl. 2 m. | |
| הֲקֵטֵּינָה | הִקַטֵּינָה | קַטֵּינָה | | 2 f. | |
| הָקֵט | הִקּוֹט, הִקֵּט | קָטוֹט | | abs. | Infin. |
| הָקֵט | הִקֵּט | קֹט | | const. | |
| מֵקֵט | | קֹטֵט | | act. | Part. |
| | נָקָט | קָטוֹט | | pass. | |

| Pôlăl. | Pôlēl. | Hŏf'ăl. | Hîf'îl. |
|---|---|---|---|
| קוֹלַל | קוֹלֵל | הוּקַל | הֵקִיל |
| קוֹלֲלָה | קוֹלֲלָה | הוּקְלָה | הֵקִילָה |
| etc. | קוֹלַלְתָּ | הוּקַלְתָּ | הֵקִילוֹתָ |
| | קוֹלַלְתְּ | הוּקַלְתְּ | הֵקִילוֹת |
| | קוֹלַלְתִּי | הוּקַלְתִּי | הֵקִילוֹתִי |
| | קוֹלֲלוּ | הוּקְלוּ | הֵקִילוּ |
| | קוֹלַלְתֶּם | הוּקַלְתֶּם | הֵקִילוֹתֶם |
| | קוֹלַלְתֶּן | הוּקַלְתֶּן | הֵקִילוֹתֶן |
| | קוֹלַלְנוּ | הוּקַלְנוּ | הֵקִילוֹנוּ |
| יְקוֹלַל | יְקוֹלֵל | יוּקַל | יָקִיל |
| תְּקוֹלַל | תְּקוֹלֵל | תּוּקַל | תָּקִיל |
| etc. | תְּקוֹלֵל | תּוּקַל | תָּקִיל |
| | תְּקוֹלֲלִי | תּוּקְלִי | תָּקִילִי |
| | אֲקוֹלֵל | אוּקַל | אָקִיל |
| | יְקוֹלֲלוּ | יוּקְלוּ | יָקִילוּ |
| | תְּקוֹלַלְנָה | תּוּקַלְנָה | תָּקֵלְנָה, תְּקִילֶינָה |
| | תְּקוֹלֲלוּ | תּוּקְלוּ | תָּקִילוּ |
| | תְּקוֹלַלְנָה | תּוּקַלְנָה | תָּקֵלְנָה |
| | נְקוֹלֵל | נוּקַל | נָקִיל |
| | קוֹלֵל | | הָקֵל |
| | קוֹלֲלִי | | הָקִילִי |
| wanting | קוֹלֲלוּ | wanting | הָקִילוּ |
| | קוֹלֵלְנָה | | הָקֵלְנָה |
| | | | הָקֵל |
| | — | — | הָקֵל |
| | קוֹלֵל | הוּקַל | הָקִיל |
| מְקוֹלַל | מְקוֹלֵל | | מֵקִיל |
| מְקוֹלָל | | מוּקָל | |

| Nif‘âl. | Kal (ע"ו). | Kal (ע"ע). | | | |
|---|---|---|---|---|---|
| נָקוֹל | קַל | קֵל | קָל | Sg. 3 m. | |
| נָקוֹלָה | קַלָּה | קֵלָה | קָלָה | 3 f. | |
| נְקוֹלוֹתָ | קַלְּתָ | קַלְתָּ | קַלְתָּ | 2 m. | |
| נְקוֹלוֹת | etc. | קַלְתְּ | קַלְתְּ | 2 f. | Perfect. |
| נְקוֹלוֹתִי | | קַלְתִּי | קַלְתִּי | 1 c. | |
| נָקוֹלוּ | | קֵלוּ | קָלוּ | Pl. 3 c. | |
| נְקוֹלוֹתֶם | | קַלְתֶּם | קַלְתֶּם | 2 m. | |
| נְקוֹלוֹתֶן | | קַלְתֶּן | קַלְתֶּן | 2 f. | |
| נְקוֹלוֹנוּ | | קַלְנוּ | קַלְנוּ | 1 c. | |
| יִקּוֹל | יָקִיל | יָקוּל, יָבוֹא | | Sg. 3 m. | |
| תִּקּוֹל | תָּקִיל | תָּקוּל | | 3 f. | |
| תִּקּוֹל | תָּקִיל | תָּקוּל | | 2 m. | |
| תִּקּוֹלִי | תָּקִילִי | תָּקוּלִי | | 2 f. | |
| אֶקּוֹל | אָקִיל | אָקוּל | | 1 c. | |
| יִקּוֹלוּ | יָקִילוּ | יָקוּלוּ | | Pl. 3 m. | Imperfect. |
| | תְּקוּלֶינָה | תְּקוּלֶינָה, תָּקֹלְנָה | | 3 f. | |
| תִּקּוֹלוּ | תָּקִילוּ | תָּקוּלוּ | | 2 m. | |
| | תְּקֶלְנָה | תְּקוּלֶינָה | | 2 f. | |
| נִקּוֹל | נָקִיל | נָקוּל | | 1 c. | |
| הִקּוֹל | קִיל | קוּל | | Sg. 2 m. | |
| הִקּוֹלִי | קִילִי | קוּלִי | | 2 f. | Imperative. |
| הִקּוֹלוּ | קִילוּ | קוּלוּ | | Pl. 2 m. | |
| | | קֹלְנָה | | 2 f. | |
| הִקּוֹל, נָקוֹל | קוֹל | קוֹל | | abs. | Infin. |
| הִקּוֹל | קִיל | קוּל | | const. | |
| | קָל | קָל | | act. | Part. |
| נָקוֹל | קוּל קִיל קָל | קוּל | | pass. | |

## Paradigm N.  Verb Lắmĕd ʾĀlĕf (ל״א)

| Hiθpăʿēl. | Hifʿil. | Piʿēl. | Nifʿāl. | Ḳăl. | |
|---|---|---|---|---|---|
| הִתְקַטֵּא | הִקְטִיא | { קִטֵּא / קִטָּא } | נִקְטָא | { קָטָא / קָטָא } | Sg. 3 m. |
| הִתְקַטְּאָה | הִקְטִיאָה | קִטְּאָה | נִקְטְאָה | קָטְאָה | 3 f. |
| הִתְקַטֵּאתָ | הִקְטֵאתָ | קִטֵּאתָ | נִקְטֵאתָ | קָטֵאתָ | 2 m. |
| הִתְקַטֵּאת | הִקְטֵאת | קִטֵּאת | נִקְטֵאת | קָטֵאת | 2 f. |
| הִתְקַטֵּאתִי | הִקְטֵאתִי | קִטֵּאתִי | נִקְטֵאתִי | קָטֵאתִי | 1 c. |
| הִתְקַטְּאוּ | הִקְטִיאוּ | קִטְּאוּ | נִקְטְאוּ | קָטְאוּ | Pl. 3 c. |
| הִתְקַטֵּאתֶם | הִקְטֵאתֶם | קִטֵּאתֶם | נִקְטֵאתֶם | קָטֵאתֶם | 2 m. |
| הִתְקַטֵּאתֶן | הִקְטֵאתֶן | קִטֵּאתֶן | נִקְטֵאתֶן | קָטֵאתֶן | 2 f. |
| הִתְקַטֵּאנוּ | הִקְטֵאנוּ | קִטֵּאנוּ | נִקְטֵאנוּ | קָטֵאנוּ | 1 c. |
| יִתְקַטֵּא | יַקְטִיא | יְקַטֵּא | יִקָּטֵא | יִקְטָא | Sg. 3 m. |
| תִּתְקַטֵּא | תַּקְטִיא | תְּקַטֵּא | תִּקָּטֵא | תִּקְטָא | 3 f. |
| תִּתְקַטֵּא | תַּקְטִיא | תְּקַטֵּא | תִּקָּטֵא | תִּקְטָא | 2 m. |
| תִּתְקַטְּאִי | תַּקְטִיאִי | תְּקַטְּאִי | תִּקָּטְאִי | תִּקְטְאִי | 2 f. |
| אֶתְקַטֵּא | אַקְטִיא | אֲקַטֵּא | אֶקָּטֵא | אֶקְטָא | 1 c. |
| יִתְקַטְּאוּ | יַקְטִיאוּ | יְקַטְּאוּ | יִקָּטְאוּ | יִקְטְאוּ | Pl. 3 m. |
| תִּתְקַטֶּאנָה | תַּקְטֶאנָה | תְּקַטֶּאנָה | תִּקָּטֶאנָה | תִּקְטֶאנָה | 3 f. |
| תִּתְקַטְּאוּ | תַּקְטִיאוּ | תְּקַטְּאוּ | תִּקָּטְאוּ | תִּקְטְאוּ | 2 m. |
| תִּתְקַטֶּאנָה | תַּקְטֶאנָה | תְּקַטֶּאנָה | תִּקָּטֶאנָה | תִּקְטֶאנָה | 2 f. |
| נִתְקַטֵּא | נַקְטִיא | נְקַטֵּא | נִקָּטֵא | נִקְטָא | 1 c. |
| הִתְקַטֵּא | הַקְטֵא | קַטֵּא | הִקָּטֵא | קְטָא | Sg. 2 m. |
| הִתְקַטְּאִי | הַקְטִיאִי | קַטְּאִי | הִקָּטְאִי | קִטְאִי | 2 f. |
| הִתְקַטְּאוּ | הַקְטִיאוּ | קַטְּאוּ | הִקָּטְאוּ | קִטְאוּ | Pl. 2 m. |
| הִתְקַטֶּאנָה | הַקְטֶאנָה | קַטֶּאנָה | הִקָּטֶאנָה | קְטֶאנָה | 2 f. |
| —— | הַקְטֵא | קַטֵּא | נִקְטֹא | קָטוֹא | abs. |
| הִתְקַטֵּא | הַקְטִיא | קַטֵּא | הִקָּטֵא | קְטֹא | const. |
| מִתְקַטֵּא | מַקְטִיא | מְקַטֵּא | | קֹטֵא | act. |
| | | | נִקְטָא | קָטוּא | pass. |